CAN

REBEL T1i /

THE EXPANDED GUIDE

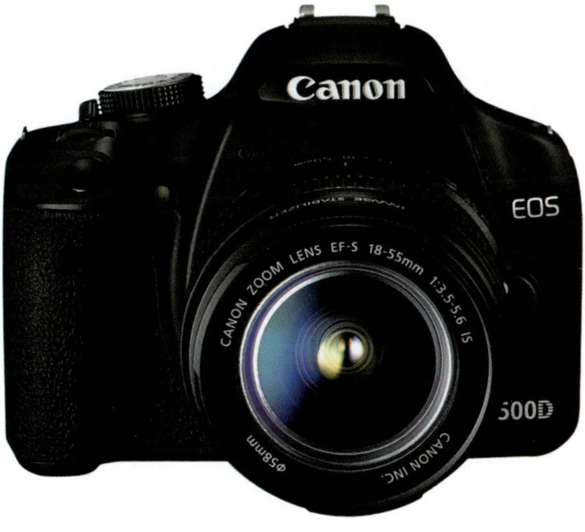

AMMONITE
PRESS

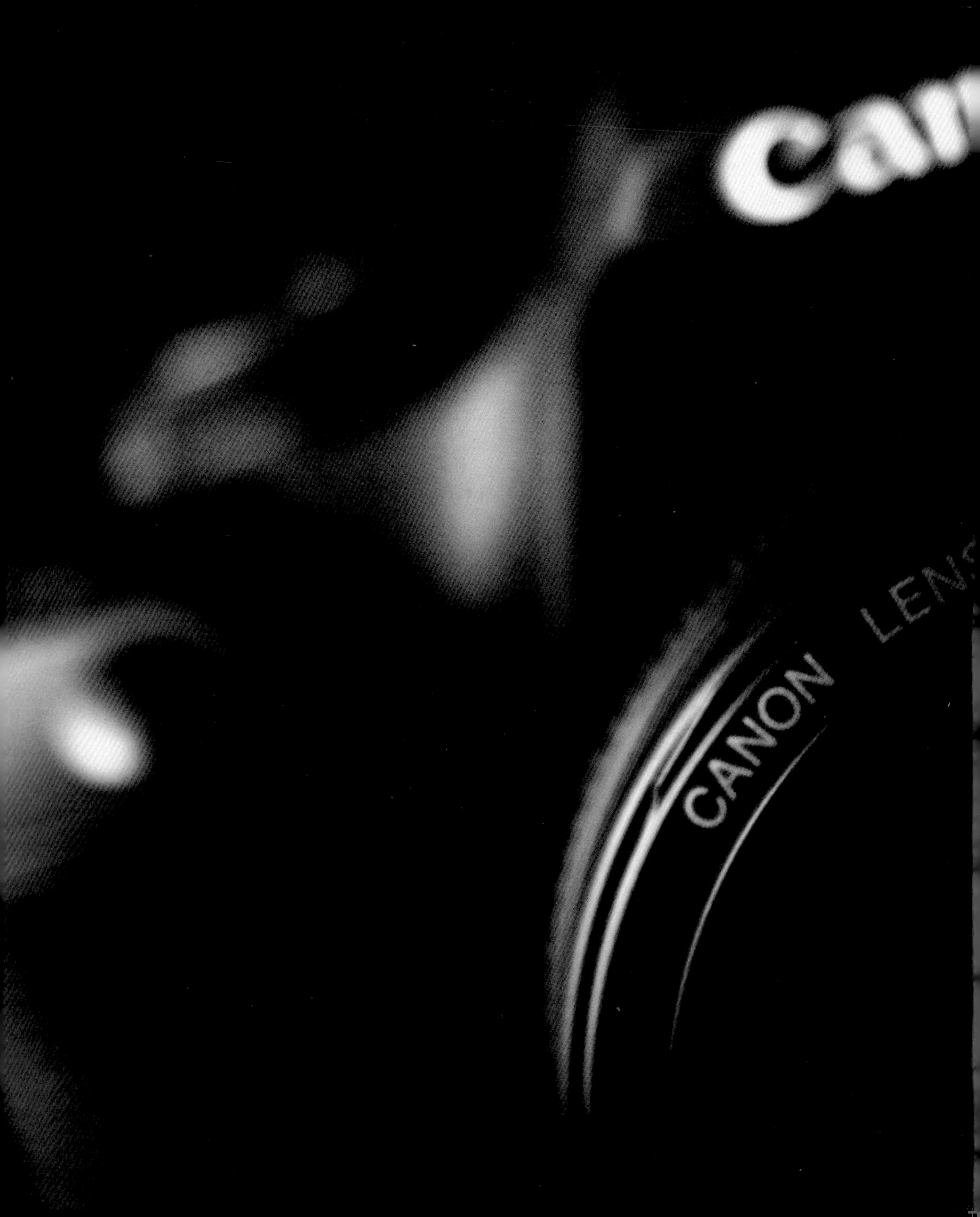
CANON

CANON REBEL T1i / EOS 500D

THE EXPANDED GUIDE

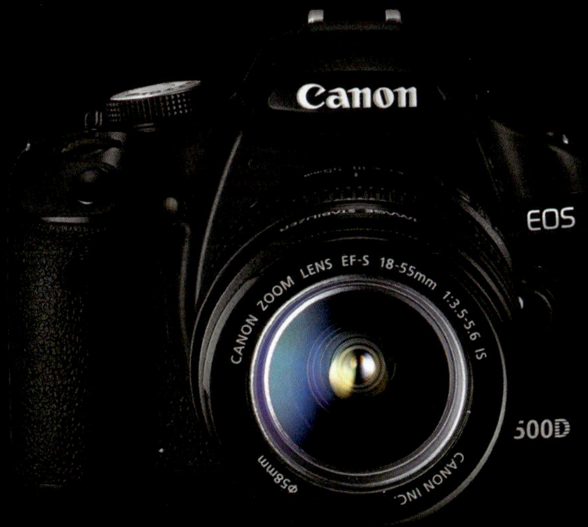

Andy Stansfield

AMMONITE
PRESS

First published 2010 by
Ammonite Press
an imprint of AE Publications Ltd
166 High Street, Lewes, East Sussex BN7 1XU, UK

ISBN 978-1-906672-47-8

British Library Cataloging in Publication Data:
A catalog record of this book is available from the British Library.

Editor: Tom Mugridge
Design: Fineline Studios

Typefaces: Frutiger and Palatino
Color reproduction by GMC Reprographics
Printed and bound in China by Everbest Printing Co. Ltd.

Contents

Chapter 1	**Overview**	8
Chapter 2	**Functions**	24
Chapter 3	**Live View & Movie mode**	122
Chapter 4	**In the field**	136
Chapter 5	**Flash**	162
Chapter 6	**Close-up**	178
Chapter 7	**Lenses**	188
Chapter 8	**Accessories**	206
Chapter 9	**Connection**	218
	Glossary	233
	Useful websites	236
	Index	238

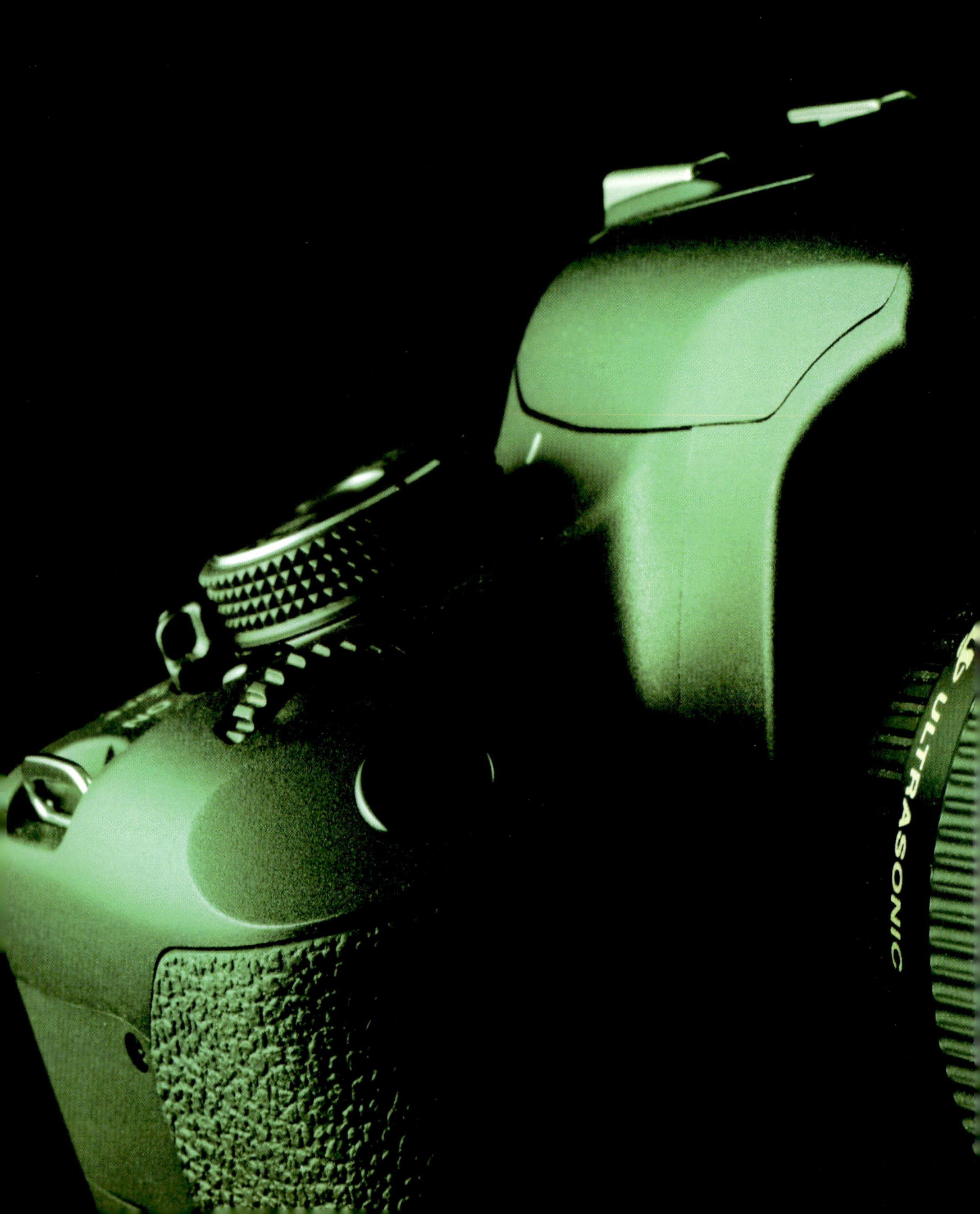
ULTRASONIC

Chapter 1

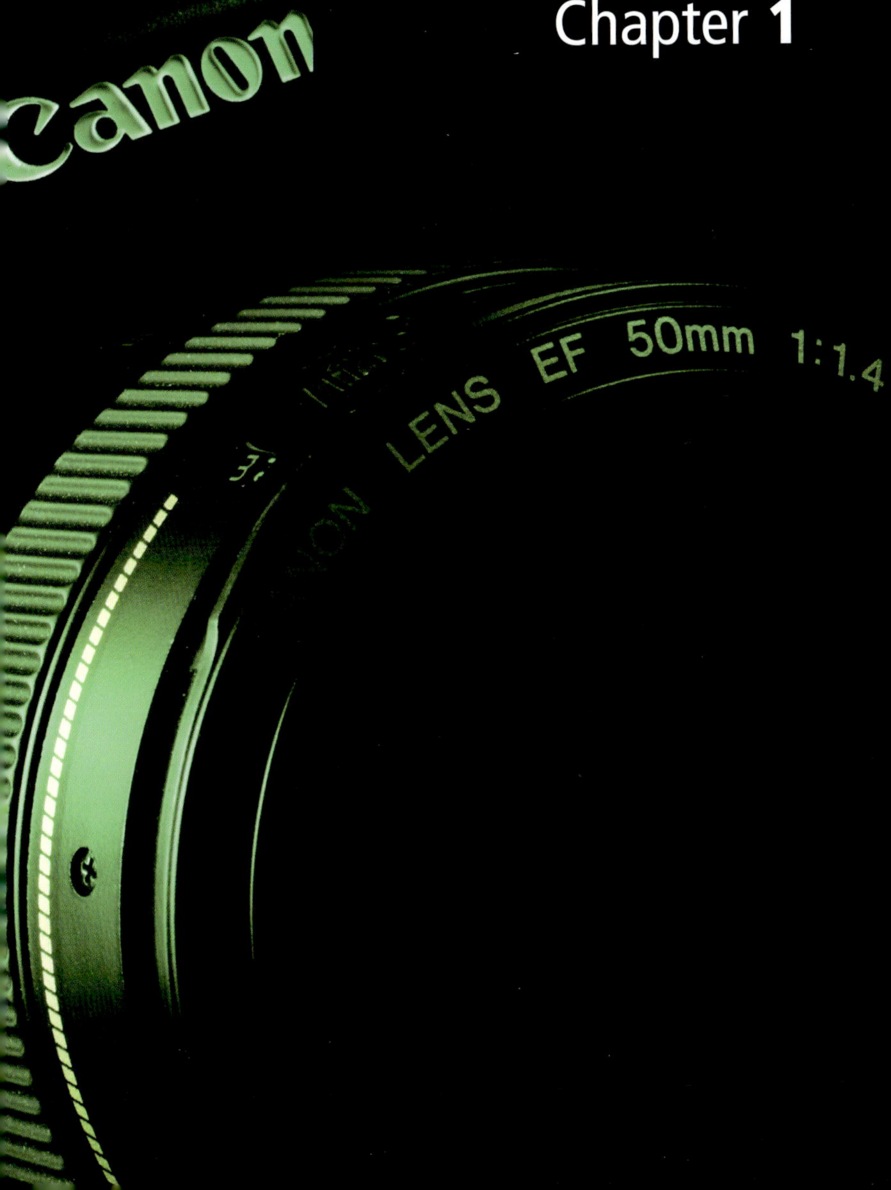

Overview

The Rebel T1i/EOS 500D is the latest and most sophisticated offering from Canon in what has become a two-tier entry-level category since the launch of the Rebel XS/EOS 1000D. Both the Rebel XS/EOS 1000D and the range that includes the 450D, 500D, and so on are characterized by their small lightweight bodies compared with the rest of Canon's model range.

Today's wide range of Canon digital SLRs has evolved from the EOS D30, which was launched with the new millennium and represented the first all-Canon DSLR after a brief partnership with Kodak. Many, but by no means all, new developments have been launched first in the professional-level 1D series before being passed down to the entry-level and enthusiast-level ranges.

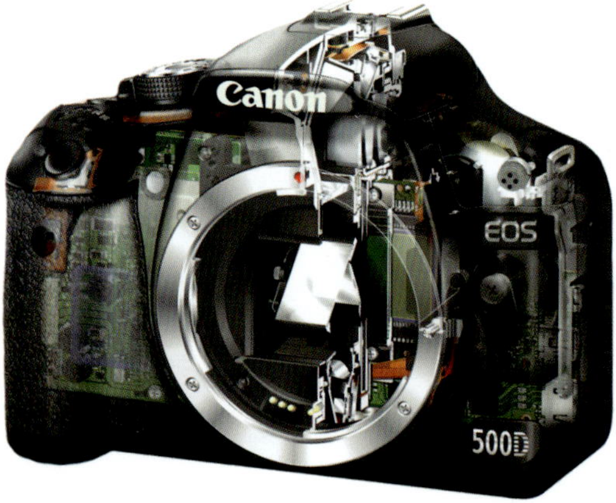

First announced in the spring of 2000, the D30 offered a resolution of just over 3 megapixels, 3-point autofocus and a burst of three JPEGs. Its monitor was just 1.8in (4.5cm) and could only be used for reviewing images already captured.

By comparison, the Rebel T1i/500D boasts 15 megapixels, a self-cleaning sensor, a much larger monitor enabling the use of Live View for detailed composition and for shooting movies, adjustable Picture Styles, and a staggering maximum ISO of 12,800—which practically allows you to capture a black cat in a coal cellar.

The professional EOS-1D series is also leaping ahead in specification, but if you want 21 megapixels, 10 frames per second or 45 AF points you should expect a significantly higher outlay. These are not the only improvements but they illustrate the progress Canon have made in terms of speed, convenience, and flexibility in the digital SLR market.

EOS history

Back in the mid-1980s, when camera and lens designers were suddenly making huge inroads in forging new links between electronic and optical components, Canon designers were preempted by autofocus SLRs from first Minolta, then Nikon. An intense two-year period of research and development followed for Canon, who saw that these new cameras would ultimately form the basis of an extensive and flexible system, so every aspect of the camera needed to be stylish as well as practical.

As a result, early EOS models were designed with three criteria in mind: first, the introduction of an AF system should not increase the price point; second, the camera should be capable of shooting sports events handheld with a 300mm f/2.8 lens or similar; and third, autofocus capability should match exposure sensitivity in low-light situations.

In March 1987, Canon put their ideas to the test with the launch of the first EOS model, the EOS 650. EOS stood for Electro Optical System, but Eos was also the Greek goddess of the dawn, described by the ancient writer Hesiod as "Eos, who brings light to all the mortals of this Earth." Fanciful perhaps, but appropriate for the camera that heralded the most successful series of developments in the history of photography. Ironically, the goddess Eos was the daughter of two Titans. Minolta and Nikon, maybe?

During the next two years, new models appeared in the form of the EOS 620 and the EOS 630, but the most significant launch was reserved for the EOS-1, which was specifically designed to lure professionals away from other manufacturers' models.

To support this drive to attract the high-end user, Canon also had to develop its lenses and worked hard to reach the forefront of lens technology. In particular, Canon needed to develop a superfast autofocus system that would work in all lighting conditions with the large-aperture lenses favored by press and sports photographers.

EF 200mm f/2 L IS
Lenses such as this EF 200mm, with its 5-stop image stabilization, demand almost instantaneous autofocus.

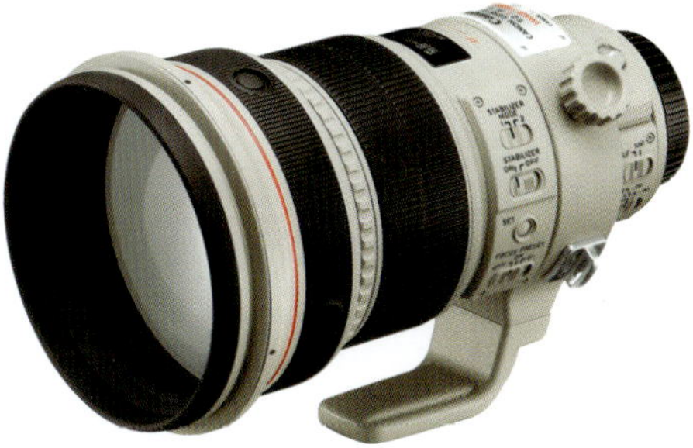

By late 1994, Canon were ready to introduce a new top-of-the-range model in the form of the EOS-1N, which introduced much quieter operation, 5-point AF, and a 16-zone evaluative metering system. Its high-speed sister, the EOS-1N RS, boasted a drive rate of ten frames per second, a figure which other manufacturers still find it hard to beat, even today. While Canon continued to improve its amateur SLRs with innovations such as eye-control focusing, the EOS-1N served professionals well for half a decade.

A new flagship model, the EOS-3, was launched in November 1998, by which time the key areas of metering and autofocus were undergoing rapid development and Canon were about to embark on a decade of model upgrades that took place every 18–24 months. The EOS-3 utilized a 21-zone metering system that was linked to AF points, of which there were eventually 45. This increased the speed of operation further, especially when combined with the eye-control system. A top shutter speed of 1/8000 sec was also included, along with a claimed lifetime of at least 100,000 shutter operations.

The EOS-1V was introduced in the spring of 2000 with high-speed continuous shooting of up to nine frames per second and 20 Custom Functions that could be tailored to each individual. The EOS D30, also launched in 2000, brought into play

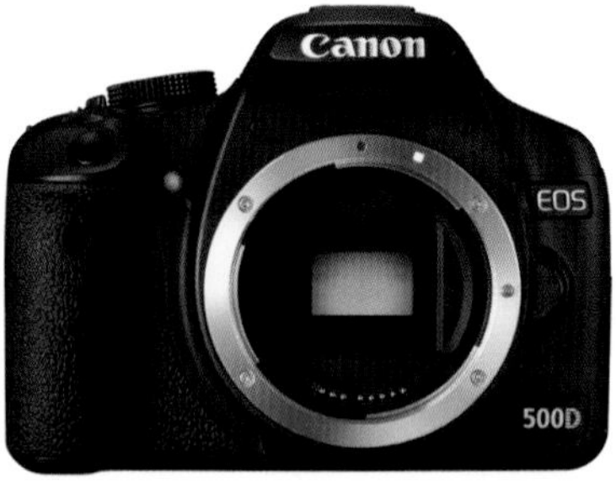

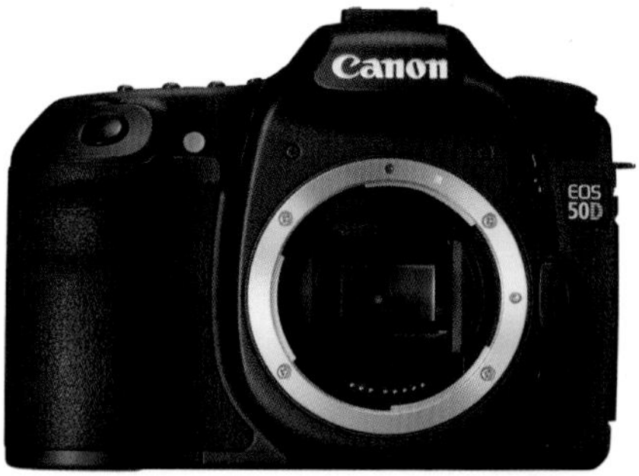

an affordable digital SLR aimed at the nonprofessional enthusiast. With its Canon-developed CMOS sensor, the EOS D30 could boast the smallest and lightest body in this sector of the market.

The EOS D30 also heralded a new approach to photography in which those with little experience could access the capabilities of a complex tool using the now-familiar Basic Zone settings indicated by symbols on the Mode Dial. More foolproofing was added in the form of a 35-zone evaluative metering system and E-TTL (electronic through-the-lens) metering for its built-in flash. Canon RAW image files could now also be selected instead of JPEG files.

The EOS-1D was introduced in 2001, followed in 2002 by the EOS-1Ds. These digital versions of the renowned professional camera took specifications and speed to staggering new levels, and recent updates have continued the trend. Today's users can expect to find superfast processors like the DIGIC IV, an Integrated Cleaning System on the camera sensor, sophisticated exposure adjustments like Highlight Tone Priority, and phenomenally high ISO capability with much less noise than might be expected, even on the entry-level models.

Those interested in the history of camera technology are advised to visit Canon's fascinating website at www. canon.com/cameramuseum.

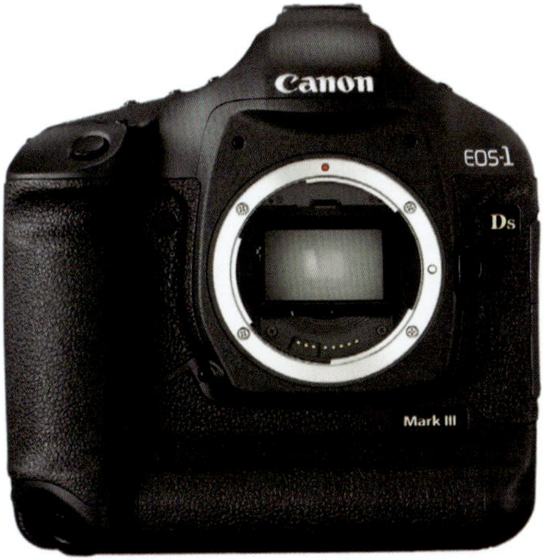

ONE SIZE DOES NOT FIT ALL
Three Canon cameras are shown here in proportion to their actual size: the entry-level Rebel T1i/EOS 500D (far left), the enthusiast-level EOS 50D (center), and the professional EOS 1Ds Mk III.

Main features

Body

Dimensions: 128.8 × 97.5 × 61.9mm
Weight: 480g
Construction: stainless steel/plastic
Lens mount: EF and EF-S
Operating environment: 32–104°F (0–40°C) at maximum 85% humidity

Sensor & processor

The Canon Rebel T1i/EOS 500D uses the same DIGIC IV processor that is found in the EOS 50D and 5D Mk II. The self-cleaning image sensor is a 22.3 × 14.9mm CMOS type with 15.1 effective megapixels.

Focusing

Three different autofocus modes including predictive autofocus can be selected to suit static or moving subjects: One Shot, AI Focus, or AI Servo. Automatic and manual selection of the seven AF points is possible. The AF system's working range is from EV -0.5 to EV 18 at 73°F (23°C) at ISO 100. Autofocus lock is possible in One Shot mode and when using flash an AF-assist beam is triggered if selected within the Custom Functions. Autofocus is not possible on lenses slower than f/5.6, or effectively slower than f/5.6 when using a teleconverter.

Exposure

The 35-zone silicon photocell sensor provides four full-aperture TTL metering modes: Evaluative (linked to any AF point), Partial (9% at center), Spot (4% at center), and Center-weighted Average metering. The metering range is EV 1 to EV 20 at 73°F (23°C) at ISO 100 using a 50mm f/1.4 lens. Both exposure compensation and 3-shot auto-exposure bracketing are possible to a maximum of +/- 2 stops using either ½- or ⅓-stop increments. Automatic ISO setting can be selected between ISO 100 and 1600. Alternatively, in Creative Zone modes manual settings can be used in 1-stop increments between ISO 100 and 3200 (expandable to 6400 or 12800).

File types and sizes

JPEG file sizes range from large/fine 4752 × 3168 pixels to small/normal 2352 × 1568 pixels, with a choice of fine or normal for each of the large, medium, or small settings. RAW files are recorded as 4752 × 3168 pixels. Simultaneous recording of 14-bit RAW and large/fine JPEG files is also possible in Creative Zone modes. Both sRGB and Adobe RGB color spaces are supported.

Flash

Using the E-TTL II metering system, the Canon Rebel T1i/EOS 500D's built-in flash has a guide number of 13 (meters) at ISO 100 and synchronization is 1/200 sec. Automatic and manual modes are provided along with selectable red-eye reduction. Flash exposure compensation, flash bracketing, and second-curtain synchronization are all supported. Wireless multiple flash is possible with EX series Speedlites.

LCD monitor

The 3in (7.6cm) TFT LCD monitor provides easier review of images already captured due to its size and seven selectable levels of brightness. It can be used in Live View mode for composing and checking fine detail, when it will be of greatest benefit to those working on a tripod in stable lighting conditions. Manual focus or three AF modes (Quick mode, Live mode and Live Face Detection mode) are possible in Live View mode. Two different grid overlays can also be selected. Magnification of ×5 and ×10 plus vertical and horizontal scrolling of the magnified portion of the image assist in the checking process when focusing manually.

The LCD monitor's display of shooting information and its image review function can both be customized in order to preserve battery power.

Custom Functions

A total of 13 Custom Functions are supported, providing a total of 39 different settings.

Memory card

SD card or SDHC card.

Software

ZoomBrowser EX/ImageBrowser, PhotoStitch, EOS Utility including Remote Capture, Picture Style Editor, Digital Photo Professional (for RAW image processing).

Full features and camera layout

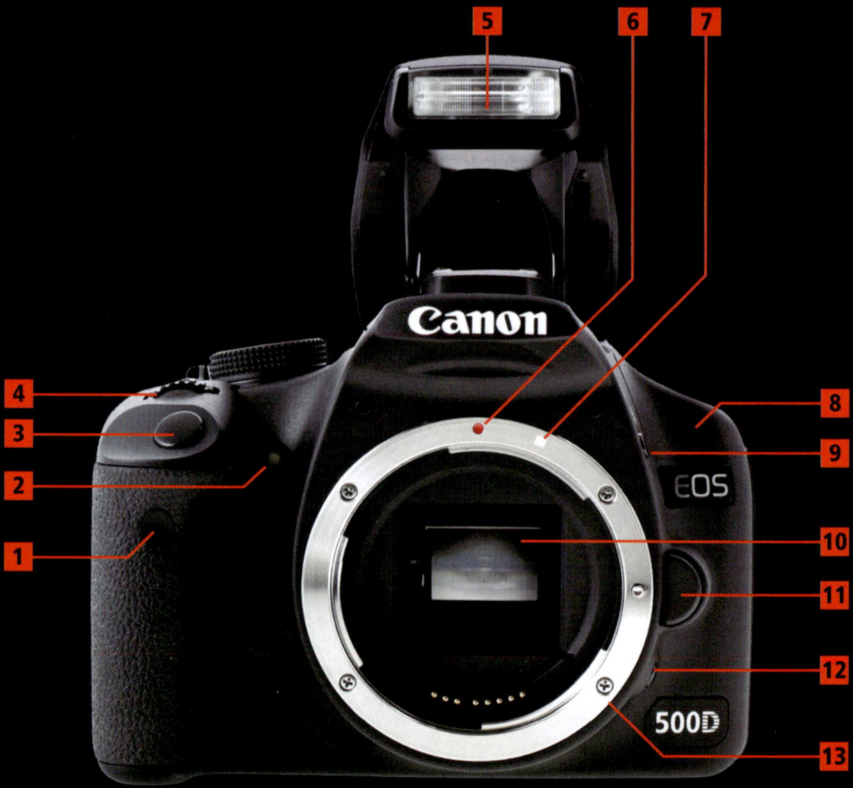

FRONT OF CAMERA

1 Remote control sensor
2 Self-timer light
3 Shutter release button
4 Main Dial
5 Built-in flash
6 EF lens mount index
7 EF-S lens mount index
8 Microphone
9 Flash pop-up button
10 Reflex mirror
11 Lens release button
12 Depth of field preview button
13 Lens mount

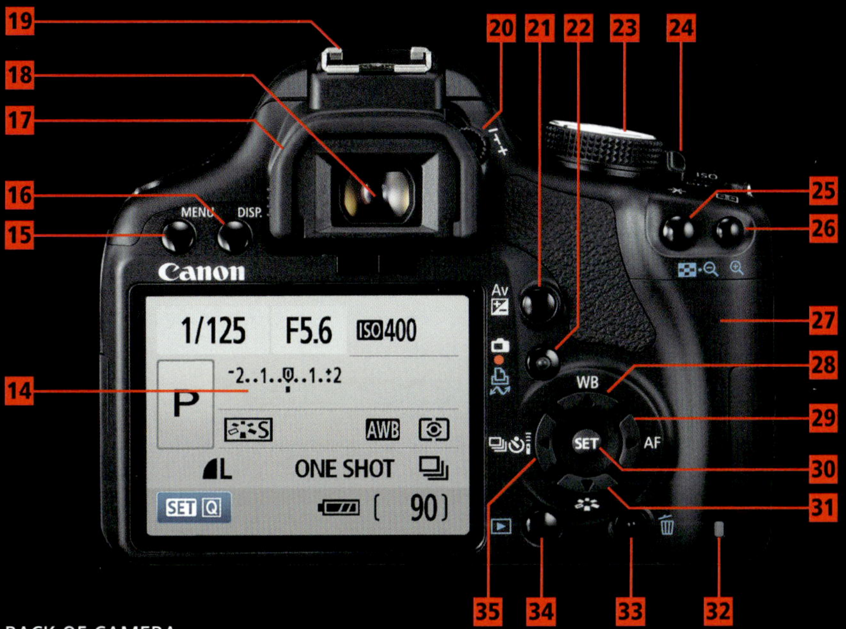

BACK OF CAMERA

14 LCD monitor

15 MENU button

16 Shooting settings display button

17 Eyecup

18 Viewfinder eyepiece

19 Hotshoe

20 Diopter adjustment

21 Aperture/Exposure compensation button

22 Live View shooting/Movie shooting/ Print/Share button

23 Mode Dial

24 Power on/off switch

25 AE lock/FE lock/Reduce/Index button

26 AF point selection/Enlarge button

27 Speaker

28 White balance selection button

29 AF mode selection button

30 SET button

31 Picture Style selection button

32 Access lamp

33 Erase button

34 Playback button

35 Drive mode selection button

TOP OF CAMERA

36 Focal plane mark
37 Camera strap eyelet
38 Lens release button
39 Hotshoe
40 Shutter release button
41 Main Dial
42 ISO selection button
43 Camera strap eyelet
44 Power on/off switch
45 Mode Dial
46 Diopter adjustment

LEFT SIDE

47 Remote control terminal
48 Audio/video out/Digital terminal
49 HDMI mini out terminal

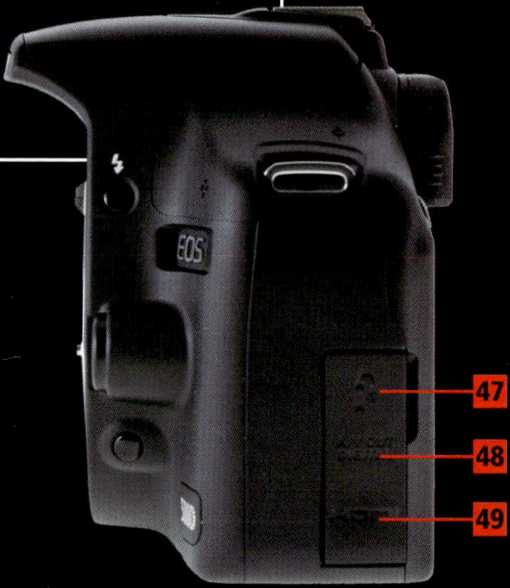

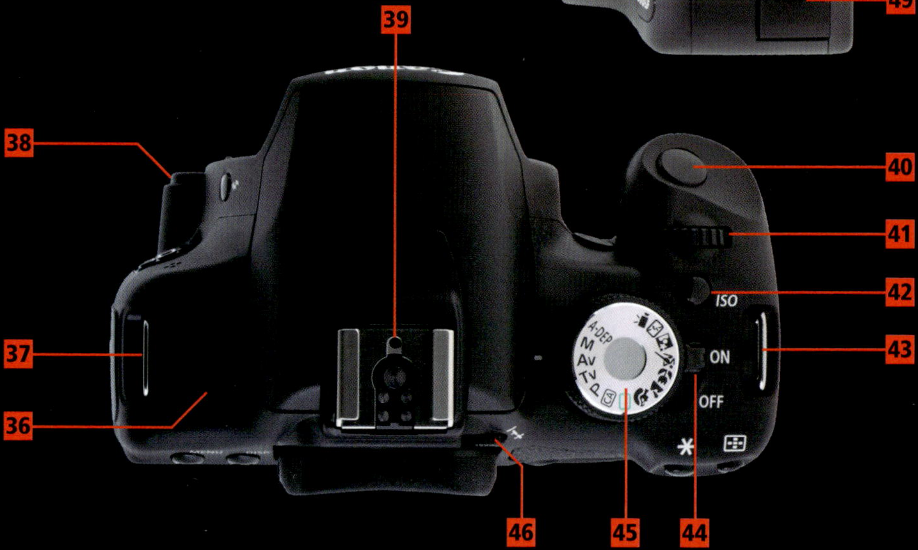

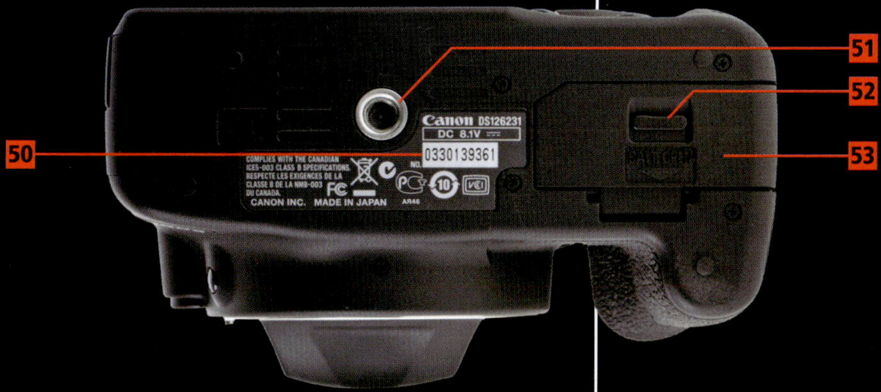

BOTTOM OF CAMERA

50 Camera serial number

51 Tripod socket (¼in)

52 Battery compartment lock release

53 Battery compartment

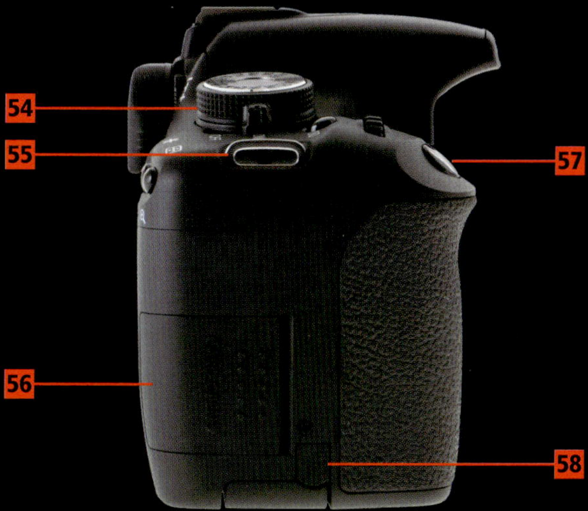

RIGHT SIDE

54 Mode Dial

55 Camera strap eyelet

56 Memory card cover

57 Shutter release button

58 DC cord hole

Viewfinder display

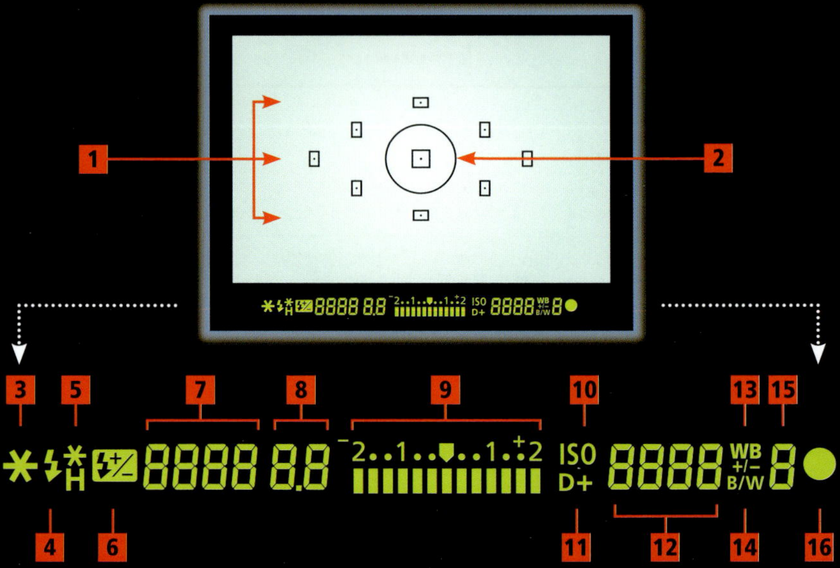

1 Focus points

2 Spot metering circle

3 AE lock/AEB in progress

4 Flash ready/improper FE lock indicator

5 High-speed sync/Flash exposure lock/ Flash exposure bracketing in progress indicator

6 Flash exposure compensation

7 Shutter speed/Flash exposure lock/ Busy indicator/Built-in flash recycling/ Card full indicator/ Card error indicator/ No card indicator

8 Aperture value

9 Exposure level indicator/Exposure compensation indicator/Auto exposure bracketing display/Red-eye reduction lamp-on indicator

10 ISO indicator

11 Highlight tone priority indicator

12 ISO speed

13 White balance correction

14 Monochrome shooting

15 Maximum burst indicator

16 Focus confimation indicator

Quick Control Screen

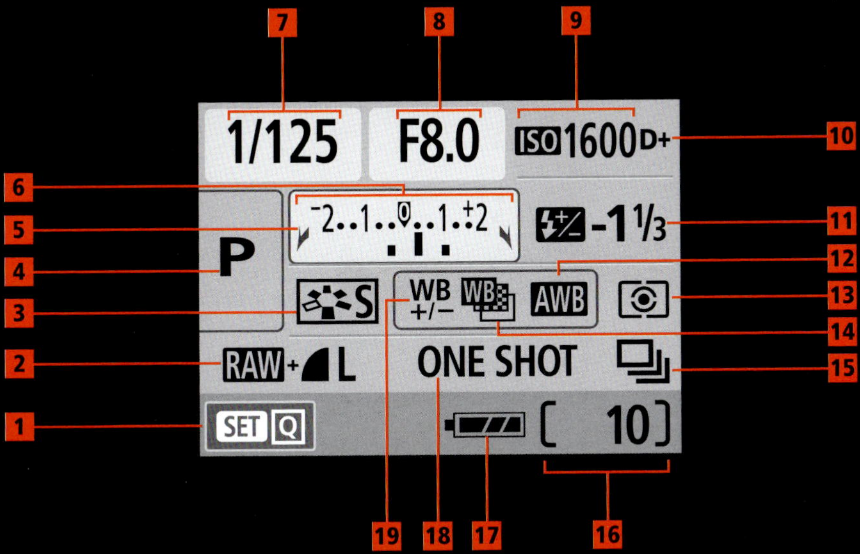

1 Quick Control icon
2 Image format, size, and quality
3 Picture style
4 Shooting mode
5 Main dial pointer
6 Exposure level indicator/Exposure compensation indicator/Auto exposure bracketing display
7 Shutter speed
8 Aperture
9 ISO speed
10 Highlight tone priority
11 Flash exposure compensation indicator
12 White balance preset
13 Metering mode
14 White balance bracketing
15 Drive mode
16 Shots remaining on card/Shots remaining during white-balance bracketing/Self-timer countdown/ Bulb exposure time
17 Battery check
18 AF mode
19 White balance correction

Menu displays

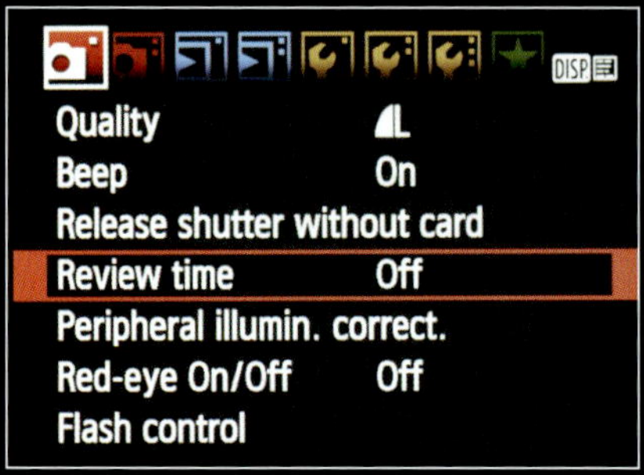

SHOOTING MENU 1
Quality
Beep
Release shutter without card
Review time
Peripheral illumination correction
Red-eye On/Off
Flash control

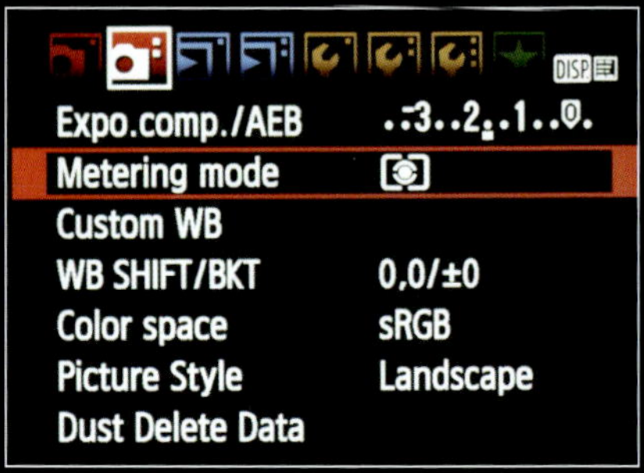

SHOOTING MENU 2
Exposure compensation/
Auto exposure bracketing
Metering mode
Custom white balance
White balance shift/bracketing
Color space
Picture Style
Dust Delete Data

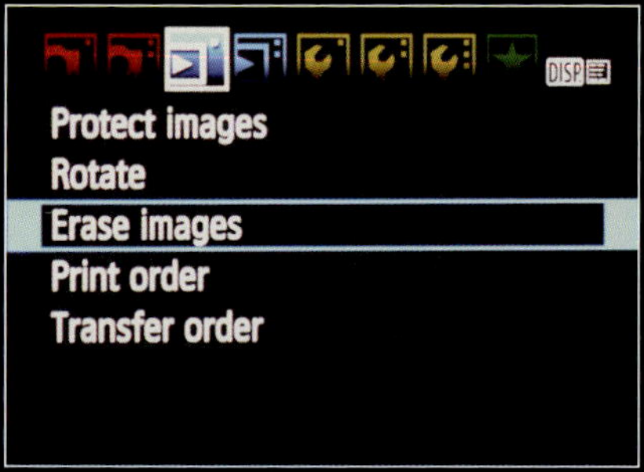

PLAYBACK MENU 1
Protect images
Rotate
Erase images
Print order
Transfer order

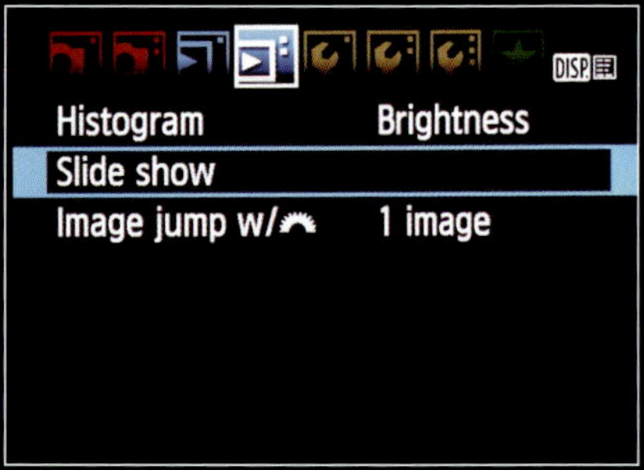

PLAYBACK MENU 2
Histogram
Slide show
Image jump with Main Dial

Note: Some menu items are not displayed in Basic Zone modes (see pages 81–3).

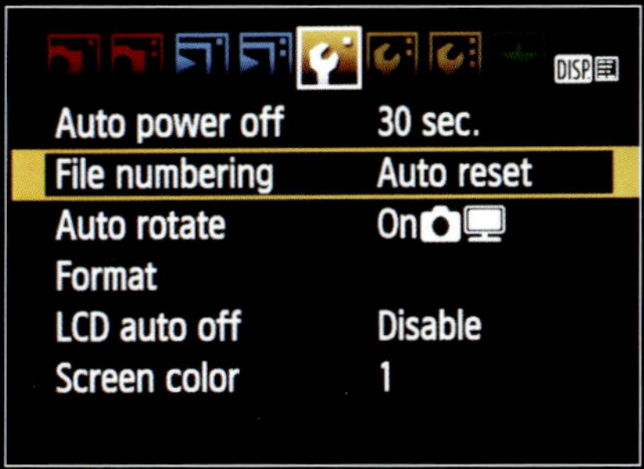

SET-UP MENU 1
Auto power off
File numbering
Auto rotate
Format
LCD auto off
Screen color

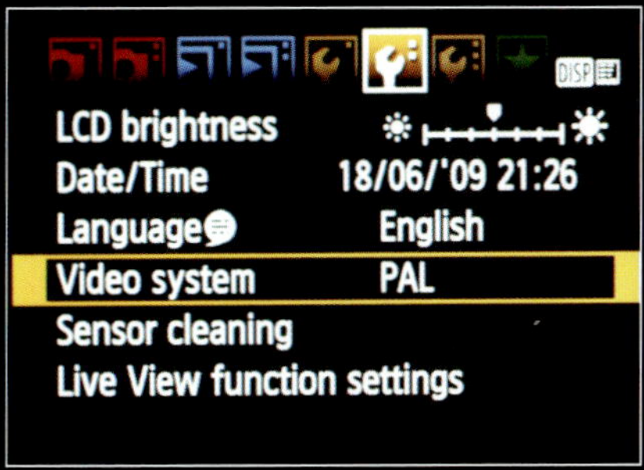

SET-UP MENU 2
LCD brightness
Date/Time
Language
Video system
Sensor cleaning
Live View function settings

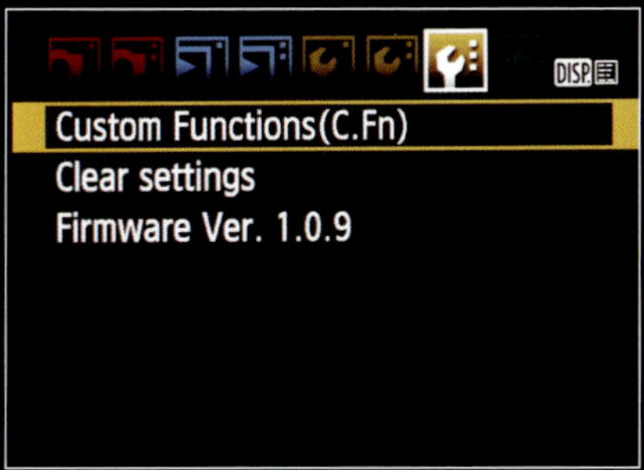

SET-UP MENU 3
Custom Functions
Clear settings
Firmware version

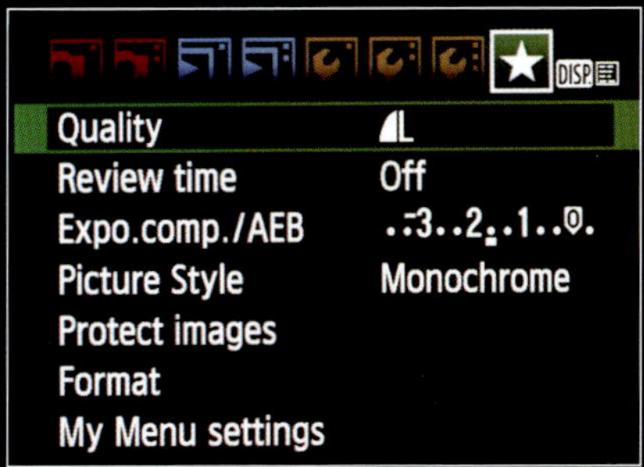

MY MENU
This menu can be customized to include up to six of your most frequently adjusted settings, enabling you to access them quickly and easily.

Function availability table

Mode Dial			Basic Zone								Creative Zone					Movie shooting
			[Full Auto]	[Portrait]	[Landscape]	[Close-up]	[Sports]	[Night Portrait]	[Flash Off]	CA	P	Tv	Av	M	A-DEP	[Movie]
Quality	JPEG		○	○	○	○	○	○	○	○	○	○	○	○	○	○
	RAW		○	○	○	○	○	○	○	○	○	○	○	○	○	○
	RAW + JPEG		○	○	○	○	○	○	○	○	○	○	○	○	○	○
ISO speed	Auto		●	●	●	●	●	●	●	●	○	○	○	○	○	●
	Manual		-	-	-	-	-	-	-	-	○	○	○	○	○	-
Picture Style	Standard		●	-	-	●	●	●	●	○	○	○	○	○	○	○
	Portrait		-	●	-	-	-	-	-	○	○	○	○	○	○	○
	Landscape		-	-	●	-	-	-	-	○	○	○	○	○	○	○
	Neutral		-	-	-	-	-	-	-	-	○	○	○	○	○	○
	Faithful		-	-	-	-	-	-	-	-	○	○	○	○	○	○
	Monochrome		-	-	-	-	-	-	-	○	○	○	○	○	○	○
	User Defined		-	-	-	-	-	-	-	-	○	○	○	○	○	○
White balance	Auto WB		●	●	●	●	●	●	●	●	○	○	○	○	○	○
	Preset WB		-	-	-	-	-	-	-	-	○	○	○	○	○	○
	Custom WB		-	-	-	-	-	-	-	-	○	○	○	○	○	○
	WB Correction		-	-	-	-	-	-	-	-	○	○	○	○	○	-
	WB Bracketing		-	-	-	-	-	-	-	-	○	○	○	○	○	-
Auto Lighting Optimizer			●	●	●	●	●	●	●	●	○	○	○	-	○	●
	Peripheral illumination correction		○	○	○	○	○	○	○	○	○	○	○	○	○	○
	Long exposure noise reduction		●	●	●	●	●	●	●	●	○	○	○	○	○	●
AF	One-shot		-	●	●	●	-	●	-	-	○	○	○	○	●	●
	AI Servo		-	-	-	-	●	-	-	-	○	○	○	○	○	-
	AI Focus		●	-	-	-	-	-	●	●	○	○	○	○	○	-
	AF point selection	Auto	●	●	●	●	●	●	●	●	○	○	○	○	●	○
		Manual	-	-	-	-	-	-	-	-	○	○	○	○	-	○
	AF-assist beam		●	●	-	●	-	●	-	●	○	○	○	○	○	-

Mode Dial		Basic Zone								Creative Zone					Movie shooting
		[Full Auto]	[Portrait]	[Landscape]	[Close-up]	[Sports]	[Night Portrait]	[Flash Off]	CA	P	Tv	Av	M	A-DEP	[Movie]
Metering mode	Evaluative	●	●	●	●	●	●	●	●	○	○	○	○	○	-
	Partial	-	-	-	-	-	-	-	-	○	○	○	○	○	-
	Spot	-	-	-	-	-	-	-	-	○	○	○	○	○	-
	Center-weighted average	-	-	-	-	-	-	-	-	○	○	○	○	○	-
Exposure	Program shift	-	-	-	-	-	-	-	○*	○	-	-	-	-	-
	Exposure compensation	-	-	-	-	-	-	-	○*	○	○	○	-	○	○
	AEB	-	-	-	-	-	-	-	-	○	○	○	○	○	-
	AE lock	-	-	-	-	-	-	-	-	○	○	○	-	○	-
	Depth-of-field preview	-	-	-	-	-	-	-	-	○	○	○	○	○	-
Drive	Single	●	-	●	●	-	●	●	○	○	○	○	○	○	●
	Continuous	-	●	-	-	●	-	-	○	○	○	○	○	○	-
	Self-timer Remote control	○	○	○	○	○	○	○	○	○	○	○	○	○	○
	Self-timer 2 sec	-	-	-	-	-	-	-	-	○	○	○	○	○	-
	Self-timer Continuous	-	-	-	-	●	-	-	-	○	○	○	○	○	-
Built-in flash	Auto	●	●	-	●	-	●	-	○	-	-	-	-	-	-
	Manual	-	-	-	-	-	-	-	○	○	○	○	○	○	-
	Flash off	-	-	●	-	●	-	●	○	-	-	-	-	-	●
	Red-eye reduction	○	○	-	○	-	○	-	○	○	○	○	○	○	-
	FE lock	-	-	-	-	-	-	-	-	○	○	○	○	○	-
	Flash exposure compensation	-	-	-	-	-	-	-	○*	○	○	○	○	○	-
Color space	sRGB	●	●	●	●	●	●	●	●	○	○	○	○	○	●
	Adobe RGB	-	-	-	-	-	-	-	-	○	○	○	○	○	-
Live View Shooting		-	-	-	-	-	-	-	-	○	○	○	○	○	●

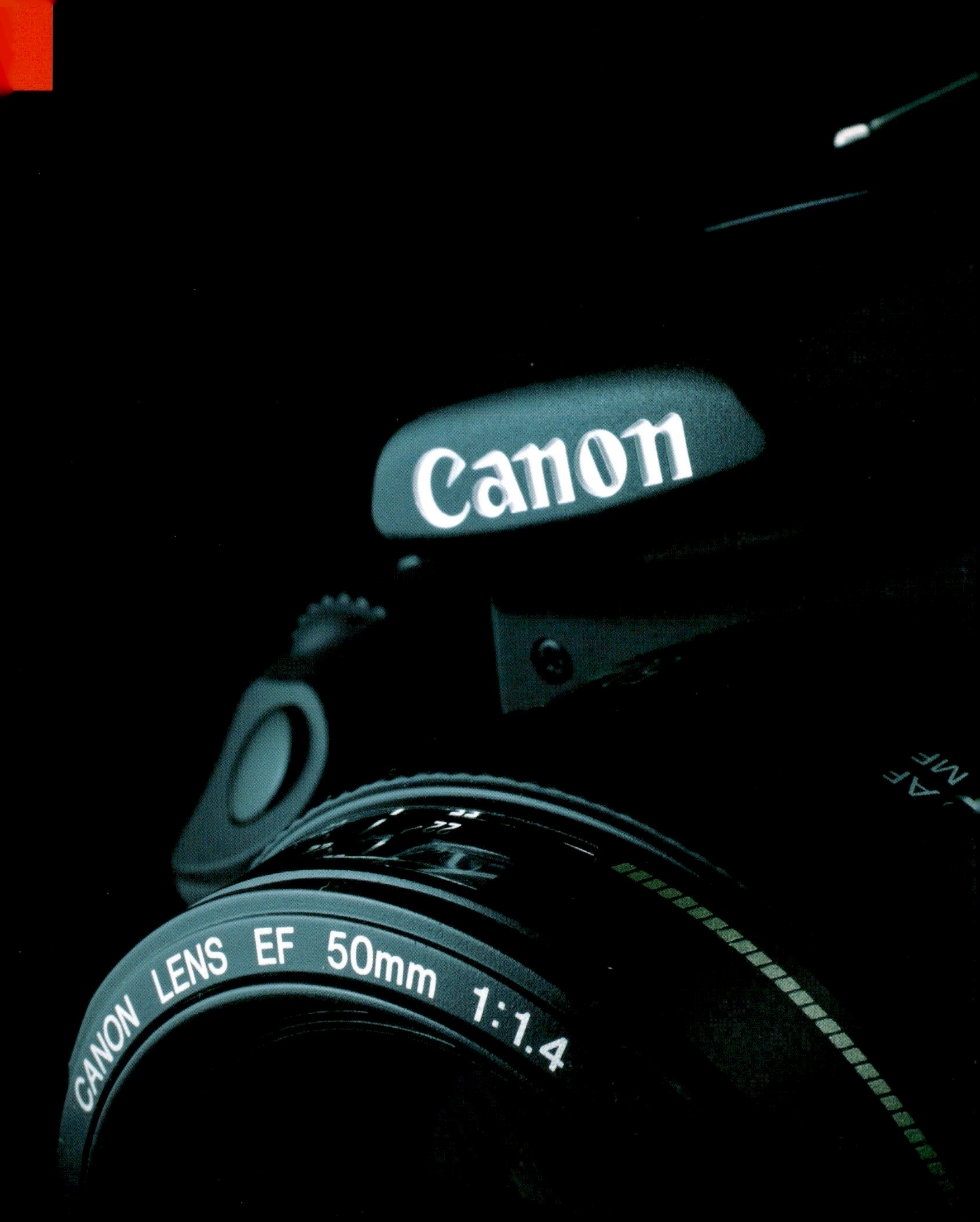
Canon
CANON LENS EF 50mm 1:1.4

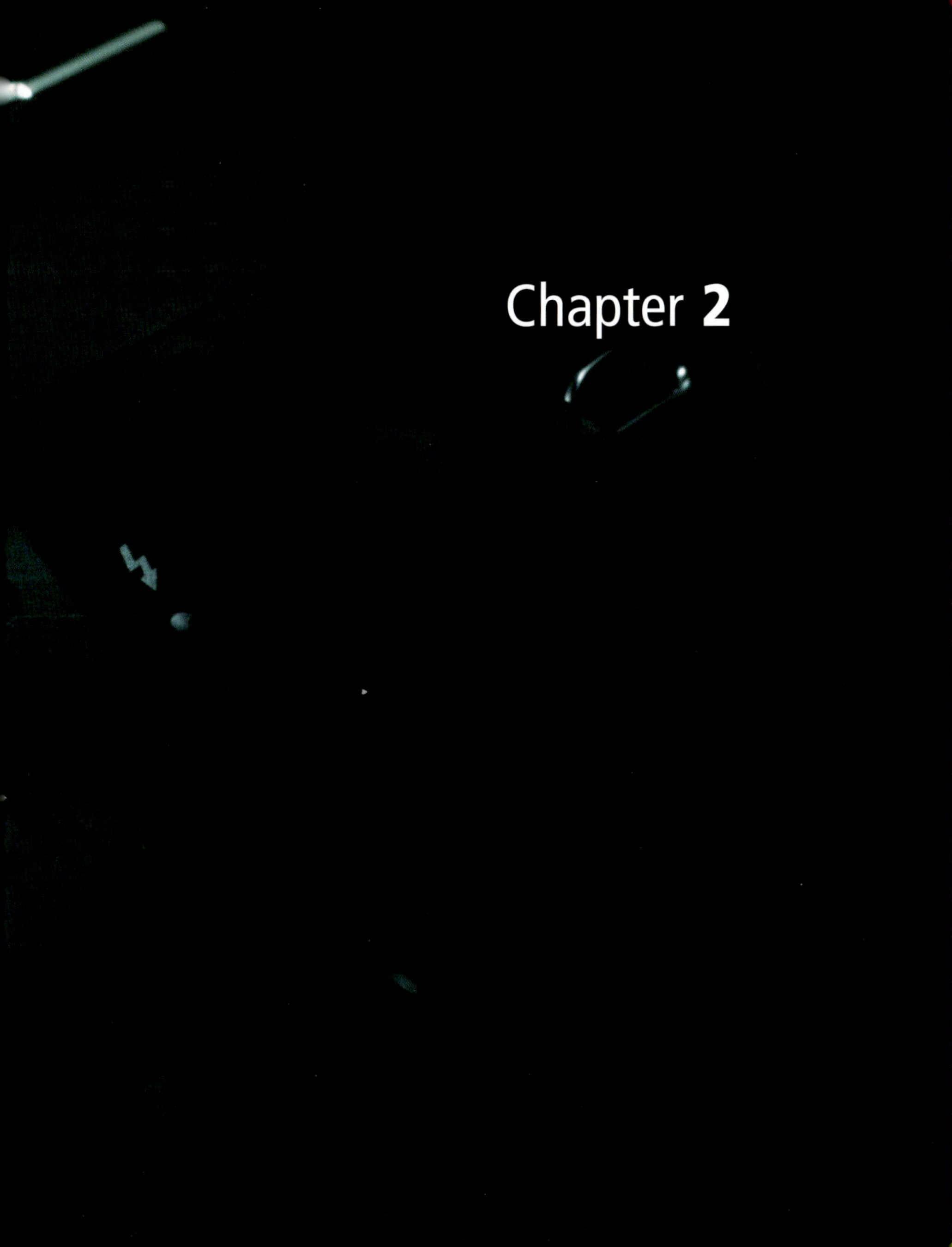

Chapter 2

Functions

Anyone making the transition from a compact digital camera to the Rebel T1i/EOS 500D may at first feel slightly daunted by the large array of buttons and dials. Fortunately, Canon offer Full Auto and Program modes that you can work with while you're getting to know the camera's functions better.

Those upgrading from other Canon digital SLRs will be familiar with many of the design concepts of the Rebel T1i/EOS 500D, if not the actual placement of the controls.

This chapter will explore the camera's full potential, step by step, by presenting basic information first and examining more complex issues in subsequent sections.

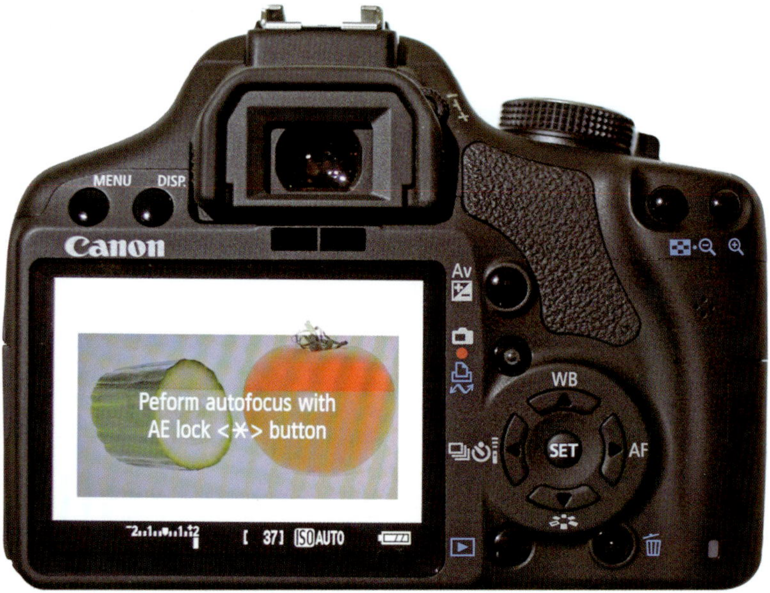

Camera preparation

Attaching the strap

Use a camera strap at all times to ensure the safety of your camera. To attach it, pass the end of the strap through either the left or right eyelet at the top of the camera. Pass the end of the strap through the buckle under the length of strap that is already threaded through the buckle. Repeat the operation on the other side of the camera. Pull the strap lightly to remove most of the slackness, position the buckle as desired, then pull more firmly so that the strap will not loosen within the buckle. The eyepiece cover is also attached to the strap.

Fitting and removing a lens

Remove the rear body cap of the lens to be fitted, along with either the camera body cap or the lens already fitted to the camera. This is done by depressing the lens-release button while turning the cap or lens anticlockwise as it is facing you.

Canon EF and EF-S lenses can be used on the Rebel T1i/EOS 500D. For EF-S lenses, align the white mark on the lens to be fitted with the white mark on the camera's lens mount, insert into the camera, and turn clockwise until you hear a faint click. For an EF lens, align the red marks. Check that the AF/MF switch on the lens is set to the desired position.

After removing a lens, ensure that the lens cap is fitted and put it down safely with the rear end up. Fit the rear lens cap as soon as possible. Avoid touching the lens contacts, as dirty contacts can cause a malfunction.

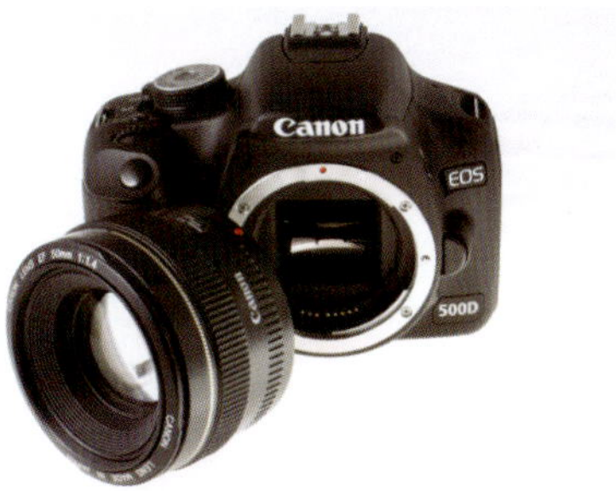

Common errors

Before you attempt this operation, always make sure that the risk of dropping either camera or lens is minimized. Make certain that dust or sand will not be blown into the camera while changing lenses.

Inserting and removing a memory card

1) Make sure the camera is switched to **OFF** and that the access lamp on the back of the camera is not illuminated.

2) With the camera facing away from you, the SD card slot cover is on the right side of the camera body. To open it, slide the cover toward you with firm finger pressure and it will swing outward on its hinges.

3) To remove a memory card, press the card into the camera and it will spring part way out, making it easy to remove.

4) To insert an SD card, slide it into the camera's slot with its label side facing you until you hear a faint click and the card stays fully inserted. When it is pushed halfway in you will start to feel some resistance as the card works against the spring. This is normal.

5) Press the cover shut and slide it forward until it snaps into position.

To prevent shooting without a CF card inserted, see 📷 Shooting menu 1.

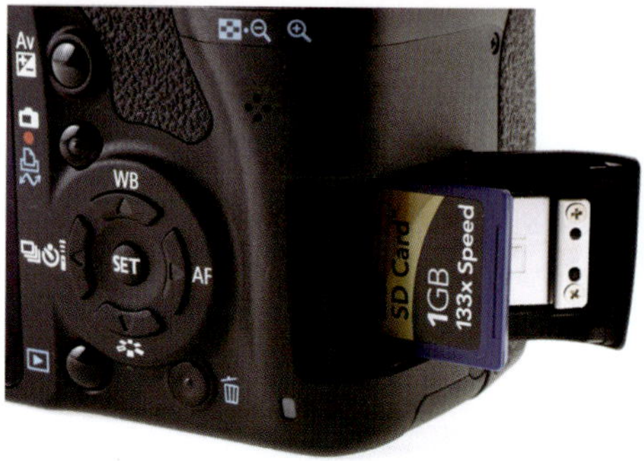

Common errors

When the red access lamp on the back of the camera is lit or blinking, it indicates that images are being processed—this may include being written, read, erased, or transferred to another device. Do not remove the battery or SD card or open the card slot cover when the red access lamp is illuminated or blinking. Any of these actions is likely to damage image data and may cause other camera malfunctions.

Warning!

Inserting the memory card incorrectly may damage the camera.

Inserting the battery

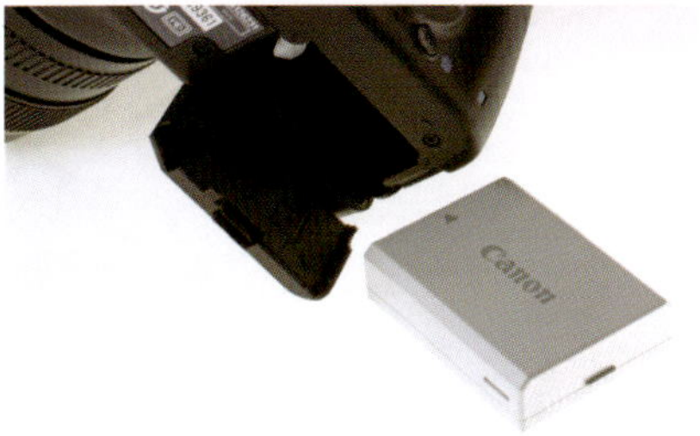

Turn the camera upside down and locate the battery compartment on the right side. Using a fingernail, release the catch and open the compartment. With the projecting battery contacts downward, press the battery against the hinged white plastic catch on the left of the battery compartment and insert the battery until it locks in position. Shut the battery compartment cover until there is an audible click. To remove the battery, ease the white plastic retaining clip to the side. Once it is removed, a battery should have its protective cover attached to prevent shorting.

Using AC power

By using the AC Adapter Kit ACK-E5 (available separately) you can connect the Rebel T1i/EOS 500D to an AC power outlet instead of using battery power.

1) Connect the power cord to the AC adapter first and then to the power outlet.

2) Connect the adapter's cord to the DC Coupler DR-E5.

3) Open the battery compartment, remove the battery, and insert the DC Coupler until you feel it lock in position.

4) Flick back the small rubber DC cord cover and press the cord into the notch. Close the battery compartment cover.

Battery charging

The dedicated Battery Charger LC-E5E should be used to charge the battery provided with the camera. Remove the protective cover and insert the battery into the charger. Connect the power cord to the charger and insert the plug into an AC outlet.

Recharging is indicated by a red lamp. This will turn green when the battery is fully charged. A fully discharged battery will take approximately two hours to charge.

Warning!

Never connect or disconnect the power cord while the camera is switched on.

Battery life

Battery life depends on many factors, including use of the Live View, image review, and built-in flash functions, choice of lens, auto power-off setting, and the length of time the shutter button is kept partially depressed (as when tracking a moving subject). The symbol ▬ indicates a full battery, while ▭ means it is nearly empty. The table below is a rough guide to the number of exposures you can take with a single LP-E5 battery.

Diopter adjustment

Using the Rebel T1i/EOS 500D without spectacles or contact lenses is facilitated by the eyepiece diopter adjustment. To use it, turn the knob so that the AF points in the viewfinder are sharp. If this does not provide enough adjustment, ten different versions of the Dioptric Adjustment Lens E are available separately.

Temperature	No flash	50% flash
73°F (23°C)	600 exposures	500 exposures
32°F (0°C)	500 exposures	400 exposures

Tips

The battery charger can be used abroad (100–240v AC 50/60 Hz) with a commercially available travel plug adapter. Do not attach any form of voltage transformer as this may damage the battery charger.

If your battery runs out quickly and needs frequent recharging, check the Auto power-off (Set-up menu 1) and Image review time (Shooting menu 1) settings to see if you can save power.

Even when it is not in use, your battery will gradually lose its charge. Remove it if the camera is to remain unused for a long period. Storing the battery after it is fully recharged may have a negative effect on the battery's performance.

The camera's stated operating range is 32–104°F (0–40°C) but the battery may not perform optimally in temperatures of 86–104°F (30–40°C) or 32–50°F (0–10°C).

Basic camera functions

Switching the camera on

The power switch is incorporated into the Mode Dial on the top of the camera and provides a simple on/off switch. Care should be taken not to accidentally change the Mode Dial setting when switching the camera on or off.

Sensor cleaning takes place automatically each time you turn the camera on or off. A message to this effect is displayed briefly on the LCD monitor on the back of the camera. Automatic sensor cleaning can be disabled in Set-up menu 2.

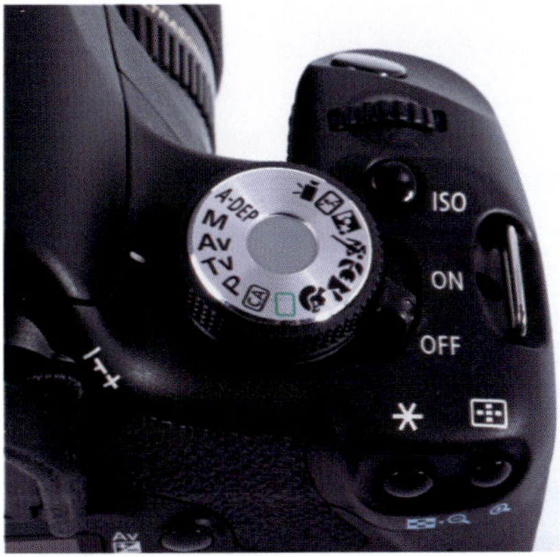

Tips

If the camera is set to power-off automatically after a set interval (Set-up menu 1), partially depressing the shutter button will fully reactivate the camera.

If the power switch is turned to **OFF** while an image file is being written, the camera will finish recording the image before turning itself off.

Common errors

The self-timer setting (indeed any Drive mode setting) is not canceled when the camera is switched off.

Always check your battery's charge level before setting out, especially if you anticipate making extensive use of flash. Even better, take a fully charged spare battery with you.

Drive mode

The Canon Rebel T1i/EOS 500D provides two frame-advance modes, Single and Continuous, and three self-timer settings.

Frame-advance in each of the Basic Zone settings is selected automatically, with **Continuous** selected in Portrait and Sports modes and **Single** in all other Basic Zone modes. Each mode allows frame-advance to be changed to self-timer.

In all Creative Zone modes, either Single or Continuous shooting is possible up to a maximum of approximately 3.4 frames per second.

Burst size when using Continuous will decrease when **2:Strong** is selected for **High ISO speed noise reduction** in the Custom Functions menu (see page 117).

Self-timer settings are available for both 2-second ⏲2 and 10-second ⏲ single-frame shots. The camera offers a useful third alternative in the form of a 10-second self-timer that provides programmable Continuous frame-advance ⏲C. This can be set to shoot 2–10 images.

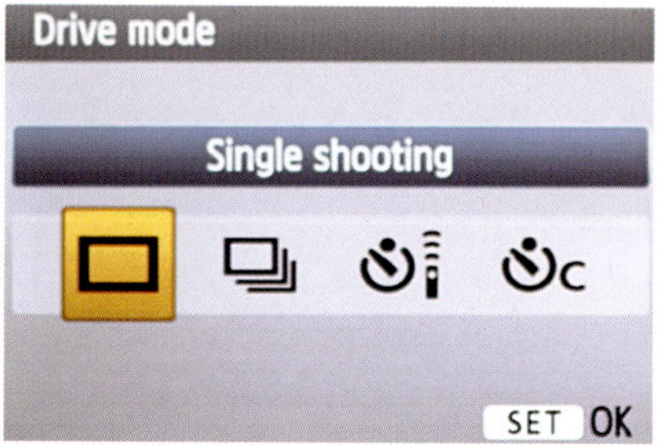

To set the Drive mode or self-timer:

1) Press the ◀ button to display the menu.

2) Use the ◀ and ▶ buttons to scroll through the selection.

3) If selecting ⏲C, use the ▲ and ▼ buttons to adjust the number of frames.

4) Press **SET** to select the desired setting.

Note
When ⏲C is selected, there is a 10-second delay between pressing the shutter release and the first exposure. Thereafter the shots are continuous, possibly with a brief delay between frames while the data is written to the memory card.

Mode Dial

The Mode Dial provides 14 different shooting modes, each of which will be explained in detail later in this chapter. These modes are divided into the Basic Zone and the Creative Zone.

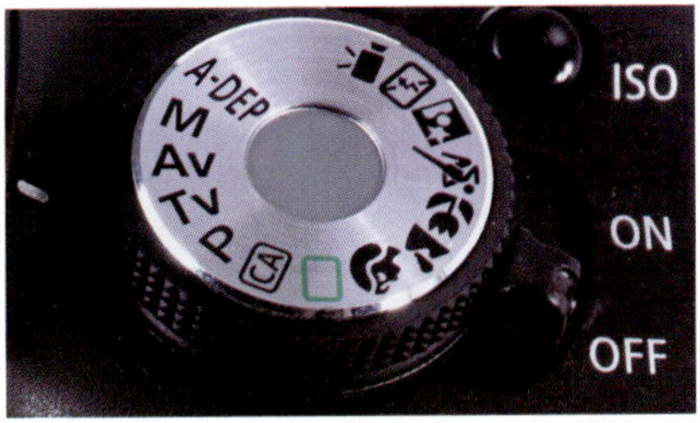

The Basic Zone provides eight fully automated modes for different types of subject, each indicated by an icon. The Creative Zone has six advanced modes offering total control of all camera settings. To select a particular mode, turn the dial until the desired mode's icon is lined up with the mark on the camera body.

Mode Dial

Basic Zone		**Creative Zone**	
Full Auto		Creative Auto	**CA**
Portrait		Program	**P**
Landscape		Shutter Priority	**Tv**
Close-up		Aperture Priority	**Av**
Sports		Manual	**M**
Night Portrait		Auto depth of field	**A-DEP**
Flash off			
Movie mode			

Operating the shutter-release button

The shutter-release button has two functions. Partially depressing it brings into play the autofocus and metering functions. Pressing it fully releases the shutter and takes the picture using the focus and exposure settings that were registered when you only partially depressed the shutter release. If the shutter-release button is fully depressed immediately, there will be a momentary delay before the picture is taken.

If you have purchased the Battery Grip BG-E5 to go with your camera, then exactly the same applies to the additional shutter-release button provided on the battery grip for vertical shooting.

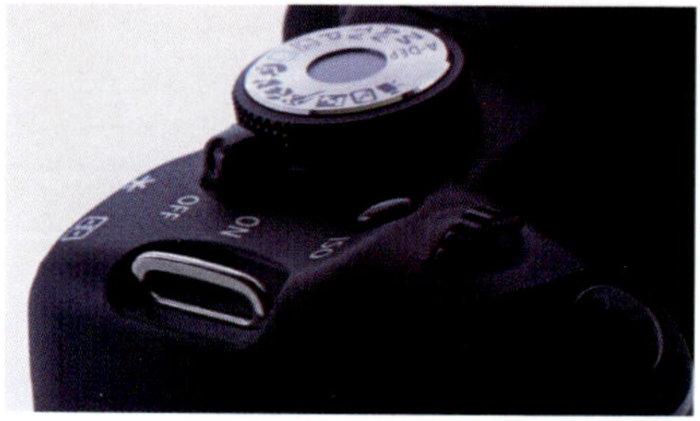

Tip
Even while menus are displayed or an image is being reviewed or recorded, the Rebel T1i/EOS 500D will immediately go to picture-taking readiness when you partially depress the shutter-release button (unless the buffer is full). This means you will very rarely miss an opportunity to take a picture.

Operating the Main Dial

The Main Dial next to the shutter-release button is used for adjustments to the settings required for shooting. It is used sometimes on its own, and on other occasions after depressing a button to select the function you wish to adjust.

In **P** mode the Main Dial used on its own will adjust both aperture and shutter speed while retaining the equivalent exposure. Used on its own in **Tv** and **M** modes, the Main Dial adjusts the shutter speed, and in **Av** mode it will adjust the aperture.

Holding down the **Av+/-** button while rotating the Main Dial will set the amount of exposure compensation in any Creative Zone mode—except in Manual mode, when it only adjusts the aperture.

All of these functions are explained in more detail later in this chapter.

Focusing

The Rebel T1i/EOS 500D accepts EF and EF-S lenses, both of which are equipped with an AF/MF switch so you can change to manual focusing. This may be necessary in very low light or when focusing on something with insufficient contrast for an AF point to latch onto. It may also be useful when photographing landscapes to obtain maximum depth of field, or when taking extreme close-ups—especially if you are using the ×5 or ×10 magnification facility in Live View mode.

The camera is equipped with nine AF points which may function as a group or can be selected singly (see page 68). Three AF modes cover most eventualities:

One Shot mode

When you partially depress the shutter release button the camera will focus just once on the subject. It will not refocus until you withdraw the pressure and partially depress the shutter-release button again.

When focus is achieved, both the green ● focus confirmation light and the red AF point(s) that achieved focus will be visible in the viewfinder. There will also be a **beep** unless this has been switched off in Shooting menu 1. If you continue to hold down the shutter-release button, focus will be locked and you will be able to recompose your photograph.

AI Servo mode

This facility is particularly useful when the camera-to-subject distance keeps changing. While you partially depress the shutter-release button, the camera will continue to readjust focus automatically. The exposure settings will be fixed at the moment the picture is taken.

When AF point selection is automatic and AI Servo is selected, the camera will use the center AF point first to achieve focus. It is therefore necessary to place your subject centrally at the start or focus may track the wrong subject. If the subject moves away from the center AF point during focus tracking, tracking will continue as long as the subject is covered by an alternative AF point.

In AI Servo mode, the **beep** will not sound and the ● focus confirmation light will not be displayed in the viewfinder.

AI Focus

In AI Focus mode, the Rebel T1i/EOS 500D will automatically switch between One Shot and AI Servo modes according to subject movement. If focus is achieved using One Shot mode but the subject starts to move, the camera will shift to AI Servo mode and track the subject provided you keep the shutter-release button partially depressed.

Unlike with AI Servo mode fully selected, if focus is achieved while AI Servo is active in AI Focus mode, then the **beep** will sound, but more softly than normal. However, the ● focus confirmation light still does not light up in the viewfinder.

Tip

If focus cannot be achieved, the ● focus confirmation light will blink and you will not be able to take a picture even if you fully depress the shutter-release button. Under these circumstances, select the center AF point in one of the Creative Zone modes or, if in a Basic Zone mode, reposition the camera and try again or switch the lens to manual focus.

Depth of field preview

The depth of field preview button is located on the left side of the front of the camera, just below the lens release button. Pressing this button will stop the lens down to the currently selected aperture, providing a more accurate impression of the range of acceptable focus. A smaller aperture will provide greater depth of field but the viewfinder will appear increasingly dark as you stop down. Exposure will be locked while the depth of field preview button is depressed.

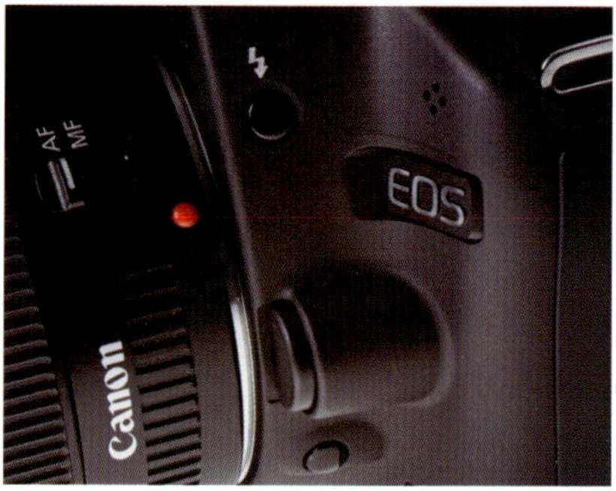

ISO setting

The ISO speed is the sensor's sensitivity to light and effectively governs the combined exposure values of aperture and shutter speed. A higher ISO speed enables a faster shutter speed and is therefore more useful in low light. However, higher ISO speeds produce more "noise," especially when shooting in a hot environment. The slower the ISO speed, the crisper the final image.

In **P**, **Tv**, **Av**, **M**, and **A-DEP** modes the ISO can be set manually in the range 100–3200, expandable to 6400 and (H) 12800. However, if Highlight tone priority is enabled the range is limited to ISO 200–3200. Auto ISO can also be selected in these shooting modes but it will be limited to a range of 100–1600, except in **M** when it will be fixed at ISO 400.

In all other modes ISO is automatically set in the range 100–1600 (except in Portrait when it will be fixed at ISO 100) and cannot be overridden.

1) To set the ISO speed, press the **DISP** button followed by the **ISO** button next to the Main Dial. The ISO setting screen will be displayed on the LCD monitor.

2) Use the ▲ and ▼ buttons (or rotate the) to select the desired ISO and press **SET** to save the setting. The setting is shown both in the viewfinder and on the LCD monitor.

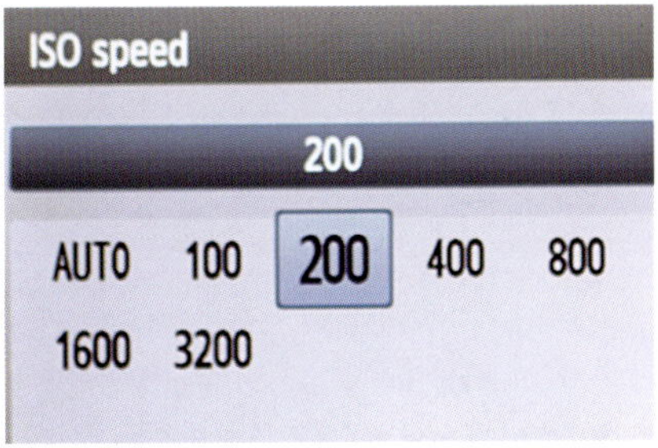

Tips

Doubling the ISO figure is equivalent to a one-stop reduction in exposure.

When Auto ISO is selected and the shutter button is partially depressed, the ISO speed chosen by the camera will be displayed temporarily in the viewfinder and on the LCD monitor.

Manually set ISO speeds use 1-stop increments. Auto ISO speeds will only be displayed with 1-stop increments but may actually use ⅓-stop increments, in which case the more accurate figure will be recorded in the image data.

Increasing the ISO speed also increases the effective range of a built-in or external flash.

Built-in flash

The built-in flash operates automatically in all Basic Zone modes except Landscape, Sports, and No Flash modes, in which it is disabled. In Creative Zone modes it can be raised and activated by pressing the small button on the front of the camera, just above the lens-release button. When the built-in flash is active and charged, the ϟ Flash symbol will appear in the viewfinder at bottom left.

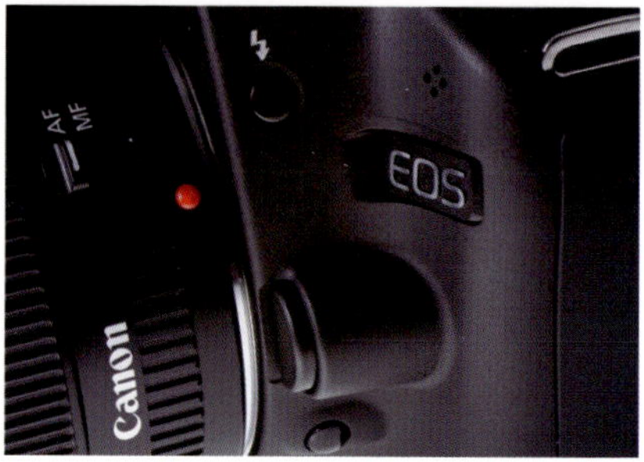

When the flash is recycling, ϟ **buSY** will be displayed in the viewfinder and **BUSY** ϟ on the LCD monitor.

In **P** mode a shutter speed of 1/60–1/200 sec will be selected automatically.

In **Av** mode the shutter speed can adjusted using C.Fn-3 (see page 116) to one of the following three settings: Auto, 1/60–1/200 sec auto, or 1/200 sec fixed.

In **M** the flash sync speed can be set within the range 30–1/200 sec or bulb. If **bulb** is selected, you are advised to enable **Long exp. noise reduction** via the Custom Functions menu (see page 117).

Red-eye reduction can be enabled via Shooting menu 1 in all modes except , , , and .

The Rebel T1i/EOS 500D also supports high-speed flash synchronization with EX Speedlites. The ϟH symbol will be displayed in the viewfinder in conjunction with shutter speeds exceeding 1/200sec. In **Av** mode flash sync must be set to **Auto** using C.Fn-3 (see page 116).

Metering modes

The Rebel T1i/EOS 500D provides four different metering modes which cover any eventuality:

Evaluative metering

This system is capable of coping with a wide range of lighting situations including backlighting and takes readings from 35 different zones. Evaluative metering is used for all Basic Zone modes.

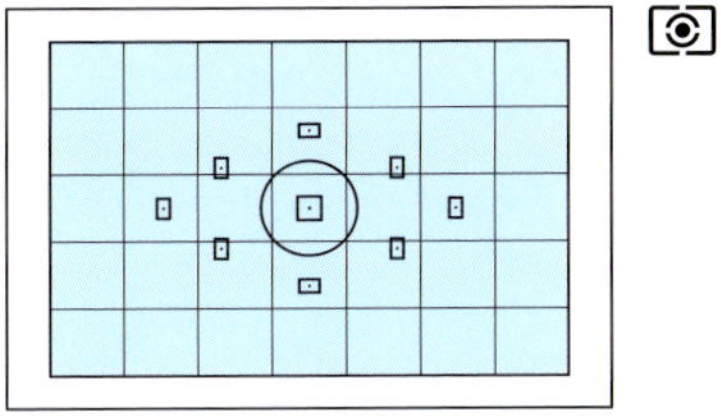

Center-weighted average metering

This metering system gives added bias to readings taken from the center of the frame, then averages readings from the whole area. This mode is only selectable in Creative Zone modes.

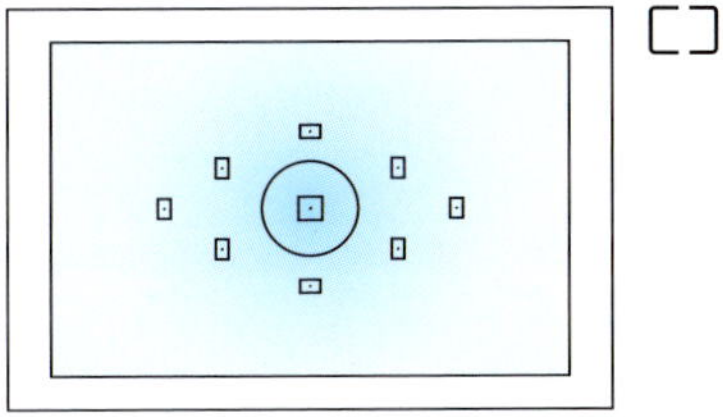

Partial metering

This mode takes readings from just 9% of the frame at the center and is especially useful in cases when the background is significantly brighter than the subject. It can also be used, in effect, as a spot meter with a larger than normal "spot." Only selectable in Creative Zone modes.

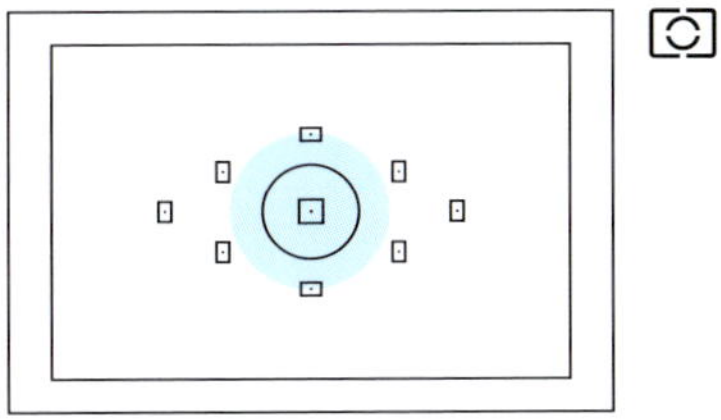

Spot metering

Spot metering mode takes readings from just 4% of the frame and is useful when metering from a small area of midtone equivalent to 18% gray or for a biased result such as when shooting a silhouette against a sunset.

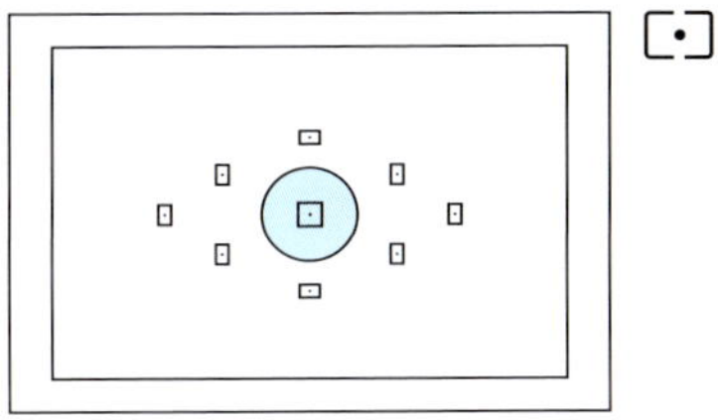

White balance presets

Press the **WB** button on the back of the camera to select Auto WB AWB or one of six predetermined settings, or to set up a Custom WB setting. The correct setting from the examples below is the Daylight setting. Not available in Basic Zone modes or Creative Auto.

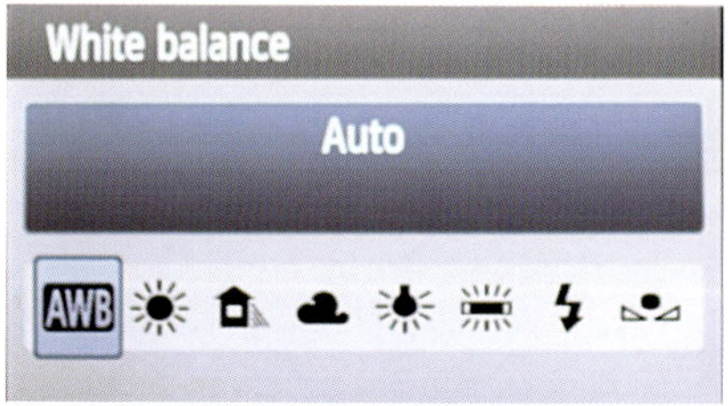

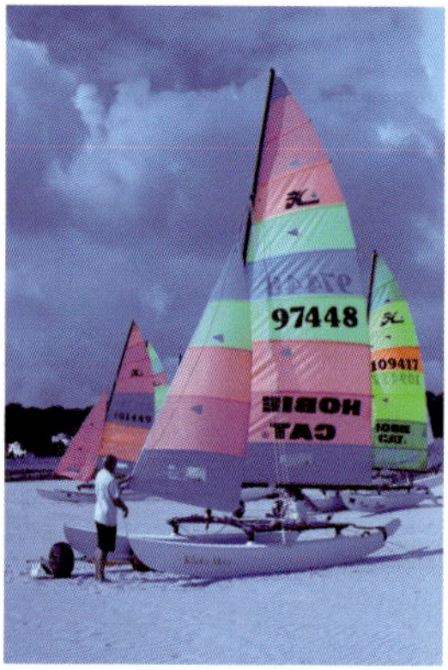

Min color temp. 2500°K

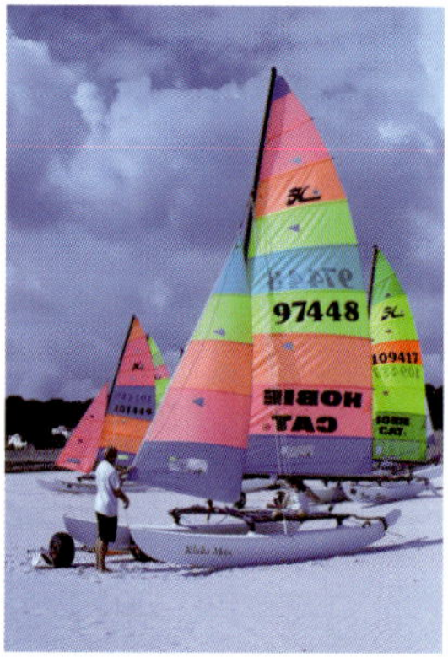

Tungsten 3200°K

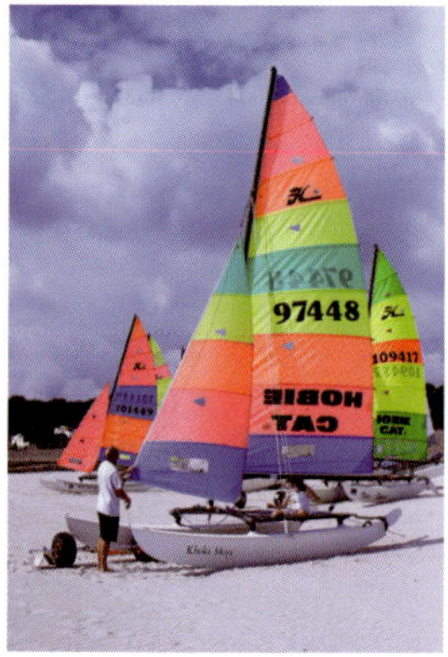

White fluorescent 4000°K

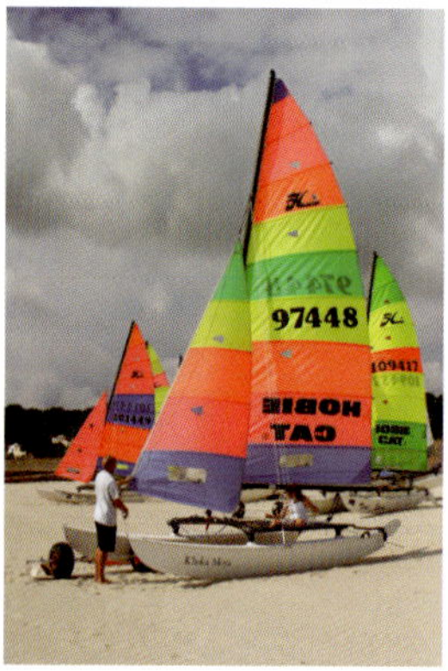

Daylight 5200°K

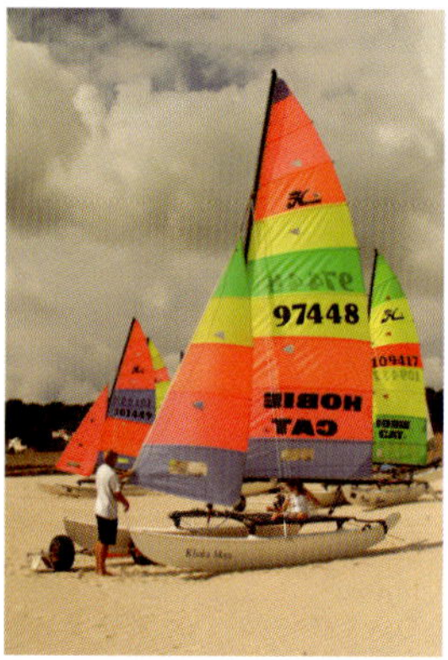

Shade 7000°K

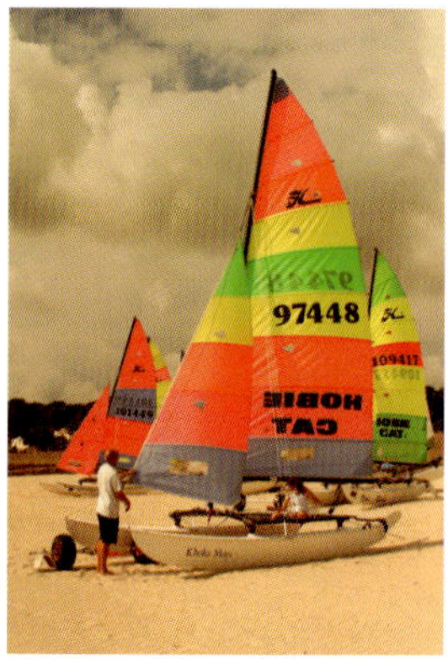

Max color temp. 10,000°K

Image playback

Using Shooting menu 1, immediate automatic playback of an image can be disabled or enabled for a duration of 2, 4, or 8 seconds, or displayed indefinitely.

All the images on the memory card can be manually reviewed by pressing the ▶ Playback button on the back of the camera. The first image to be shown will be the most recent or the last viewed. Use the ◀ and ▶ buttons to scroll through the images one at a time.

Press the **DISP** button to change the display style. The styles available are Single image, Single image with file-quality setting, Shooting information with either Brightness or RGB histogram (selectable in ▶ Playback menu), or both histograms with limited shooting information. When any histogram display is selected, the Automatic highlight alert will cause overexposed or very bright areas to blink. You may need to shoot the image again, reducing the exposure.

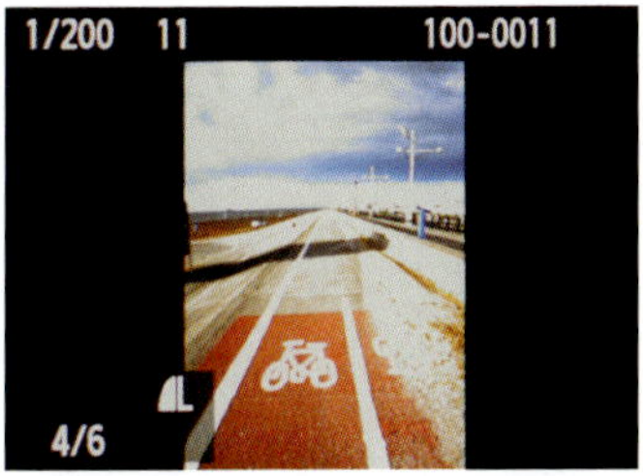

Single image with file-quality setting

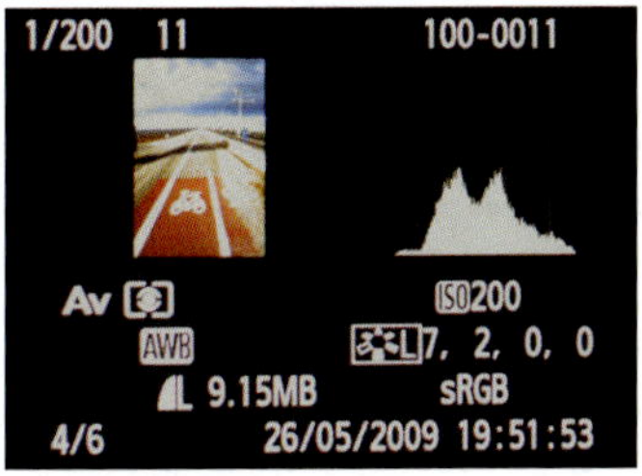

Shooting information with Brightness histogram

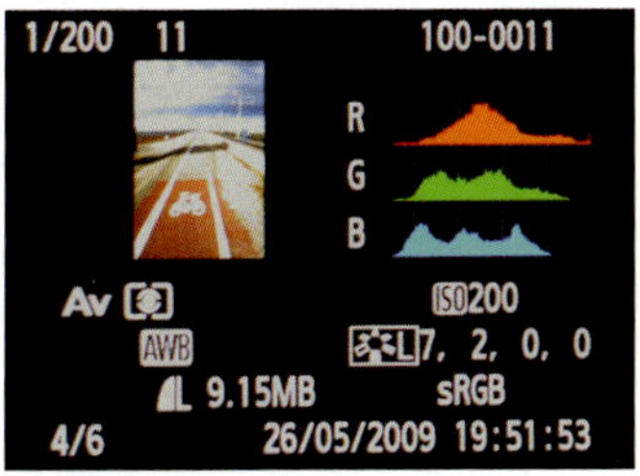

Shooting information with RGB histogram

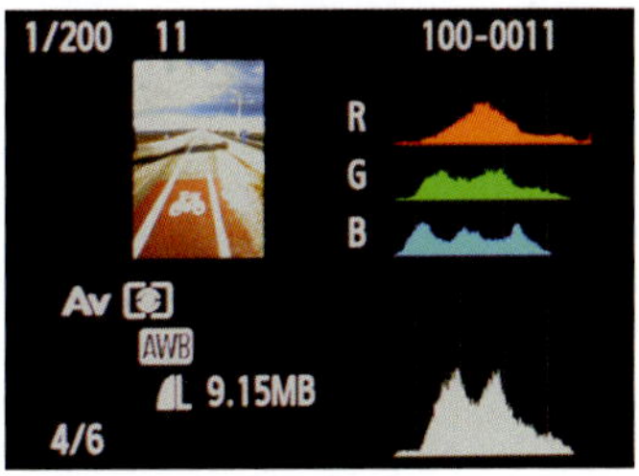

Both histograms with limited shooting information

Magnifying or reducing images during playback

During image playback you can zoom into the image by repeatedly pressing the ⊡/⊕ button. Use the ◀▶▲▼ buttons to move around the magnified image. The ✱/⊞•⊖ button zooms out again in steps; alternatively, you can return to the full image view after zooming in by pressing the ▶ Playback button once.

If the ✱/⊞•⊖ Reduce button is pressed while an unmagnified image is displayed, the LCD monitor will display four images. If pressed a second time, nine images will be displayed. This multidisplay is referred to as the index display. The current image is highlighted in blue. To select a different image, use the ◀▶▲▼ buttons (or the Main Dial, depending on the selected setting for the Jump function).

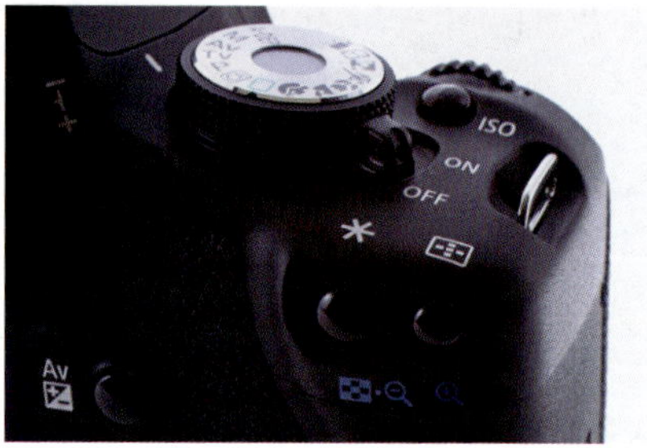

To exit playback, press the ▶ Playback button again.

Jump

You can set the Jump function to jump 1, 10, or 100 images at a time during playback, or to jump to the next date, movie, or still image.

With an image displayed in playback, press the ▲ button and scroll through the choices using the ▲ or ▼ buttons. Press **SET** to save your setting. Use the Main Dial during playback to operate the Jump facility.

Alternatively, the Jump setting can be adjusted in ▶: Playback menu 2.

Tips

If automatic review is active, the magnification function described above is not possible.

In ▶: Playback menu 2 you can select **Slide show** to run a slide show of images on the memory card. To pause Auto Play, press the **SET** button; press it again to resume the slide show. Press **MENU** to stop the slide show. During Auto Play the Auto power-off function will not work.

Rotating images

To rotate all portrait format images automatically, enable Auto Rotate in ͳT˙ Set-up menu 1. To rotate a single image during playback, press **MENU** and select ▶˙ Playback menu 1. Select **Rotate** and press **SET**. The display will return to Playback mode. Press **SET** again. The currently displayed image will rotate. Pressing **SET** repeatedly will rotate the image through different orientations.

Deleting images

Method 1

To delete a selected image during playback:

1) Press the 🗑 Erase button.

2) Confirm deletion by highlighting **Erase** and pressing **SET**. Alternatively, select **Cancel** and press **SET** to return to playback mode.

Method 2

To delete selected or all images via the menu system:

1) Press **MENU** and use the Main Dial to select ▶˙ Playback menu 1.

2) Use the ▲ or ▼ buttons to select **Erase images** and press **SET**.

3) Select either **Select and erase images** or **All images on card** and press **SET**.

4) To delete all the images on the card, select **All images on card** and press **SET**. A **Cancel/OK** option appears. Press **SET** to cancel or **OK** to erase the images.

5) To delete only selected images, choose **Select and erase images** and press **SET**.

6) Use the /🔍 and ✱/•🔍 buttons to choose between one, three, or nine images to be displayed.

7) Press ▲ or ▼ to add a white tick to a box above the highlighted image. Scroll through the images on the card using the ◀ and ▶ buttons and tick all those you wish to erase.

8) When your selection of images to erase is complete, press 🗑 Erase. A **Cancel/OK** option appears. Press **SET** to cancel or **OK** to erase the images.

FUNCTIONS

Protecting images

1) Press **MENU**. Select [▶] Playback menu 1 and then **Protect images**.

2) Use the [⊞]/⊕ and ✱/[⊞]•⊖ buttons to choose whether the monitor displays one, three, or nine images.

3) Select the image to be protected and press **SET**. A key symbol will be displayed at the left of the folder number at the top of the monitor screen. This indicates that the currently highlighted image is locked and cannot be deleted.

4) To remove protection from an image, select it and press **SET** again. The key symbol will disappear and the image is no longer protected.

Camera settings display

Normally, when the **DISP** button is pressed, the LCD monitor displays the Quick Control Screen (also known as the Shooting Settings display) for the mode selected on the Mode Dial. However, if the **DISP** button is pressed while one of the menus is displayed, the LCD monitor shows a summary of the current camera settings. It is not possible to make any adjustments to the settings from this screen.

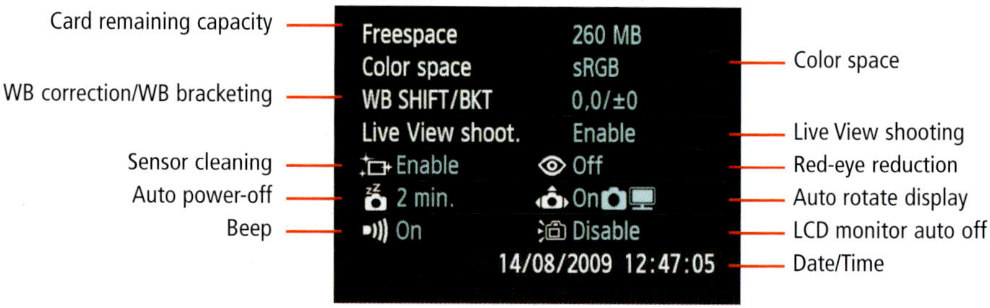

Exposure modes—the Basic Zone

The settings on the Mode Dial fall into two groups, one on either side of the green rectangle that identifies Full Auto mode. The group that makes use of symbols, and which includes Full Auto mode, is known as the Basic Zone. The other settings on the dial, which are denoted by letters of the alphabet, are known as the Creative Zone. In the Basic Zone, camera adjustments are extremely limited as it is assumed that, by selecting the appropriate symbol on the Mode Dial (e.g. Portrait mode), the photographer will want to use the camera for a specific purpose for which settings are predetermined by the manufacturer.

Photographic styles

Good images are rarely created by accident, at least not on a consistent basis. Certainly the best photographs are the product of, if not forethought and planning, then at least a sense of purpose. It is that intention, even if it is subconscious and intuitive in nature, that lies behind the concept of the Basic Zone.

The Basic Zone is primarily intended for those photographers who know what kind of images they want to achieve but do not yet have a deep understanding of the principles behind photography in general, and exposure in particular, nor breadth of experience. The latter can only be gained in time and with repeated experience of similar photographic situations.

Each symbol in the Basic Zone represents a photographic style. The Basic Zone symbols indicate automatic settings that, in general terms, will suit each of the following styles: Portrait, Landscape, Close-up, Sports, Night Portrait, and No Flash.

The settings for Full Auto mode are obviously a compromise. The Basic Zone assumes that, having determined either the nature of the subject or the style required, the user can select an appropriate mode, but thereafter all the decisions will be taken by the camera. This is typified by two of the three focus modes, AI Focus and AI Servo, in which AI stands for Artificial Intelligence.

The Auto Lighting Optimizer, a recent addition from Canon, adjusts predominantly dark or low-contrast images automatically in Basic Zone modes. The autofocus point is also selected automatically according to the position of what the camera deems to be the main subject. Full details for each Basic Zone mode can be found on the following pages.

Full Auto mode

Full Auto mode is a blessing for the less experienced photographer in situations where there is insufficient time to think carefully about camera settings and where lighting (and therefore exposure) is changeable; a children's party or family outing, for example. Basically, the camera does the thinking for you. This is often thought of as a basic mode but there is nothing basic about it at all, as it takes into account most of the settings over which you could have some control if you chose. The panel opposite indicates the various settings which the camera will select and which you cannot override. The built-in flash will automatically pop up into position if required and the AF-assist beam will be used to aid focusing in low light levels.

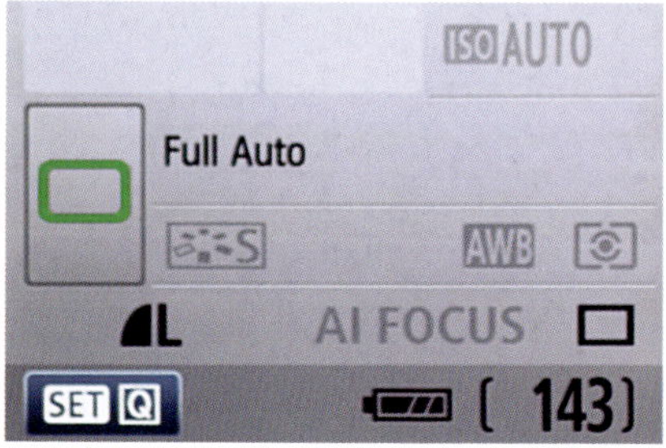

Tips
Full Auto mode is ideal for shooting scenes with average tones in favorable light, but when you need more control over your results, it is time to move on. Program mode is the next logical step up as it selects most of the settings for you but permits you to override them.

When you lock focus using partial pressure on the shutter release, the red AF point(s) illuminated when focus is achieved do not remain lit. However, the green focus indicator ● in the bottom right of the viewfinder does remain illuminated to indicate that focus is locked while you recompose your picture.

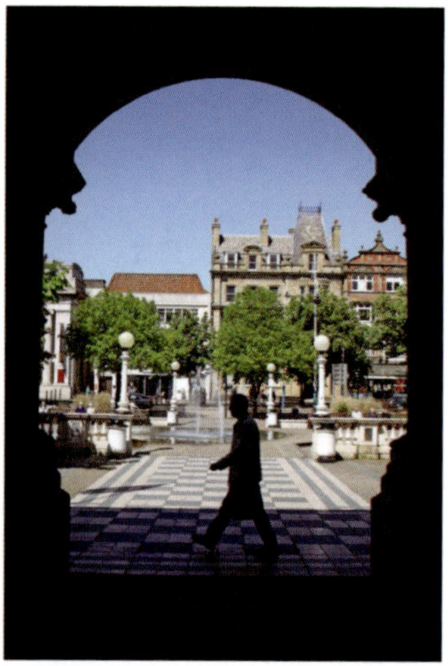

GRAB SHOT
Full Auto mode is ideal when you see a situation about to unfold but don't have time to consider camera settings.

Full Auto mode	
Quality setting	Six JPEG settings; RAW; RAW+Large/fine JPEG
Exposure settings	Evaluative metering; shutter speed and aperture are chosen to suit the light levels and subject; Auto ISO; Standard Picture Style; Auto White Balance; Auto Lighting Optimizer; Long exposure noise reduction; selectable Peripheral illumination correction
Focus settings	Automatic AF point selection in AI Focus mode (the camera will automatically select AI Servo mode if it detects subject movement and will track it if you keep the shutter button partially depressed)
Frame advance	Single frame advance; self-timer (10 sec and continuous)
Flash	Automatic flash and automatic fill-in flash; red-eye reduction; AF-assist beam, effective up to 13ft (4m); first-curtain sync
Notes	Full Auto is easy to use and gives pleasing results in situations where the action and lighting are less challenging.

Using Full Auto mode

1) Turn the Mode Dial to ▭.

2) Aim the camera at your subject. Focusing may be easier by placing the center AF point over the main subject. You can recompose the picture later.

3) Lightly press the shutter button to achieve focus. The in-focus Indicator ● and automatically selected AF points will illuminate briefly. Exposure settings (aperture and speed) will appear at the bottom of the viewfinder on the left; the automatically selected ISO speed and available burst settings on the right.

4) In low light levels, the built-in flash will pop up and the flash symbol ϟ will show at the bottom left of the viewfinder. The built-in flash may also operate in bright conditions to reduce shadows.

5) Retain light pressure on the shutter button to keep the focus locked and recompose the picture before depressing the button fully to take the photograph.

6) After a very brief delay, the captured image will display on the LCD monitor for two seconds unless the review function has been adjusted or switched off.

Creative Auto mode

Creative Auto mode adopts the same default settings used by Full Auto mode but introduces the possibility of overriding certain settings. It offers an intermediate step between Full Auto mode and Program mode.

The two adjustable settings which mark a new approach from Canon are, first, the option to adjust the degree of background blur and, second, the ability to adjust overall image brightness. Each of these adjustments is achieved using a +/-2 sliding scale on the Quick Control Screen. The background-blur scale adjusts the selected aperture in order to change the depth of field, with the corresponding shutter speed changing accordingly—in effect providing the same function as Program Shift in Program mode. However, the function is presented simply, with a desired result in mind (a more- or less-blurred background) without touching on the technicalities of aperture and depth of field.

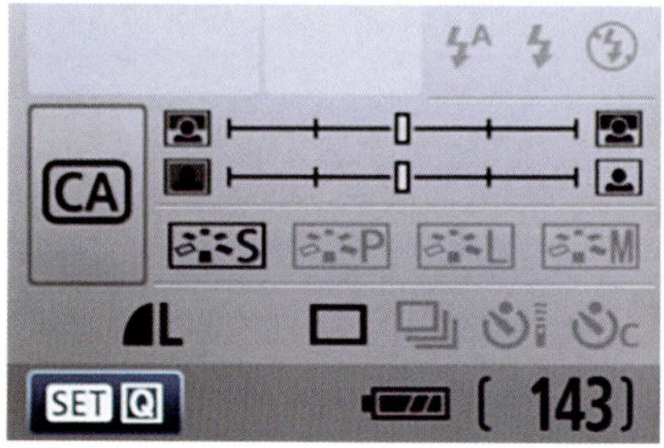

The brightness scale is essentially a means of providing exposure compensation, again concentrating on the desired result while avoiding the need to explain the business of exposure and the relative properties of aperture and shutter speed.

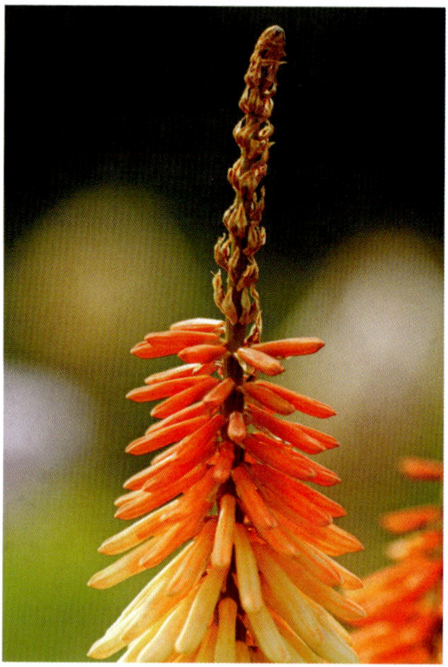

BACKGROUND BLUR
Creative Auto mode allows you to adjust the degree of background blur. This is especially useful for isolating detail.

Creative Auto mode

Quality setting	Six JPEG settings; RAW; RAW+Large/fine JPEG
Exposure settings	Evaluative metering using 35 different zones; shutter speed and aperture are set automatically but can be adjusted to increase or decrease background blur or overall brightness; Auto ISO; Picture Styles: Standard, Portrait, Landscape, or Monochrome; Auto White Balance; Auto Lighting Optimizer; Long exposure noise reduction; Peripheral illumination correction
Focus settings	Automatic AF point selection in AI Focus mode (will automatically switch to AI Servo mode if linear subject movement is detected, tracking the subject as long it is covered by the AF points and you continue to partially depress the shutter button)
Frame advance	Single frame advance; continuous; self-timer (10 sec and continuous)
Flash	Automatic flash and automatic fill-in flash; red-eye reduction; AF-assist beam, effective up to 13ft (4m); first curtain sync.

Using Creative Auto mode

1) Turn the Mode Dial to **CA**. Display the Quick Control Screen (press **DISP** if it is not displayed automatically).

2) Press **SET**. One of the selectable functions will be highlighted. Use the ◀▶▲▼ buttons to select a different function, then rotate the Main Dial to change the setting.

3) Aim the camera at your subject. Focusing may be easier by placing the center AF point over the main subject. You can recompose the picture later.

4) Lightly press the shutter button to achieve focus. The in-focus indicator ● and automatically selected AF points will be illuminated in the viewfinder. The exposure settings (aperture and speed) will appear at the bottom of the viewfinder.

5) In low light levels the built-in flash will pop up (unless it was deactivated in step 2) and the flash symbol ϟ will appear in the viewfinder. The flash may also operate in bright conditions to reduce shadows.

6) Follow steps 5–6 on page 47.

Portrait mode

Traditionally, portraits tend to be head-and-shoulders images with a vertical orientation (hence the term "portrait format"). However, there are plenty of portrait situations that benefit from landscape orientation, particularly when photographing someone in the context of their activity or profession.

Perspective and choice of lens or zoom setting are particularly important with portraits, as it is all too easy to distort the subject's features. Wide-angle lenses make the features closest to the camera look disproportionately large, while longer telephotos tend to "flatten" facial features. The traditional favorite for head-only portraits is a fast lens of around 85mm focal length (approx. 50mm on the Rebel T1i/EOS 500D due to its crop factor of 1.6) with a 50mm lens (approx. 30mm on the Rebel T1i/EOS 500D) being fine for upper-body portraits.

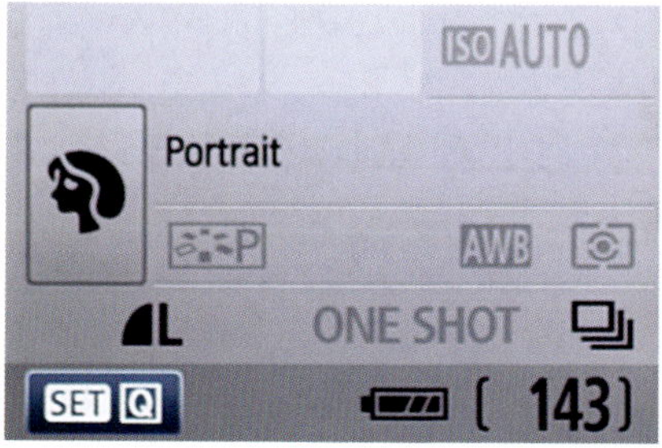

Tip
In portraits, the subject's eyes are critically important in terms of focus and clarity. If at all possible try to include "catchlights"—sharp points of light created by flash, natural, or reflected light.

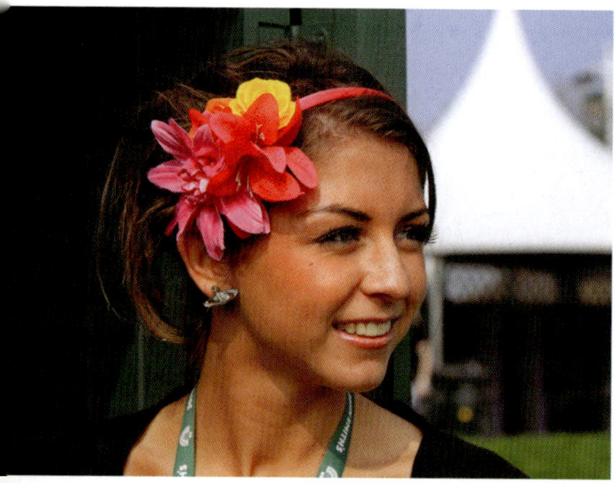

A QUESTION OF STYLE
Portraits do not have to be formal. In fact, more personality often shows through when the subject is captured off-guard.

Portrait mode	
Quality setting	Six JPEG settings; RAW; RAW+Large/fine JPEG
Exposure settings	Evaluative metering; a wide aperture is selected to blur the background, accentuating the subject; Auto ISO; Portrait Picture Style; Auto White Balance; Auto Lighting Optimizer; Long exposure noise reduction; selectable Peripheral illumination correction
Focus settings	Automatic AF point selection in One Shot focus mode
Frame advance	Continuous shooting; self-timer (10 sec and continuous)
Flash	Automatic flash and automatic fill-in flash; red-eye reduction; AF-assist beam, effective up to 13ft (4m); first curtain sync
Notes	The camera selects a color setting to improve flesh tones, plus a less sharp result than Full Auto to soften hair and wrinkles.

Using Portrait mode

1) Turn the Mode Dial to [Portrait icon].

2) Aim the camera at your subject. Pay attention to framing and to the background, which may contain distracting elements.

3) Lightly press the shutter button to achieve focus. The in-focus indicator ● and automatically selected AF points will be illuminated in the viewfinder. The exposure settings (aperture and speed), the selected ISO, and the number of burst exposures possible will also appear.

4) In low light levels the built-in flash will pop up and the ϟ flash symbol will show bottom left in the viewfinder. (When you've finished taking the photographs that are likely to require flash, push the built-in flash unit back down manually.) The built-in flash may also operate in bright conditions to reduce shadows.

5) Retain light pressure on the shutter button to keep the focus locked and recompose the picture before depressing the button fully to take the photograph.

6) After a very brief delay, the captured image will display on the LCD monitor for two seconds, unless the review function has been adjusted or switched off.

Landscape mode

While photos of family and friends tend to be the most popular subjects for less ambitious amateur snappers, there's no doubt that those who aspire to be better photographers tend to favor scenic photography in one form or another. The reasons are obvious: an unlimited supply of vistas that change all the time according to the weather, the light, seasonal variations, and our own perceptions of them depending on our mood. I have never met a serious landscape photographer who felt that he or she had run out of challenges.

A high percentage of scenic photographs are taken using wide-angle lenses (or wide zoom settings). Wide-angles maximize depth of field, encompass a broader scene, and accentuate foreground, providing a better sense of depth.

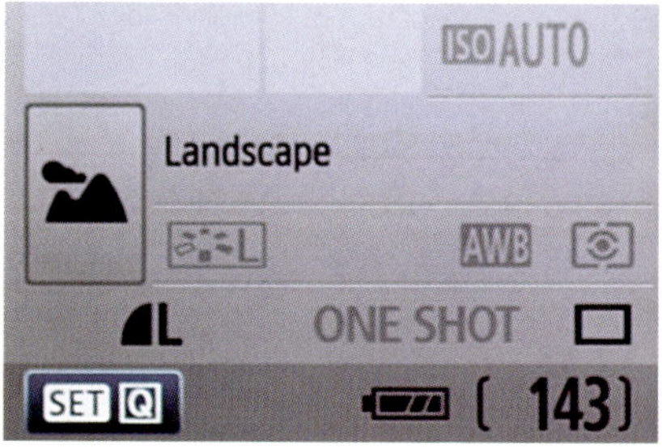

Using the camera in the vertical ("portrait") position is a simple way to accentuate foreground without using a particularly wide lens.

Common errors

Keep an eye on the shutter speed indicated in the viewfinder. If it blinks, this indicates the risk of camera shake, so use a tripod or find an alternative form of support for the camera.

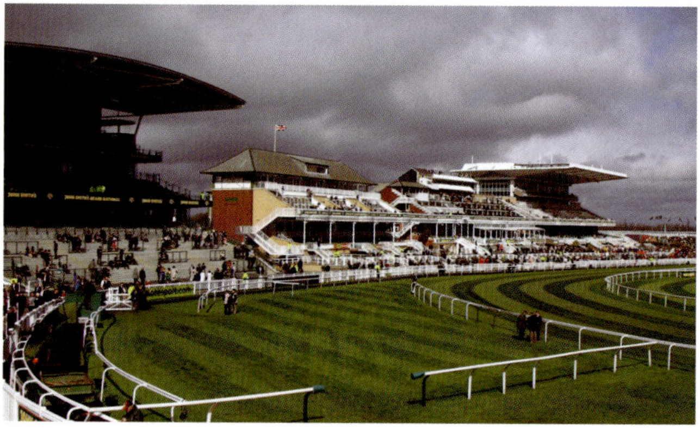

AINTREE RACECOURSE, UK
Landscape mode provides rich greens and additional depth to shadow areas.

Landscape mode	
Quality setting	Six JPEG settings; RAW; RAW+Large/fine JPEG
Exposure settings	Evaluative metering; a narrow aperture is chosen to maximize depth of field while retaining a shutter speed sufficient to permit handheld shooting; Auto ISO; Landscape Picture Style; Auto White Balance; Auto Lighting Optimizer; Long exposure noise reduction; selectable Peripheral illumination correction
Focus settings	Automatic AF point selection in One Shot focus mode
Frame advance	Single frame advance; self-timer (10 sec and continuous)
Flash	Flash and AF-assist beam are switched off
Notes	Also useful for night scenes with a tripod, because the built-in flash will be automatically disabled.

Using Landscape mode

1) Turn the Mode Dial to [landscape icon].

2) Aim the camera at your subject. Make sure you pay close attention to framing and to the foreground, which may contain distracting elements such as litter.

3) Lightly press the shutter button to achieve focus. The in-focus indicator ● will illuminate in the viewfinder. The automatically selected AF points will illuminate briefly, accompanied by a beep (unless the beep has been disabled in [camera icon] Shooting menu 1). The exposure settings (aperture and speed) appear at the bottom of the viewfinder on the left, with the automatically selected ISO speed and available burst on the right.

4) Retain light pressure on the shutter button to lock focus. You can recompose the picture before fully depressing the shutter button to take the photograph.

5) After a very brief delay, the captured image will be displayed on the LCD monitor for two seconds, unless the review function has been adjusted or switched off.

Close-up mode

The terms "close-up" and "macro" are used differently in this book. Macro, properly speaking, means a life-size image (i.e. at a magnification ratio of 1:1) and requires the use of either a special macro lens or extension tubes, plus a good understanding of depth of field, exposure, and lighting issues. More on this subject can be found in Chapter 6. For now, though, a close-up is defined as an image that is captured at the closest focusing distance of the lens being used.

As a generalization, the maximum magnification ratio of a lens tends to be between one-tenth and one-fifth life-size, but it varies enormously between lenses, even among those of similar focal lengths.

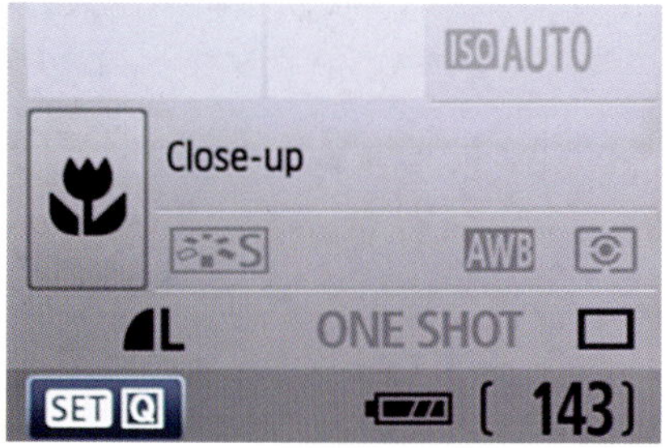

In calculating exposure, good depth of field and a higher shutter speed are traded off against each other, so any automatic settings selected by the camera will always be a compromise. This is true of all exposure modes, but the high magnification ratios involved here make it a particular concern. Good depth of field and a higher shutter speed may be necessary when shooting close-ups outdoors, but Close-up mode chooses your ISO setting for you and cannot be overridden, so you will have to rely on plenty of light, preferably diffuse light rather than strong direct light.

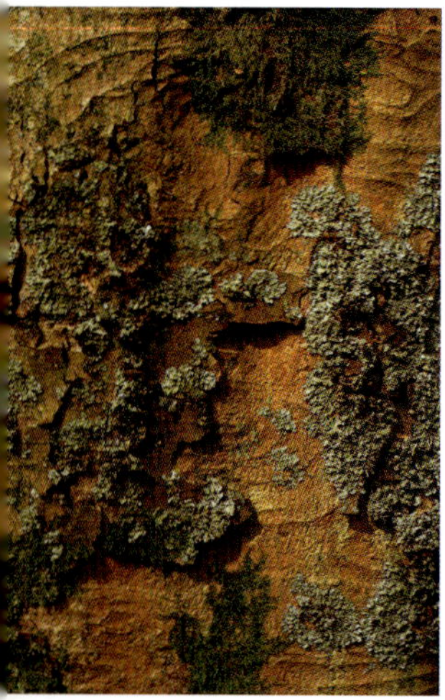

TREE BARK
The wonderful thing about close-up photography is that it teaches us to look more closely at the things around us. There is never a shortage of potential subjects.

Common errors

For close-ups, any movement of either camera or subject must be avoided. The greater the magnification, the more important this becomes, so a tripod and remote release are invaluable tools.

Close-up mode	
Quality setting	Six JPEG settings; RAW; RAW+Large/fine JPEG
Exposure settings	Evaluative metering; shutter speed, aperture and ISO are chosen to suit the light levels and subject; Standard Picture Style; Auto White Balance; Auto Lighting Optimizer; Long exposure noise reduction; selectable Peripheral illumination correction
Focus settings	Automatic AF point selection in One Shot focus mode
Frame advance	Single frame advance; self-timer (10 sec and continuous)
Flash	Automatic fill-in flash, red-eye reduction, first curtain sync, AF-assist beam
Notes	Autofocus will pick out the closest subject, so if you are photographing flowers, make sure there are no wisps of grass or other plants between the lens and the subject.

Using Close-up mode

1) Turn the Mode Dial to 🌷.

2) Aim the camera at your subject. Set your zoom lens to its longest focal length.

3) If using a tripod, set the frame advance mode to self-timer or use a remote release to minimize camera shake.

4) Lightly press the shutter button to achieve focus. If the lens cannot focus, change the camera position. (If focus still proves difficult, adjust the AF/MF switch on the lens to MF and focus manually.)
If the in-focus indicator ● blinks, you may be too close to the subject.

5) The automatically selected AF points will illuminate briefly in the viewfinder, accompanied by a beep (unless disabled in 📷 Shooting menu 1).

6) In low light levels the built-in flash will pop up and the ϟ Flash symbol will appear in the viewfinder. The built-in flash may also operate in bright conditions to reduce shadows.

7) Depress the shutter. After the Auto Review image has been displayed, press ▶ to play back the image and use the ☷/🔍 button to magnify it and check sharpness in key areas.

Sports mode

For sports, read any situation where your subject matter is on the move: that might include festivals, children at play, your pets, school events, and a host of other activities.

Like the other Basic Zone modes, Sports mode makes use of evaluative metering to select the exposure. The emphasis will be on a higher shutter speed, so unless it's very bright, you are likely to be working with a wider aperture and consequent loss of depth of field. In order to keep the moving subject in focus, the camera uses AI Servo to track your subject, provided you first focus using the center AF point then keep the subject covered by the AF points as a whole, all the time keeping the shutter release partially depressed.

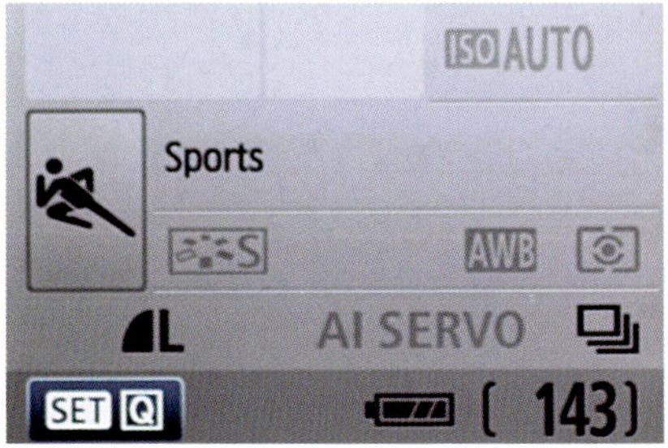

What's more, AI Servo focus mode predicts where the subject will be when the photograph is taken—a factor that is continually reassessed while focus tracking takes place. Frame advance is set to Continuous at three frames per second to help you capture that critical moment.

It is also very helpful if you can predict the action and choose a suitable vantage point accordingly. The best sports photographers are those who know in advance where they will need to be positioned to obtain the best images.

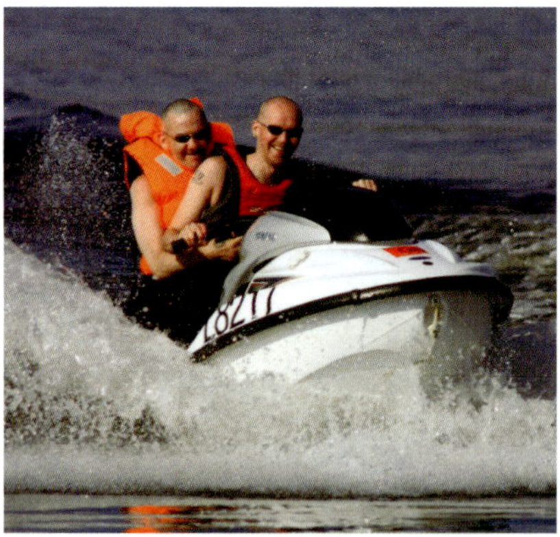

THE BEST APPROACH
Fast-moving subjects approaching at an angle give a good sense of speed while being relatively easy to capture.

Sports mode	
Quality setting	Six JPEG settings; RAW; RAW+Large/fine JPEG
Exposure settings	Evaluative metering; shutter speed, aperture and ISO are chosen to suit the light levels and subject; Standard Picture Style; Auto White Balance; Auto Lighting Optimizer; Long exposure noise reduction; selectable Peripheral illumination correction
Focus settings	Automatic AF point selection in AI Servo focus mode
Frame advance	Continuous shooting; self-timer (10 sec and continuous)
Flash	Flash and AF-assist beam are switched off
Notes	In this mode the camera uses the center AF point first to acquire focus. If the subject moves away from the center AF point, focus tracking will be acquired by one or more of the other AF points.

Using Sports mode

1) Turn the Mode Dial to .

2) Aim the camera with the center AF point on the subject.

3) Lightly press the shutter button to achieve focus while panning to keep the subject covered by the AF points. (The AF points will not light up in red as you are accustomed to.) Maintain light pressure on the shutter release.

4) Fully depress the shutter button at the desired moment.

5) Keep the shutter button depressed to take multiple photographs, panning the camera and ensuring that the subject is covered by at least one of the AF points. The exposure settings, automatically selected ISO speed, and available burst will appear in the viewfinder.

6) Depending on how many burst frames have been exposed, there will be a delay while files are written to the memory card before they can be reviewed. If Auto Review is enabled, only the final frame of a burst sequence will be displayed.

Night Portrait mode

The purpose of this mode is to achieve a well-lit subject and a well-lit background using a combination of two techniques. Exposure for the background is achieved by the camera setting a narrow aperture to create good depth of field, with a consequent low shutter speed, so that it is properly exposed for the ambient light. However, the main subject is lit by flash, which fires at a far higher speed than the shutter and freezes the subject while also providing a different quality of light. The flash itself would not reach the background and ordinarily this area of the picture would be very dark.

Night Portrait mode is especially effective with a dramatic sunset and when your subject is standing in front of an illuminated building.

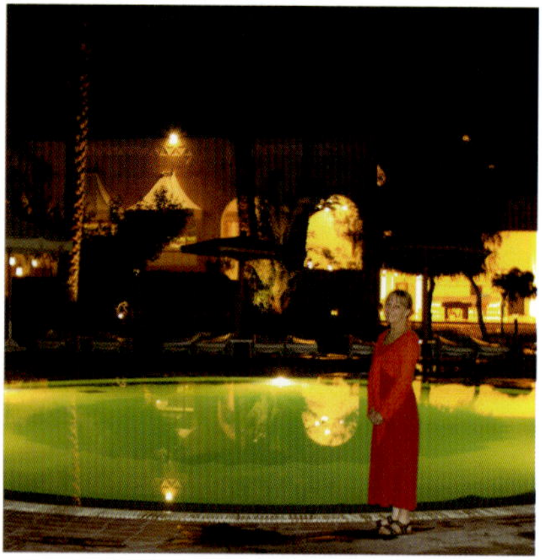

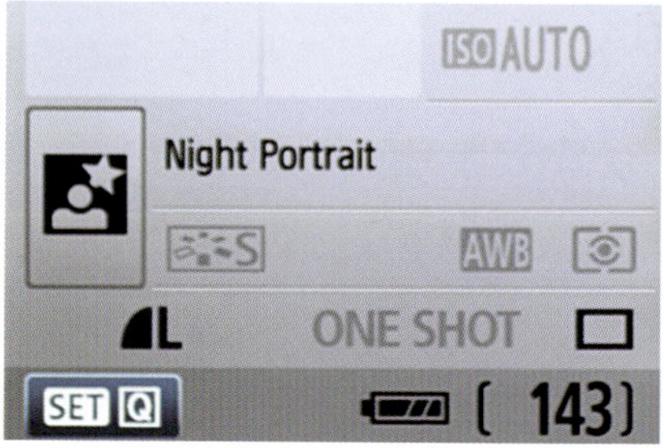

Backgrounds illuminated at night by floodlights or even domestic lighting may appear yellow in comparison with the subject. This is because the two different forms of lighting (ie. floodlights and flash) have quite different color temperatures.

Tip
Position your subjects no more than about 15ft (4.5m) from the camera, or the built-in flash may not illuminate them properly. If they are still underexposed (too dark), ask them to step forward.

HOW IT WORKS
In effect, this mode combines two exposures: a fast one using flash and a slow one without flash. This means that any subject movement will create "ghosting," so use a tripod and make sure that the subject remains quite still.

Night Portrait mode	
Quality setting	Six JPEG settings; RAW; RAW+Large/fine JPEG
Exposure settings	Evaluative metering; a narrow aperture is selected to ensure good depth of field; shutter speed and ISO are selected to suit the background; normal flash sync speed (1/200) is ignored in favor of ambient lighting; Standard Picture Style; Auto White Balance; Auto Lighting Optimizer; Long exposure noise reduction; selectable Peripheral illumination correction
Focus settings	Automatic AF point selection in One Shot focus mode
Frame advance	Single frame advance; self-timer (10 sec and continuous)
Flash	Automatic flash; red-eye reduction; first curtain sync; AF-assist beam, effective up to 13ft (4m)
Notes	The red-eye reduction function can be set to either on or off via Shooting menu 1.

Using Night Portrait mode

1) Turn the Mode Dial to  and turn the red-eye reduction function on.

2) For the best results, use a tripod and either the self-timer or remote release to minimize camera shake.

3) Aim the camera at your subject and partially depress the shutter-release button. Focusing may be easier by placing the center AF point over the main subject.

4) The in-focus indicator ● and the automatically selected AF points will illuminate in the viewfinder.

5) The built-in flash will pop up and the ⚡ flash symbol will show at the bottom left of the viewfinder. (After taking all the photographs likely to need flash, push the built-in flash back down manually.)

6) If you retain light pressure on the shutter button, focus will be locked and you can recompose the picture before fully depressing the shutter button to take the photograph.

7) The image will be displayed on the LCD monitor for two seconds unless the review function has been adjusted or switched off.

No Flash mode

No Flash mode is essentially Full Auto mode with the flash disabled, and is useful in situations where flash is not permitted or would be intrusive. With a fast maximum aperture lens such as the EF 50mm f/1.4 or EF 85mm f/1.8, this mode is a very suitable option for concerts, school plays, and similar situations.

The Rebel T1i/EOS 500D is also capable of ISO settings up to and including ISO 12800. This allows the capture of images without flash in dimly lit situations, even with slower lenses, but it is only available in Creative Zone modes—another good reason to hone your skills and move away from the Basic Zone.

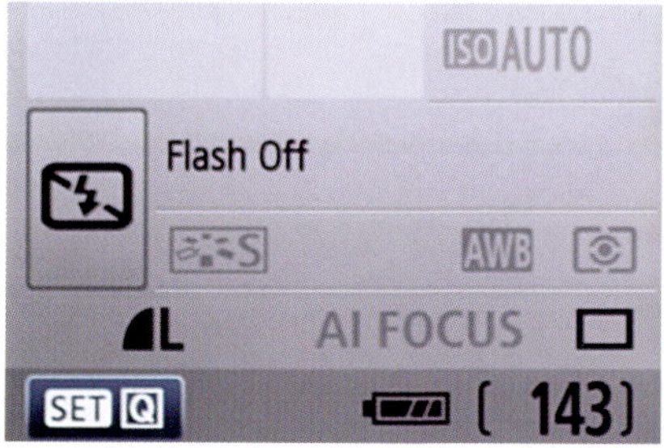

Tip
If you are in a shooting situation where flash is inappropriate, you may also wish to switch off the beep using Shooting menu 1.

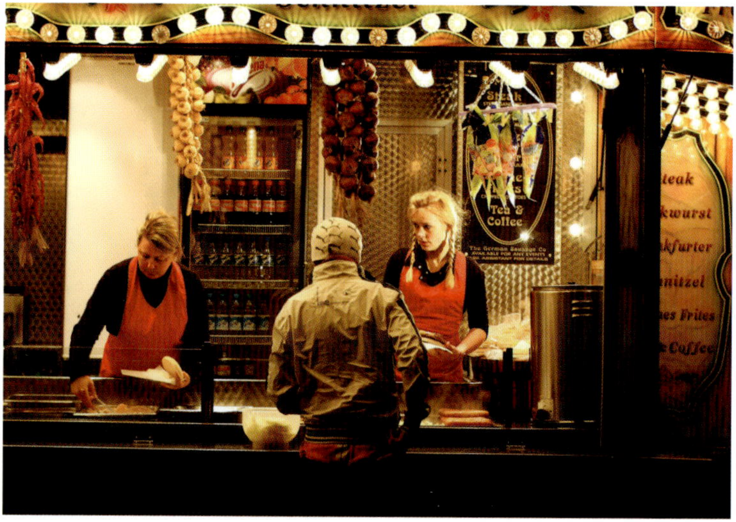

HOLD THE ONIONS
This image was captured outside a soccer stadium on a winter evening. Flash would have alerted the subjects to my presence and probably spoiled the candid nature of the shot.

No Flash mode	
Quality setting	Six JPEG settings; RAW; RAW+Large/fine JPEG
Exposure settings	Evaluative metering; shutter speed, aperture, and ISO are chosen to suit the light levels and subject; Standard Picture Style; Auto White Balance; Auto Lighting Optimizer; Long exposure noise reduction; selectable Peripheral illumination correction
Focus settings	Automatic AF point selection in AI Focus mode
Frame advance	Single frame advance; self-timer (10 sec and continuous)
Flash	Flash and AF-assist beam are switched off
Notes	The AF-assist flash function is disabled so focusing in poor light may require you to select manual focusing using the AF/MF switch on the lens.

Using No Flash mode

1) Turn the Mode Dial to .

2) Aim the camera at your subject. Focusing may be easier by placing the center AF point over the main subject. You can recompose the picture later.

3) Lightly press the shutter button to achieve focus. The in-focus indicator ● and automatically selected AF points will be illuminated in the viewfinder. The exposure settings (aperture and speed) will appear at the bottom of the viewfinder on the left, with the ISO speed and available burst on the right.

4) In low-light conditions it may be necessary to switch the lens to manual focusing, as the AF-assist flash function will not function in this mode.

5) Retain light pressure on the shutter button to keep the focus locked and recompose the picture before depressing the button fully to take the photograph.

6) After a very brief delay, the captured image will be displayed on the camera's LCD monitor for two seconds unless the review function has been adjusted or switched off.

Understanding exposure

This topic is often best explained by means of an analogy. When you're cooking something in the oven, the end product is dependent on two factors: the oven temperature and the cooking time. If you adjust one, you need to adjust the other to get the same result.

Exposure is also a product of two factors: time and aperture. The aperture is the size of the opening through which light falls onto the digital camera's sensor. The time is the shutter speed, which is measured in fractions of a second: 1/60, 1/125, 1/250, 1/500, 1/1000, etc.

The aperture (opening) itself is measured in f-stops. The larger the number, the smaller the opening. Each stop represents a halving or doubling of the adjacent stop. Thus f/11 allows half as much light in as f/8 but twice as much as f/16. The sequence runs as follows: f/2.8, f/4, f/5.6, f/8, f/11, f/16, f/22.

There is also a third factor—the ISO setting. An ISO 200 setting is only half as sensitive as ISO 400 and therefore requires twice the exposure.

LANGSTROTHDALE, UK
This photograph was taken with a shutter speed of 1/250 sec and an aperture of f/5.6, but 1/500 sec at f/4 (half the time but twice the light) or 1/125 sec at f/8 (twice the time but half the light) would also have given a correct exposure.

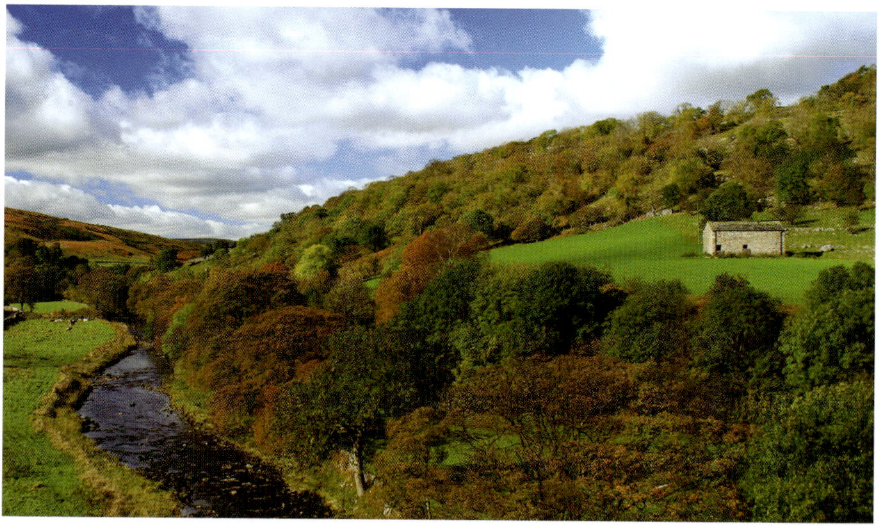

Exposure and metering

A light meter is simply a gadget that measures the quantity of light falling on it (known as an incident reading) or how much light is reflected by the subject (a reflected reading). Through-the-lens (TTL) metering makes use of reflected light readings, which means that they are more likely to be fooled by highly reflective surfaces in your shot.

How helpful a meter reading is depends on how you, or your camera, interprets the result. Any light-meter reading—from Canon's 35-zone full-frame evaluative system to that of a simple 1° spot meter—averages the readings it has taken and provides a recommended shutter speed and aperture (for a given ISO setting) that would give the correct exposure for an 18% gray card. The metering process works as follows:

1) The extent of the area to be metered is determined by the selected metering mode.

2) The camera's light meter "sees" this scene in black and white and takes the meter reading.

3) The meter suggests an exposure which would give an overall tone of 18% gray.

4) The camera user adjusts the suggested reading to account for highlight and shadow preferences.

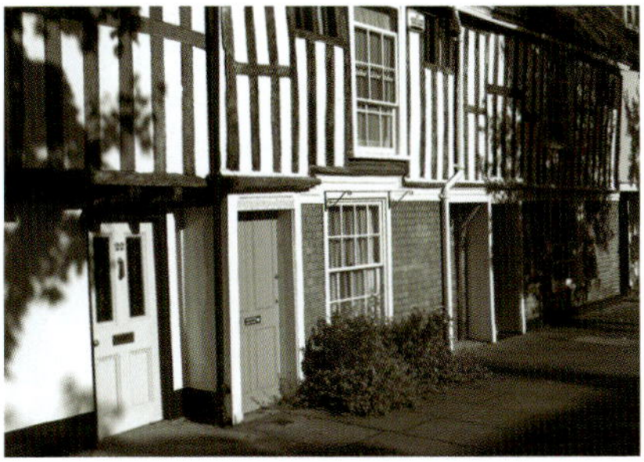

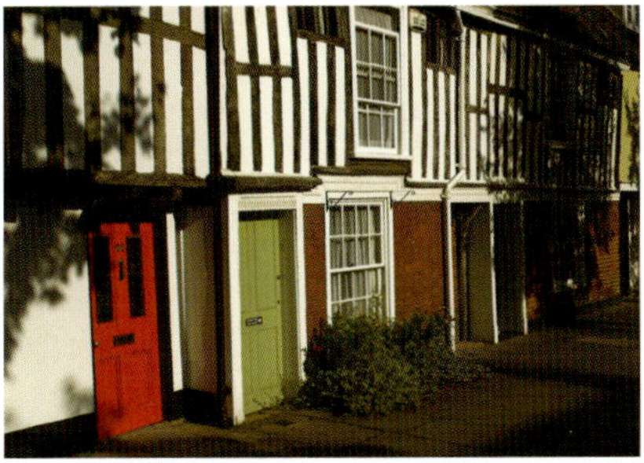

FAVERSHAM, UK
Your camera's meter works by "seeing" the selected scene as black and white tones (left) and calculating the correct exposure for an overall tone of 18% gray. The result is a range of accurately represented colors (right).

FUNCTIONS

AE Lock

The AE Lock (auto exposure lock) function is used when there is a difference between the area of the image that is to be metered and the area used to achieve focus, or when multiple frames will be taken using the same exposure. AE lock is not available in Basic Zone modes or Manual mode.

1) Focus on the subject by partially depressing the shutter-release button.

2) Press the ✱/▦•🔍 button. The ✱ icon is displayed in the viewfinder, indicating exposure lock. The setting will be overridden by pressing the ✱/▦•🔍 button again.

3) Recompose the picture and depress the shutter-release button. To take multiple shots at the locked exposure, continue to depress the ✱/▦•🔍 button while depressing the shutter-release button fully.

There are two techniques which can be employed to make life a little more certain. The first is to set exposure bracketing (see page 92). The second is to be aware of constantly changing ambient light and to adjust your camera settings while you are walking around—so that when an opportunity presents itself, the camera is already set up to achieve the correct exposure. The latter method works best of all in Manual exposure mode.

Tips

In Evaluative metering mode, AE Lock depends upon the AF point selection settings: with automatic AF point selection, AE Lock is applied to the AF point(s) which achieved focus; with manual AF point selection, AE Lock is applied to the selected AF point.

In Partial, Center-weighted, and Spot metering modes, AE Lock is applied at the center AF point.

When the lens is switched to MF (manual focus), AE Lock is also applied to the center AF point.

Common errors

One of the most frequent causes of badly exposed images is the tendency to shoot first and ask questions later. Often, you have a lot more time to get the shot than you think—enough to consider which metering mode is most likely to give the best result.

Exposure compensation

In most instances the exposure suggested by the camera will be quite adequate provided there are no bright highlights and deep shadows that contain detail which you want to retain. In these cases you can use exposure compensation to shift the overall exposure and pull in additional detail. This makes all the tones darker or lighter, depending on the option chosen.

If you have essential detail in both the bright highlights and the deep shadows, it may be beyond the capacity of the sensor to retain the necessary detail. In this case you may wish to consider using exposure bracketing (see page 92) to play safe. If you are shooting RAW files, you may have some additional latitude when the images are processed later on the computer. You may also want to investigate the use of HDR (High Dynamic Range) software.

Exposure compensation of up to +/-2 stops in ⅓- or ½-stop increments can be set in any of the Rebel T1i/EOS 500D's Creative Zone modes, regardless of which metering mode has been selected.

Tips

Exposure compensation can be applied in conjunction with Auto exposure bracketing.

Exposure compensation is not canceled when you turn off the camera. Reset compensation to zero as soon as it is appropriate.

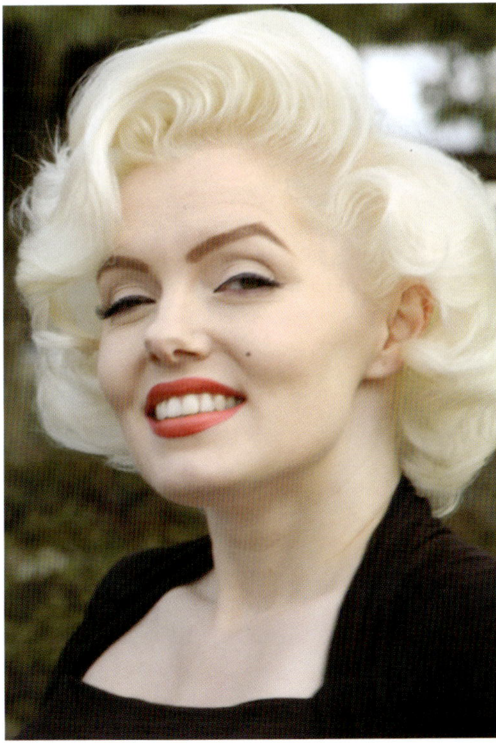

MONROE LOOKALIKE
This frame was dominated by light tones, so exposure compensation was necessary to render the skin tones correctly.

Setting exposure compensation

1) Turn the Mode Dial to any Creative Zone setting except **M** (Manual).

2) Turn the power switch to **ON**.

3) Frame your shot and partially depress the shutter-release button to obtain an exposure reading. Consider the balance between highlight and shadow and assess the likely level of compensation needed.

4) Check the exposure level indicator -2..1..•..1..+2 at the bottom of the viewfinder (or on the LCD monitor by pressing **DISP**) to check that the indicator is at the center of the exposure scale.

5) To set the level of compensation, hold down the **Av** button while rotating the Main Dial. One direction will increase the exposure and the opposite direction will decrease it, one increment at a time. The indicator -2..1..•..1..+2 will show the extent of the compensation.

6) Take the photograph and review the result. You may wish to increase or decrease the compensation and take further exposures.

7) To cancel the exposure compensation, repeat step 5 and return the indicator -2..1..•..1..+2 to the center point of the scale.

Setting the exposure compensation increment

To change the exposure compensation increment from ⅓ to ½ stop:

1) Press the **MENU** button and select Set-up menu 3.

2) Highlight **Custom Functions** and press **SET**.

3) Use the ◀ and ▶ buttons to scroll through the Custom Functions screens until you reach **C.Fn I: Exposure/1 Exposure Level Increments**.

4) Press **SET** to highlight the existing setting.

5) Press ▲ or ▼ to change to the alternative setting.

6) Press **SET** again to save the setting. Press **MENU** to exit.

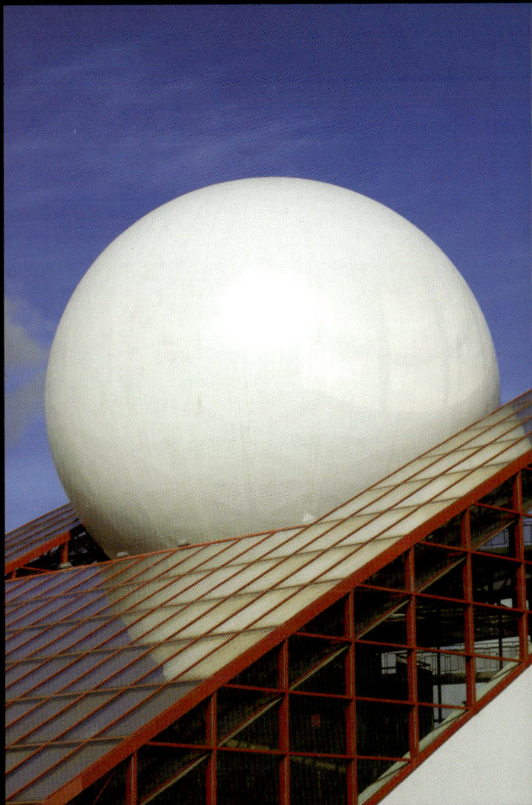

WHITE POINT
When you are faced with both bright highlights and shadows, it is usually necessary to determine which will dictate the exposure. In this case, the highlights had to be exposed correctly to prevent the white dome from burning out, but the shadowed area inside the building contained no essential detail. Evaluative metering did a good job of determining the intial exposure, but I still needed to apply compensation of ⅓ stop.

Settings
Manual exposure
ISO 100
f/8 at 1/400 sec
Evaluative metering

Using AF points

Automatic AF point selection will take place in the Basic Zone and in **A-DEP** mode, and it cannot be overridden. In the Creative Zone modes (except A-DEP), you can select any one of the nine AF points, or automatic AF point selection using all nine AF points.

Setting the AF point

1) Press the [-:-]/⊕ button. The currently selected AF point(s) will be illuminated in the viewfinder. If all nine AF points are illuminated, automatic AF point selection is the current setting.

2) Press [-:-]/⊕ and scroll through the AF points by turning the Main Dial.

3) Lightly depress the shutter release button or press [-:-]/⊕ to finalize your AF point selection.

Tips

Only one AF point can be selected at a time, except in Auto AF point selection.

In Auto AF point selection, the camera will tend to focus on the nearest object in the frame.

After pressing the [-:-]/⊕ button, pressing the **SET** button will toggle the AF point display between auto selection and the center AF point.

If focusing proves difficult in a low-contrast or low-light situation, select the center AF point—it is more sensitive than the others.

For a moving subject, select AI Servo focus mode and automatic AF point selection. Focus using the center AF point initially, and the other AF points will pick up and track the moving subject.

When the lens is set to **MF**, the AF point that achieves focus will still illuminate, the beep will sound, and the ● in-focus indicator in the viewfinder will be illuminated.

AF-assist beam

In low-light conditions, when the built-in flash is deployed automatically in Basic Zone modes, or is deployed manually in Creative Zone modes, it fires a brief burst of flashes to illuminate the subject and aid focusing prior to taking the picture. The maximum effective distance for this feature is about 13ft (4m) with the built-in flash. If an external Speedlite is attached, the Speedlite will perform the AF-assist beam function instead and can be used over greater distances due to its higher guide number (see page 166).

The AF-assist beam can be enabled or disabled in C.Fn-8. These settings apply to both the built-in flash and to an external Speedlite. It is also possible to make this function work only with an attached Speedlite. However, if the Speedlite's own AF-assist beam Custom Function is set to "disabled," it will override the camera settings and the Speedlite will not fire.

AF lock

Maintaining light pressure on the shutter-release button will lock focus so that you can recompose the image, safe in the knowledge that your main subject will be sharply focused.

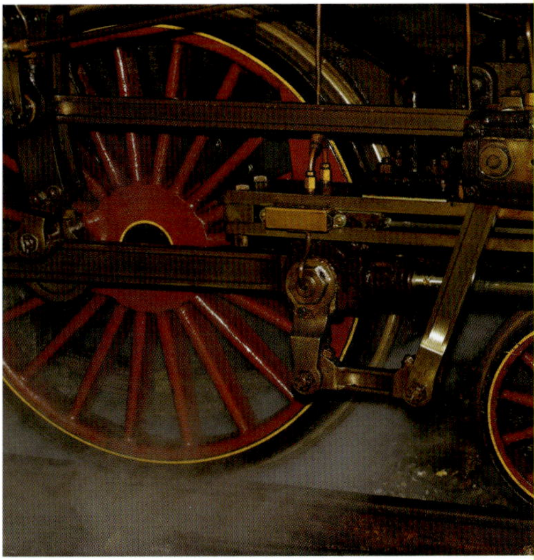

LOCOMOTIVE
Flash exposures of essentially dark subjects such as this locomotive are made much easier with the aid of the AF-assist beam.

Exposure modes—the Creative Zone

Canon's Creative Zone modes allow the photographer absolute control over every function on the camera, creating a seemingly infinite range of permutations. What really matters, though, is that you can set up the camera for virtually any situation—from the unhurried shooting of a still life using a tripod and Live View (see Chapter 3) to capturing the fast action of sports events.

Somewhere between the two extremes, most photographers will work within their comfort zones at first and gradually expand their horizons and try new techniques.

(P) Program AE mode

Program AE mode automatically sets the shutter speed and aperture. The specific combination can be adjusted but only as a combination and not individually. You could change 1/250 at f/8, for example, to 1/1000 at f/4 or to any other combination giving the same effective exposure. This is referred to as Program Shift. However, full control is available over AF mode, drive mode, built-in flash, and other functions, so it is still a flexible mode and is perhaps the next step up the learning curve from Full Auto.

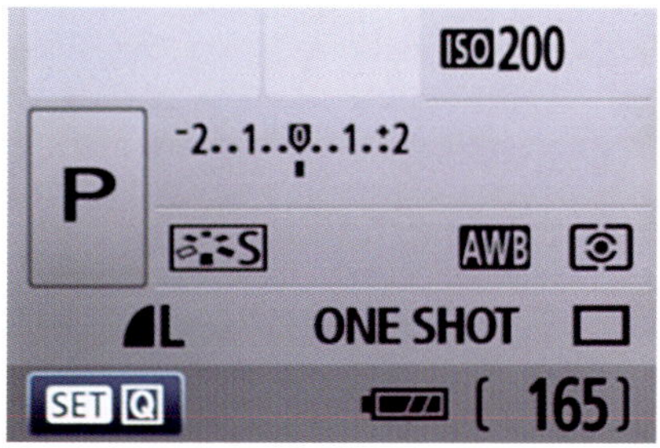

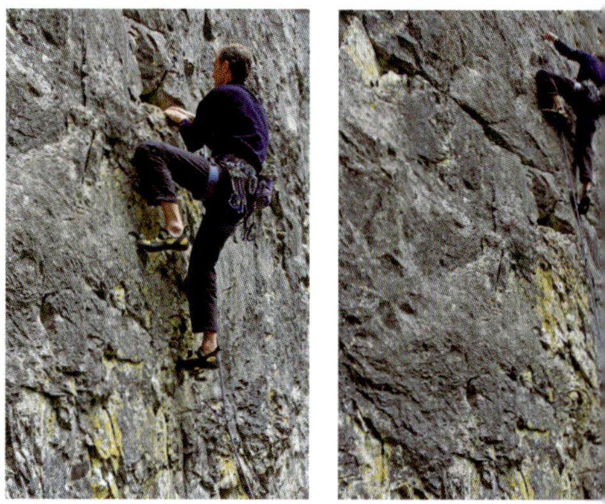

ROCK CLIMBING
This is a classic situation for Program mode with a zoom lens: one moment you want to be ready for action (left), a momentary slip resulting in a dramatic fall; the next, you want great depth of field (right). By rotating the Main Dial, a different combination of shutter speed and aperture can be selected almost instantaneously.

Program AE mode	
Quality settings	Six JPEG settings; RAW; RAW+Large/fine JPEG
Exposure settings	The camera determines a combination of shutter speed and aperture. The combination can be changed using Program Shift. Evaluative metering using 35 different zones; Partial metering; Spot metering; Center-weighted metering; Exposure compensation; Auto exposure bracketing; Exposure increment adjustment; ISO expansion; High ISO noise reduction; Long exposure noise reduction; six preset Picture Styles plus three user-defined styles; Auto lighting optimizer; Highlight Tone Priority; Peripheral illumination correction; White balance presets and shift/bracketing; Custom white balance; Flash sync speed adjustment
Focus settings	One Shot; AI Servo; AI Focus; automatic/manual AF point selection
Frame advance	Single frame; continuous; self-timer (three settings)
Flash	AF-assist beam; red-eye reduction; first- and second-curtain sync; high-speed sync with selected Speedlites; flash exposure compensation; flash exposure lock; external flash function and Custom Function settings with compatible Speedlites
Notes	The least flexible of the Creative Zone modes.

Using Program AE mode

1) Turn the Mode Dial to **P**. Lightly press the shutter button to achieve focus. The automatically selected exposure settings are shown in the viewfinder.

2) To change the exposure settings using Program Shift, rotate the Main Dial until the desired combination is shown.

3) The built-in flash will not pop up automatically in Program mode, so keep an eye on the selected shutter speed. If you raise it manually, the flash symbol ϟ will show bottom left in the viewfinder.

4) Follow steps 5–6 on page 61.

(Tv) Shutter Priority AE mode

Shutter Priority mode gives the photographer the opportunity to decide on shutter speed as the single most important function. This may be in order to capture a fast-moving subject or to deliberately blur movement for pictorial effect. For the record, Tv stands for Time value.

The key factor in determining a suitable shutter speed is not the absolute speed at which the subject is traveling. What is important is the speed at which the subject is moving across the frame, and its size in relation to the area of the frame.

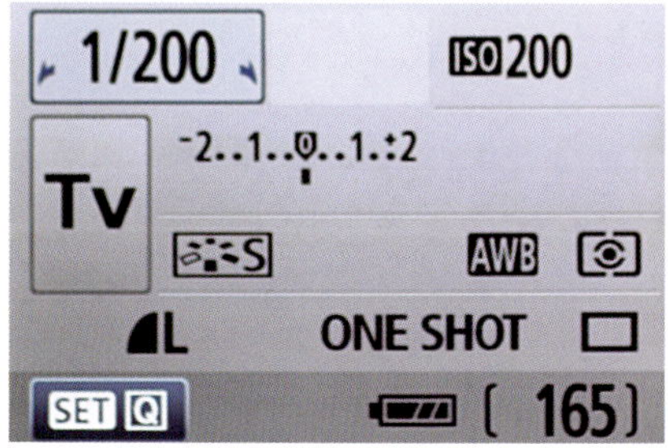

For example, a 1:1 magnification of a flower moving gently in the breeze is more likely to blur than an express train some distance away taken with a wide-angle lens.

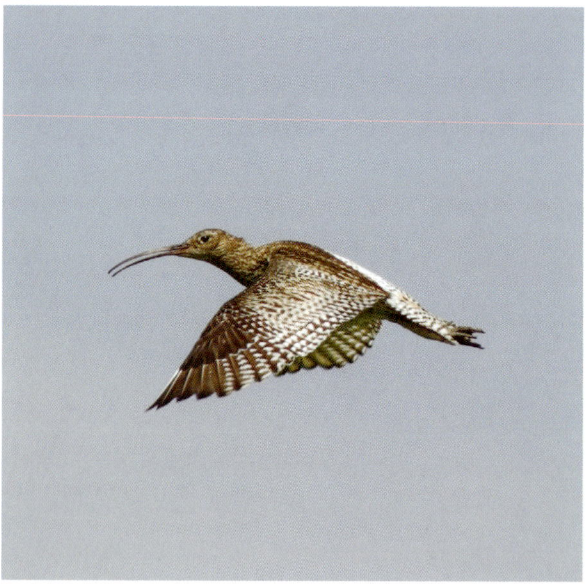

FROZEN IN FLIGHT
This curlew was captured while panning from right to left using a 300mm f/2.8 lens with a 2× extender attached. With a selected shutter speed of 1/1500 sec at ISO 400, it was easy to freeze the flight of this attractive moorland bird at the critical moment at the end of its wing beat.

Shutter Priority AE mode

Quality settings	Six JPEG settings; RAW; RAW+Large/fine JPEG
Exposure settings	The user sets the shutter speed and the camera automatically selects a suitable aperture. Evaluative metering using 35 different zones; Partial metering; Spot metering; Center-weighted metering; Exposure compensation; Auto exposure bracketing; Exposure increment adjustment; ISO expansion; High ISO noise reduction; Long exposure noise reduction; six preset Picture Styles plus three user-defined styles; Auto lighting optimizer; Highlight Tone Priority; Peripheral illumination correction; White balance presets and shift/bracketing; Custom white balance; Flash sync speed adjustment
Focus settings	One Shot; AI Servo; AI Focus; automatic/manual AF point selection
Frame advance	Single frame; continuous; self-timer (3 settings)
Flash	AF-assist beam; red-eye reduction; first- and second-curtain sync; high-speed sync with selected Speedlites; flash exposure compensation; flash exposure lock; external flash function and Custom Function settings with compatible Speedlites
Notes	Also useful in changing light conditions to avoid camera shake.

Using Shutter Priority AE mode

1) Turn the Mode Dial to **Tv** and set the desired shutter speed by rotating the [Main Dial icon] Main Dial.

2) Lightly press the shutter button to achieve focus. The in-focus indicator ● will illuminate in the viewfinder. The selected AF point(s) will also illuminate briefly, accompanied by a beep (unless disabled in [camera icon] Shooting menu 1).

3) The shutter speed and automatically selected aperture will be visible in the bottom left of the viewfinder.

4) The built-in flash will not pop up automatically. It can be raised manually if needed, when the flash symbol ϟ will show bottom left in the viewfinder.

5) Follow steps 5–6 on page 61.

(Av) Aperture Priority AE mode

This is the mode to use when you want to be sure that everything from the foreground to the background is in focus. Conversely, and especially if you use a fast telephoto lens, you can opt to use differential focus to make your subject stand out against an out-of-focus background. A wide aperture ensures narrower depth of focus and a narrow aperture (larger number) will provide greater depth of field.

Many landscape photographers switch off autofocus on their lens when using this mode with a very narrow aperture. Instead, they manually focus on a point about a third of the way into the zone they want in focus. Alternatively, they may use the depth-of-field scale on the lens, if it has one.

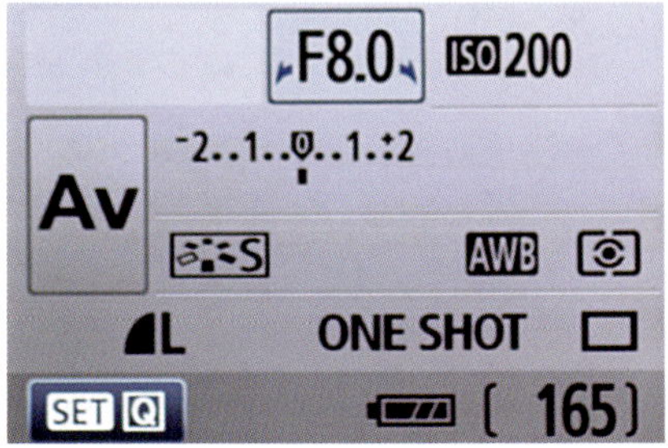

Tip

For very wide depth of field at slow ISO settings you will probably need a tripod. If you do not have a remote release, use the self-timer at its 10-second setting to minimize camera shake.

Mirror lock-up is also useful for slow exposures. The shutter has to be tripped twice—once to raise the mirror and again to record the exposure. After you have raised the mirror, allow time for any vibration to cease before tripping the shutter using a remote release.

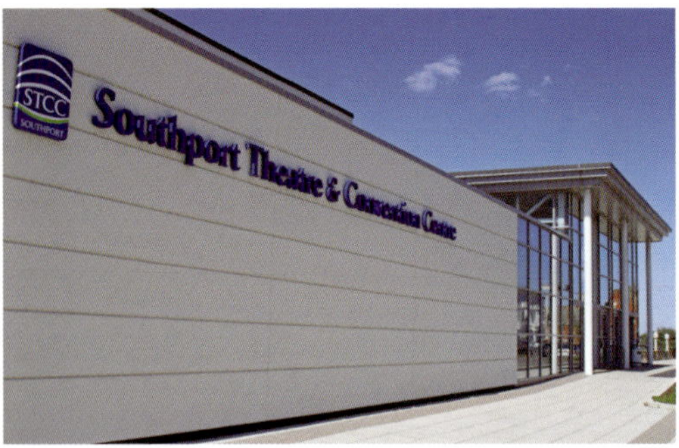

SHARP LINES
Using Aperture Priority mode, an aperture of f/8 on a 24mm lens was enough to keep the subject sharp from a few feet in front of the camera to infinity.

Aperture Priority AE mode

Quality settings	Six JPEG settings; RAW; RAW+Large/fine JPEG
Exposure settings	The user sets the aperture and the camera automatically selects a suitable shutter speed. Evaluative metering using 35 different zones; Partial metering; Spot metering; Center-weighted metering; Exposure compensation; Auto exposure bracketing; Exposure increment adjustment; ISO expansion; High ISO noise reduction; Long exposure noise reduction; six preset Picture Styles plus three user-defined styles; Auto lighting optimizer; Highlight Tone Priority; Peripheral illumination correction; White balance presets and shift/bracketing; Custom white balance; Flash sync speed adjustment
Focus settings	One Shot; AI Servo; AI Focus; automatic/manual AF point selection
Frame advance	Single frame; continuous; self-timer (three settings)
Flash	AF-assist beam; red-eye reduction; first- and second-curtain sync; high-speed sync with selected Speedlites; flash exposure compensation; flash exposure lock; external flash function and Custom Function settings with compatible Speedlites
Notes	Used to achieve maximum or deliberately reduced depth of field.

Using Aperture Priority AE mode

1) Turn the Mode Dial to **Av** and set the desired aperture by rotating the Main Dial.

2) Aim the camera at the subject and lightly press the shutter button to achieve focus. The in-focus indicator ● will illuminate briefly in the viewfinder. The selected AF point(s) will also illuminate briefly, accompanied by a beep (unless disabled in Shooting menu 1).

3) The aperture and automatically selected shutter speed will be visible in the bottom left of the viewfinder.

4) The built-in flash will not pop up automatically in Av mode. It can be raised manually if needed, when the flash symbol ϟ will show bottom left in the viewfinder.

5) Follow steps 5–6 on page 61.

(M) Manual exposure mode

This mode provides ultimate control over exposure, as the shutter speed and aperture are set independently—the camera does not choose one to fit the other. This is particularly useful at times when the camera's meter may be fooled by the luminosity or reflectivity of the subject matter, and when the desired effect is other than an averagely toned scene.

There are occasions when a particularly bright high-key image is required—for example, a soft-focus portrait of a bride in her wedding dress. Sometimes what might normally be deemed an underexposed result is needed, typically in reportage images.

Another factor to bear in mind with the Rebel T1i/EOS 500D is that it offers a monochrome option, including the simulated use of

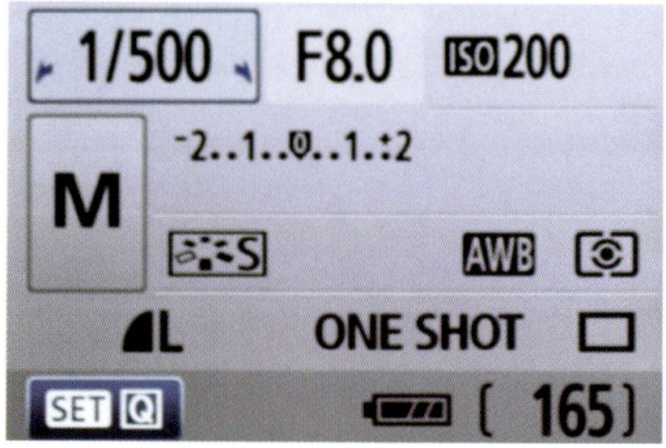

black-and-white filters. Traditionally, metering for slide film has always been based on the highlights, whereas metering for black-and-white photography has been based on the shadows. However, with the Rebel T1i/EOS 500D in Manual mode you can adopt different midtones to suit different styles of photography. You can also use Picture Styles (see pages 98–102) to fine-tune your way of working.

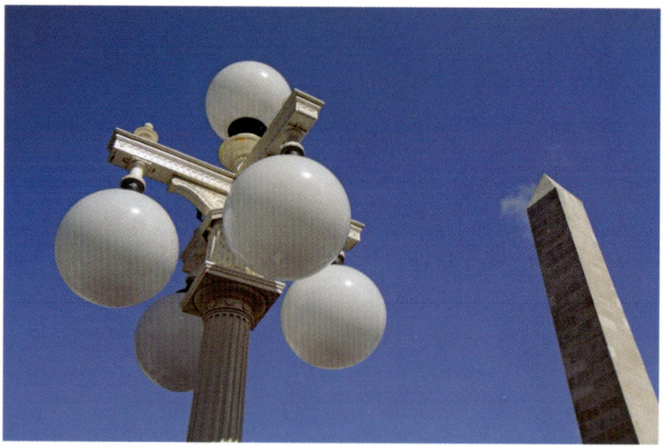

PRECISION
For subjects like this, when a very precise exposure is required, Manual mode combined with spot metering guarantees a pleasing result.

Manual exposure mode

Quality settings	Six JPEG settings; RAW; RAW+Large/fine JPEG
Exposure setting	The user sets both the aperture and the shutter speed independently of one another. Evaluative metering using 35 different zones; Partial metering; Spot metering; Center-weighted metering; Auto exposure bracketing; Exposure increment adjustment; ISO expansion; High ISO noise reduction; Long exposure noise reduction; six preset Picture Styles plus three user-defined styles; Highlight Tone Priority; Peripheral illumination correction; White balance presets and shift/bracketing; Custom white balance; Flash sync speed adjustment
Focus settings	One Shot; AI Servo; AI Focus; automatic/manual AF point selection
Frame advance	Single frame; continuous; self-timer (three settings)
Flash	AF-assist beam; red-eye reduction; first- and second-curtain sync; high-speed sync with selected Speedlites; flash exposure compensation; flash exposure lock; external flash function and Custom Function settings with compatible Speedlites.

Using Manual exposure mode

1) Turn the Mode Dial to **M** and set the desired metering mode.

2) Lightly press the shutter button to achieve focus. The in-focus indicator ● and the selected AF point(s) will be illuminated in the viewfinder.

3) Rotate the Main Dial to adjust the shutter speed.

4) Press the **Av** button with your thumb while rotating the Main Dial with your index finger to adjust the aperture until the exposure-level mark is centered on the scale in the viewfinder.

5) If metering from a selected area, take the reading and adjust as necessary to center the exposure level mark again.

6) The built-in flash will not pop up automatically in Manual mode. It can be raised manually if needed.

7) Follow steps 5–6 on page 61.

(A-DEP) Automatic Depth of Field AE mode

Using the data provided by the AF points, this mode automatically selects an aperture and shutter speed that will maximize depth of field. It will attempt to give the photographer as fast a shutter speed as possible within the constraints of its objective: in other words, it won't give you f/11 when f/5.6 will do.

So what are the advantages of A-DEP mode over Aperture Priority with the depth-of-field preview button? First of all, it takes away the need to think about selecting a suitable aperture for each photograph. Secondly, it is extremely useful in situations demanding a very narrow aperture which would render the viewfinder image very dark when previewing the depth of field. Its main disadvantage is the loss of control over aperture and shutter speed.

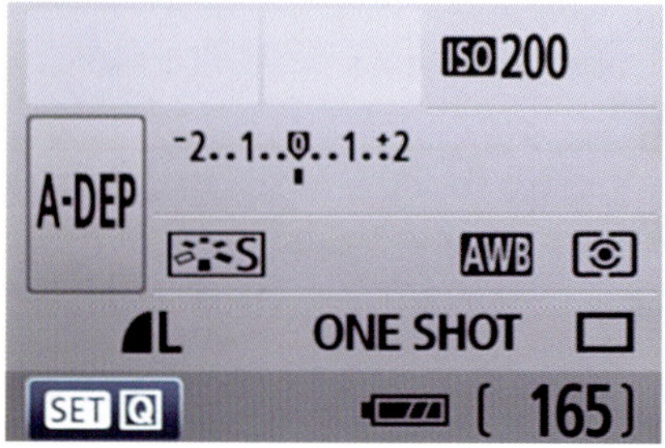

Tips

If the automatically selected aperture produces a shutter speed that is too slow, increase the ISO setting or select Auto ISO.

If you are shooting in RAW, you can use exposure compensation to gain a couple of stops by shooting at the wrong exposure and rescuing the image on the computer later.

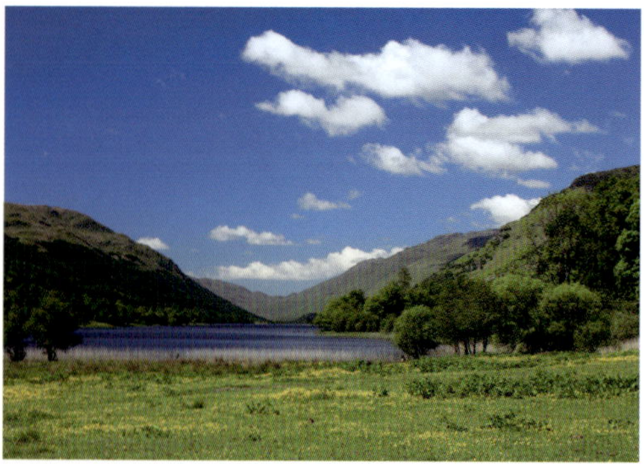

ROB ROY COUNTRY
This mode is useful for landscapes like this, the setting for Sir Walter Scott's famous Scottish novel. If a foreground feature demands sharp focus, however, Aperture Priority mode is a safer option.

Automatic Depth of Field AE mode

Quality settings	Six JPEG settings; RAW; RAW+Large/fine JPEG
Exposure settings	Evaluative metering using 35 different zones; Partial metering; Center-weighted metering; Spot metering; Exposure compensation; Auto exposure bracketing; Auto lighting optimizer; Exposure increment adjustment; ISO expansion; High ISO noise reduction; Long exposure noise reduction; six preset Picture Styles plus three user-defined styles; Highlight Tone Priority; Peripheral illumination correction; White balance presets and shift/bracketing; Custom white balance; Flash sync speed adjustment
Focus settings	One Shot; AI Servo; AI Focus; automatic/manual AF point selection
Frame advance	Single frame; continuous; self-timer (three settings)
Flash	The results will be the same as when using Program mode (see pages 70–1) and depth of field may be lost
Notes	Useful to make sure that key elements of the image are in focus, but control of aperture and shutter speed is lost. Effectively acts like Program mode but without the option of Program Shift.

Using A-DEP mode

1) Turn the Mode Dial to **A-DEP** and select the metering mode.

2) Lightly press the shutter button to achieve focus. The in-focus indicator ● and AF points that have achieved focus will illuminate briefly in the viewfinder.

3) If the briefly illuminated AF points do not pick out the areas of the image that are the most important, change position relative to the subject.

4) If you retain light pressure on the shutter button, focus will be locked and you can recompose the picture before fully depressing the shutter button to take the photograph. However, in recomposing the image you may lose focus on critical elements of the subject.

5) After a very brief delay, the captured image will display on the LCD monitor for two seconds unless the review function has been adjusted or switched off.

Menu options

The Rebel T1i/EOS 500D's menu screens are displayed on the LCD monitor on the back of the camera. The eight menu tabs consist of two Shooting menus, two Playback menus, three Set-up menus, and a customizable My Menu for quick access to your most frequently changed options. Each category is represented by a symbol and is color-coded to make identification easier.

The currently selected item on any menu is highlighted in the same color as its parent menu category. For example, the Playback menu symbol is blue, so Playback menu items are also highlighted in blue.

When a menu item is selected, a secondary menu may be displayed. This is sometimes followed by a third menu or a Cancel/OK dialog box, as described below.

Selecting menu options

1) Press the **MENU** button and then use the Main Dial or ◀ and ▶ buttons to scroll through the menus until you reach the one you want.

2) Use the ▲ and ▼ buttons to highlight the desired menu item. To select it, press the **SET** button.

3) If secondary menus or confirmation dialog boxes are displayed, you may need to use the ◀ ▶ ▲ ▼ buttons, the Main Dial, or the **SET** button in different ways, usually indicated on screen.

4) Once a setting has been changed, press **SET** to save the new setting.

5) To exit at any stage, press the **MENU** button to go back one level and repeat the process if necessary.

Note
If you are shooting in any of the Basic Zone modes, some menu options are not available and will not be displayed. These options are "grayed out" in the Menu summary tables on pages 81–3.

Menu summary

Menus or selected functions shaded in gray are not accessible in Basic Zone modes.

Shooting menu 1 (Red)	Options
Quality	◢L ▟L ◢M ▟M ◢S ▟S RAW+◢L RAW
Beep	Off / On
Release shutter w/o card	On / Off
Review time	Off / 2 sec / 4 sec / 8 sec / Hold
Peripheral illumination correction	Enable / Disable
Redeye on/off	On /Off
Flash control	Flash firing Built-in flash functions External flash functions External flash Custom Functions Clear external flash Custom Functions

Shooting menu 2 (Red)	Options
Exposure compensation/AEB	Bracketing in ⅓ or ½ stop increments, +/-2 stops
Metering mode	Evaluative / Partial / Spot / Center-weighted
Custom White Balance	Manual setting of white balance
WB Shift/Bracketing	White balance correction and/or bracketing
Color space	sRGB / Adobe RGB
Picture Style	Standard / Portrait / Landscape / Neutral / Faithful / Monochrome / 3 User-defined styles
Dust Delete Data	Obtains data used to erase dust spots

Playback menu 1 (Blue)	Options
Protect images	Prevent deletion of highlighted image(s)
Rotate	Rotate highlighted image(s)
Erase images	Erase highlighted image(s)
Print order	Specify images to be printed
Transfer order	Specify images to be transferred to computer

Playback menu 2 (Blue)	Options
Histogram	Brightness / RGB
Slide show	All images / movies / stills / by date / repeat / display each image for 1, 2, 3, or 4 secs.
Image jump with	Movies / stills / by date / 1, 10, or 100 images

Set-up menu 1 (Yellow)	Options
Auto power off	30 sec / 1 min / 2 min / 4 min / 8 min / 15 min / Off
File numbering	Continuous / Auto reset / Manual reset
Auto rotate	On / On / Off
Format	Initialize and erase data on memory card
LCD auto off	Enable / Disable
Screen color	Four color scheme settings

Set-up menu 2 (Yellow)	Options
LCD brightness	Seven levels of brightness
Date / Time	Set date and time
Language	25 languages to select from
Video system	NTSC / PAL
Sensor cleaning	Auto cleaning / Clean now / Clean manually
Live View function settings	Live View shoot: Disable / Enable Grid display: Off / On / Grid 1 / Grid 2 Metering timer: 4 sec / 16 sec / 30 sec / 1 min / 10 min / 30 min

Set-up menu 3 (Yellow)	Options
Custom Functions	C.Fn I-1: Exposure level increments C.Fn I-2: ISO expansion C.Fn I-3: Flash sync in Av mode C.Fn II-4: Long exp. noise reduction C.Fn II-5: High ISO noise reduction C.Fn II-6: Highlight tone priority C.Fn II-7: Auto lighting optimizer C.Fn III-8: AF-assist beam firing C.Fn III-9: Mirror lock-up C.Fn IV-10: Shutter/AE lock button C.Fn IV-11: Assign SET button C.Fn IV-12: LCD display when power on C.Fn IV-13: Add orig. decision data
Clear settings	Clear all camera settings / Clear all Custom Function settings Delete copyright information
Firmware version	Display / update current firmware

My Menu (Green)	Options
My Menu settings	Register frequently used menu items and Custom Functions

My Menu

For faster access, you can register a combination of up to six menus that you use on a regular basis in My Menu, and choose the order in which they are displayed.

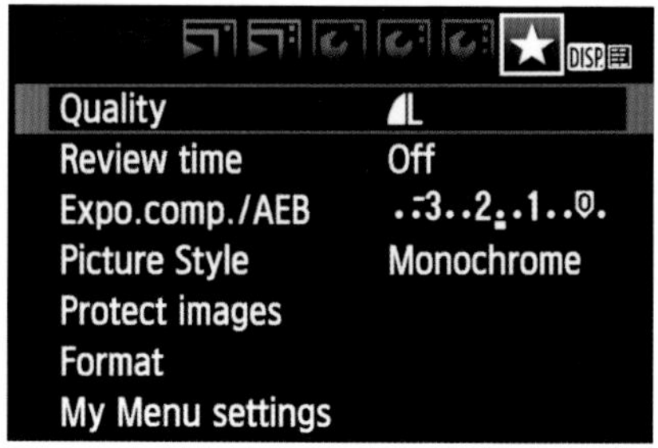

1) Press the **MENU** button and select ★ My Menu. Press **SET**.

2) Select **Register** and press **SET**.

3) Using the ▲ and ▼ buttons, scroll through the list of features to an item you wish to include. Press **SET**, then **OK** when the dialog box is displayed.

4) Repeat the process for up to six items and press the **MENU** button to exit to My Menu settings.

5) To change the order in which the menu items are listed, select **Sort**.

6) Use the ▲ and ▼ buttons to highlight an item and press **SET**. Change its position using the ▲ and ▼ buttons. Press **SET**.

7) Repeat steps 6 and 7 as necessary. Press **SET** to exit to **My Menu settings**.

Tips

You can easily delete a single item or all of the items registered to My Menu from the **My Menu settings** screen.

The final item on the My Menu settings screen is **Display from My Menu**. If this is enabled, My Menu will be displayed every time you press **MENU** rather than the last menu viewed.

The camera is dispatched from the factory with a set of default settings. These can be restored at any time by selecting any Creative Zone mode, then choosing Set-up menu 3 and selecting **Clear all camera settings**.

Shooting menu 1

The Rebel T1i/EOS 500D has two Shooting menus, which use red highlighting to differentiate them from other menus. The two Shooting menus control all the basic shooting-related functions including the quality of the files recorded, auto exposure bracketing, white balance and color options, and Picture Styles.

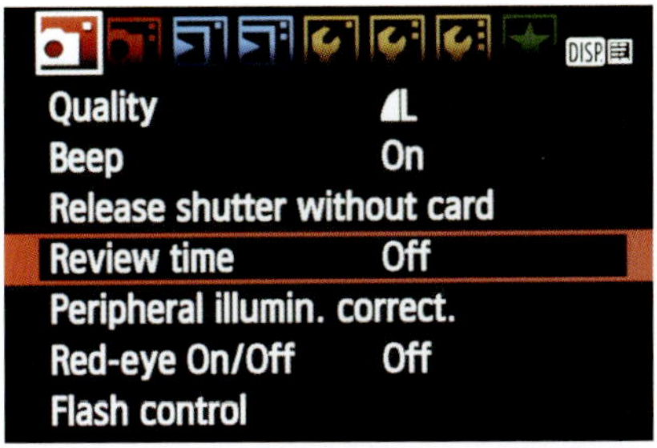

Setting file quality

The Canon Rebel T1i/EOS 500D has eight different file-quality settings. There are six JPEG options, a RAW setting, and the option to record both RAW and Large/fine JPEG files simultaneously.

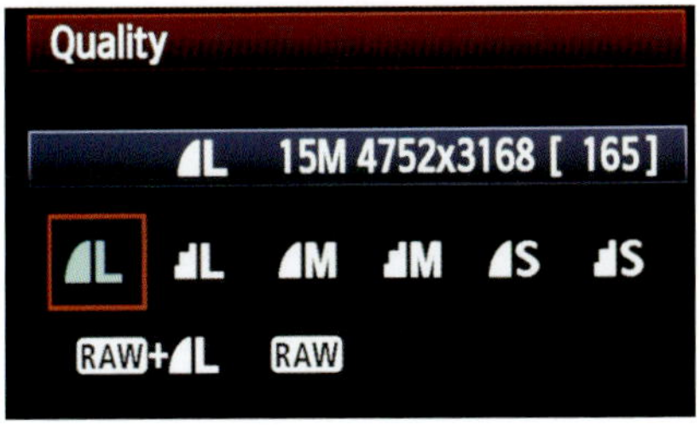

JPEG files, especially the smaller JPEG options, will take up much less space on your memory card, but will be of lower quality. They will also write faster so you won't need to wait while the buffer empties, as may happen when shooting RAW files. The burst size (the maximum number of shots you can take before the buffer is full) is also significantly increased.

As the camera performs a number of processing tasks on JPEGs compared with RAW files, far less post-processing is required. The disadvantage of shooting JPEGs is that you have far less control over the recorded image than is the case with a RAW file. JPEG is also a compressed format, which means that there is some loss of quality. The smaller the file, the greater the compression and the greater the loss of picture quality.

Using RAW files suits those who require the highest-quality images and are prepared to use computer software to bring those images to fruition. With the advent of Picture Styles, however, some of the post-processing can be avoided, which makes shooting RAW a much more viable option for those who are less interested or less skilled in post-processing techniques.

File-quality settings

	Quality	Pixels	File-size (approx.)	Shots per 2GB card (approx.)	Maximum burst
L	High quality JPEG	15.1Mp	5Mb	370	170
L			2.5Mb	740	740
M	Medium quality JPEG	8Mp	3Mb	620	610
M			1.6Mb	1190	1190
S	Low quality JPEG	3.7Mp	1.7Mb	1090	1080
S			0.9Mb	2040	2030
RAW	High quality	15.1Mp	20.2Mb	91	9
RAW + L	High quality	15.1Mp	20.2+5Mb	72	4

Based on Canon's testing standards with a 2GB card, ISO 100, and Standard Picture Style.
The file size, number of possible shots, and maximum burst will will vary depending on the subject, brand of memory card, ISO speed, Custom Functions, and other settings.

Beep

The beep is very useful to confirm focus, especially if you wear spectacles and have difficulty getting your eye right up to the viewfinder. However, the beep can also be an unwelcome distraction in situations such as a church or museum, so you can choose to turn it off.

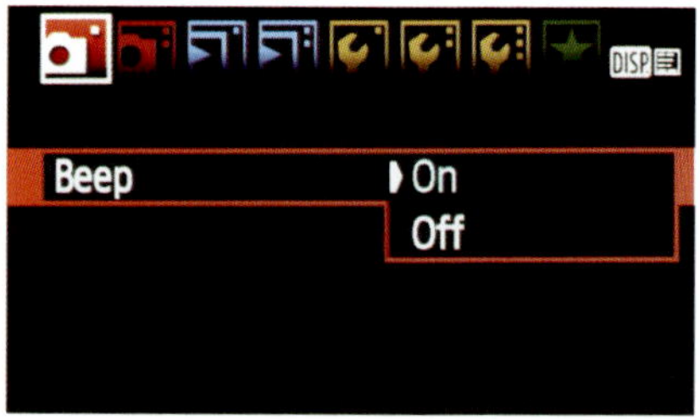

Release shutter without card

With this function you can choose to allow the camera to function without a memory card installed. This facility might be used when capturing a large number of images direct to your computer.

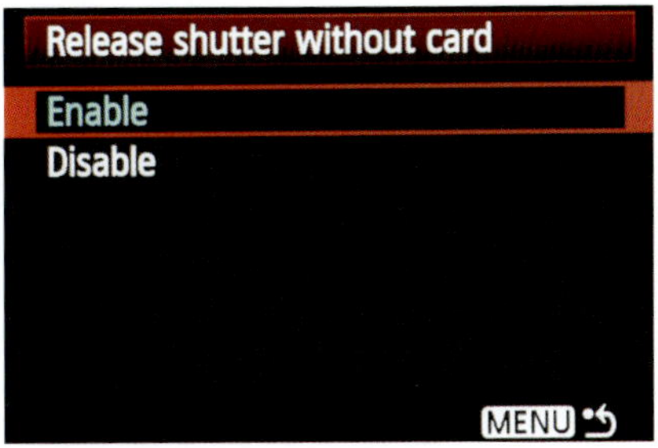

Review time

After shooting, the camera will display the image on the monitor for 2, 4, or 8 sec, or for as long as you like if you select **Hold**. Alternatively, if want to conserve battery power and review images later, you can turn the review function off.

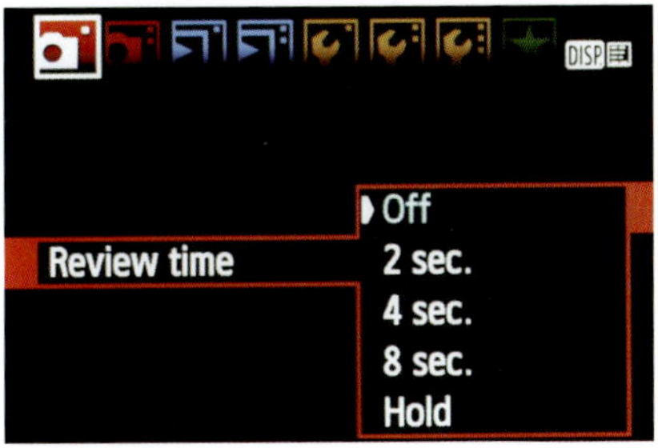

Peripheral illumination correction

Light fall-off at the four corners of the image is corrected in-camera for JPEG files. (RAW images can be corrected using the Digital Photo Professional software provided with the camera.)

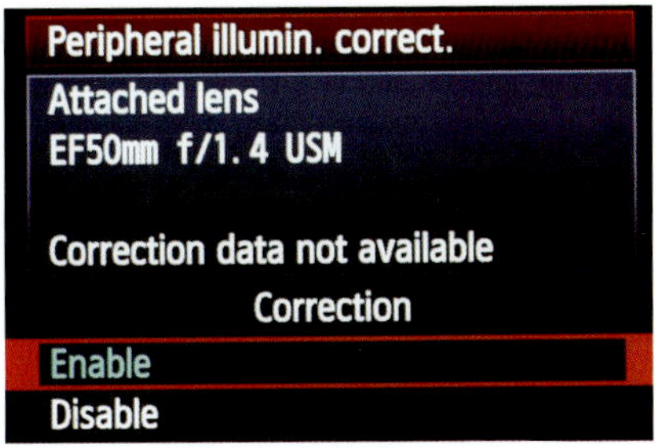

Red-eye On/Off

This feature can be used in any mode except Landscape, Sports, and No Flash modes in the Basic Zone. Red-eye reduction works by emitting a pre-exposure burst of flash which narrows the blood vessels in the eye. Bear in mind that this will warn a subject of your intention, so it may not be appropriate for candid shooting.

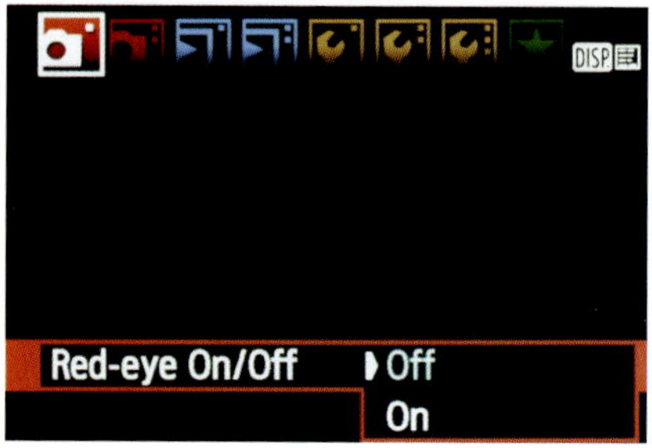

Flash control

This menu enables you to change a variety of settings for both the built-in flash and an external flash, provided the latter is a Canon EX Speedlite that permits the setting of functions on the camera. Flash control is not available in Basic Zone modes.

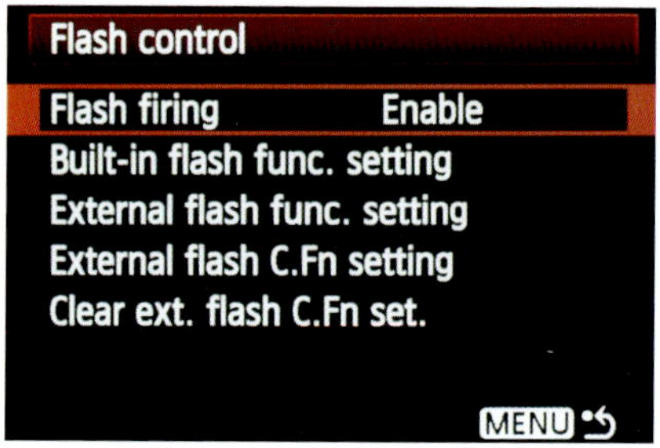

Flash firing

The first option in the Flash control menu is simply to enable or disable flash firing. If flash firing is disabled, then neither the built-in flash nor an external flash will fire. They will continue to provide an AF-assist beam as long as this is not disabled too.

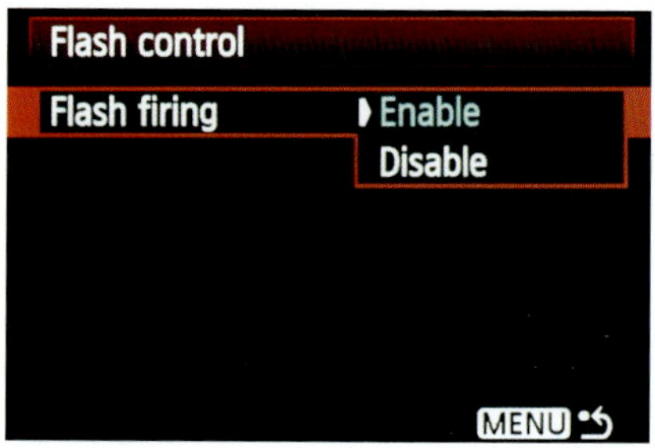

Built-in flash functions

On this screen you can adjust the settings for shutter synchronization, flash exposure compensation, and flash metering mode within E-TTL II.

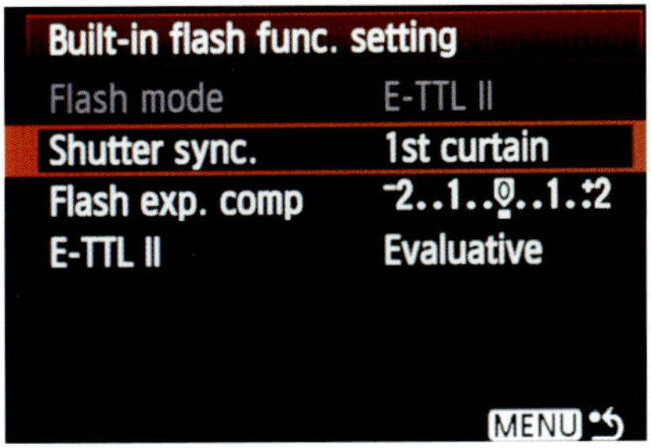

The top line of the menu shows the flash mode: either E-TTL II or Manual flash. The flash mode is fixed as E-TTL II for the built-in flash. The synchronization can be set to first curtain or second curtain (see pages 171–2). The default setting is first-curtain flash, which is generally considered to be "normal" flash exposure.

Flash exposure compensation works in exactly the same way as exposure compensation for the camera. SImply highlight the **Flash exp.comp.** setting and use the ◀ button to reduce the exposure or the ▶ button to increase it. Compensation can be set in either ½- or ⅓-stop increments, depending on the increment set in the Custom Functions menu (see page 116).

E-TTL II metering can be set to either **Evaluative** or **Average**.

Evaluative metering compares the data obtained by the metering burst with the exposure levels under ambient lighting in order to extrapolate the best flash exposure. Readings are taken from the entire frame without bias toward any AF points covering the main subject. Distance information, which is provided by compatible lenses, is also factored into these calculations.

Average metering simply calculates the flash exposure based on readings across the frame without taking into account the ambient lighting and may require some flash exposure compensation.

External flash functions

The settings available depend on the Speedlite being used, but they would normally include flash mode, first- or second-curtain synchronization, flash exposure bracketing, flash exposure compensation, and flash metering mode. Any functions displayed in pale gray have to be set on the flash itself.

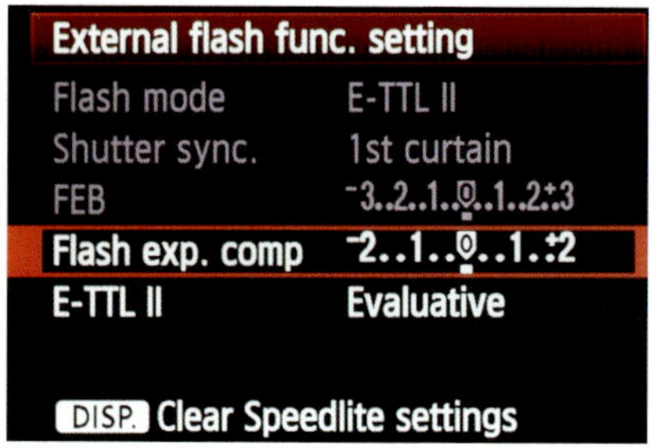

To clear all Speedlite settings, press **DISP**.

External flash & Clear external flash Custom Function settings

These functions operate in much the same way as the above external flash settings except that you have direct access to the Speedlite's custom functions.

Common problems

Clearing the Speedlite settings using the DISP button will also return all built-in flash settings to their default values.

Flash exposure compensation is not canceled when the camera is switched off. Make sure you zero the setting as soon as appropriate.

Tip
Lenses equipped to transmit distance data to the camera will provide the most accurate exposure. However, distance data is not transmitted when the Speedlite is used in bounce mode or when multiple Speedlites are used. With EX Speedlites which are set to TTL, or EZ/E/EG/ML/TL Speedlites which are set to TTL or A-TTL, the flash will fire at full output only.

Shooting menu 2

Shooting menu 2 gives access to settings which control exposure, color, contrast, and sharpness. The process for selecting menu options is described on page 80.

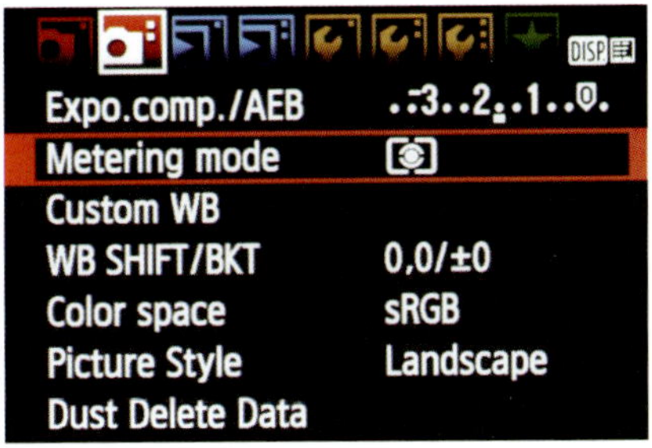

> **Note**
> This menu cannot be accessed in Basic Zone modes.

Exposure compensation/Auto exposure bracketing (AEB)

This function permits either exposure compensation or bracketing, or both combined, and is very useful when you're not quite sure how the balance between highlights and shadows will work out. In some situations there is no such thing as "correct" exposure, and the intended use for the image also plays a part in the decision. Images to be viewed only on a computer can afford to be slightly darker because they don't rely on reflected light like pictures in a book or magazine.

Exposure compensation

Method 1: Press **DISP**. Hold down the **Av+/-** button and rotate the Main Dial to adjust exposure compensation.

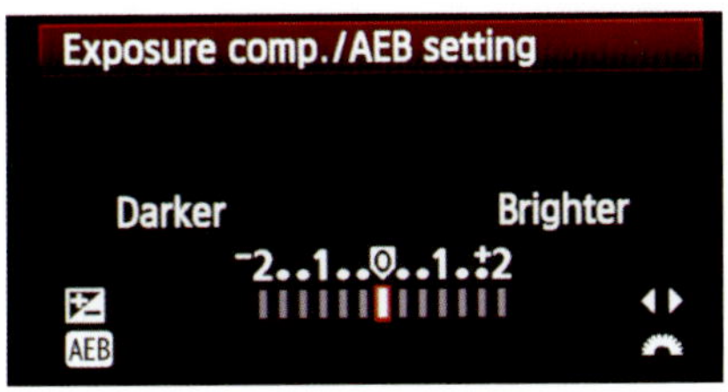

Method 2: Press **MENU**. Select Shooting menu 2 and **Exp. Comp./AEB**. Press **SET**. Use the ◀ or ▶ buttons to adjust compensation. (This method is also used to select bracketing.)

Auto exposure bracketing (AEB)

Three bracketed exposures will be taken, one either side of the optimum exposure, up to +/- 2-stops. Increments will be either ⅓ or ½ stop depending on the increment selected in Custom Function 1 (see page 116). The scale in the viewfinder shows additional indicator marks either side of the central indicator to show the level of over- and underexposure. This information is also shown on the scale in the Display screen. The default order in which the shots are taken is: normal, underexposed, then overexposed.

To activate AEB, press **MENU**. Select Shooting menu 2 and **Exp. Comp./AEB**. Press **SET**. Use the ◀ or ▶ buttons and/or rotate the Main Dial to adjust the bracketing interval. Press **SET**.

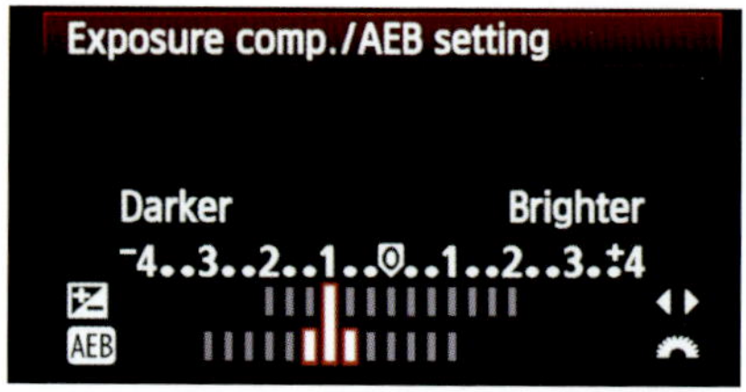

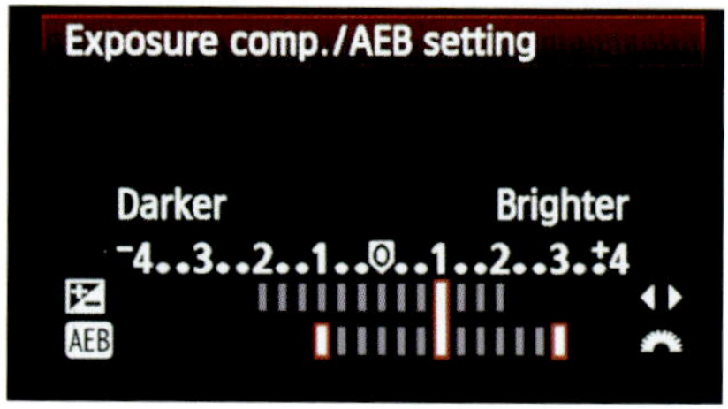

To cancel AEB, follow the same procedure but return the indicator on the scale to its central position.

Tips

Unlike Auto exposure compensation, Auto exposure bracketing is canceled when the camera is turned off.

AEB can be used with both single and continuous drive modes. It cannot be used with flash or bulb exposures, but Flash exposure bracketing can be set on certain Speedlites.

Auto exposure bracketing can be combined with Auto exposure compensation. The compensated setting will be the "normal" exposure of the three taken.

If the Auto Lighting Optimizer function is enabled, AEB may not prove effective.

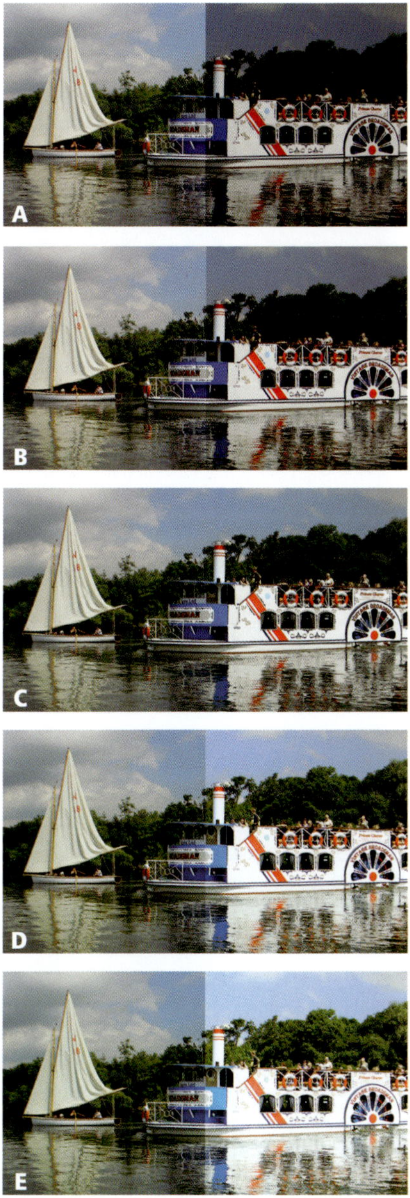

PADDLE STEAMER

This subject contains a full range of tones. Image C is the "correct" exposure. Split images A and B demonstrate underexposure by 1 stop and ½ stop respectively. Image D shows overexposure by ½ stop and image E by 1 stop. Bracketing by ⅓ or ½ stop would be sufficient to achieve a successful result in this instance.

Tip

AEB is not available in Basic Zone modes. Once selected in a Creative Zone mode, it will be retained when you change to any other Creative Zone mode.

Metering mode

Four different metering modes cover any eventuality: Evaluative, Partial, Spot, and Center-weighted.

Evaluative metering makes uses of 35 different zones covering the entire frame area. This is set automatically in all Basic Zone modes and is reasonably foolproof, even with backlit subjects.

Partial metering is suited to strong backlit subjects and concentrates on the center of the frame.

Spot metering is useful for precision metering of a selected tone to be used as the midpoint.

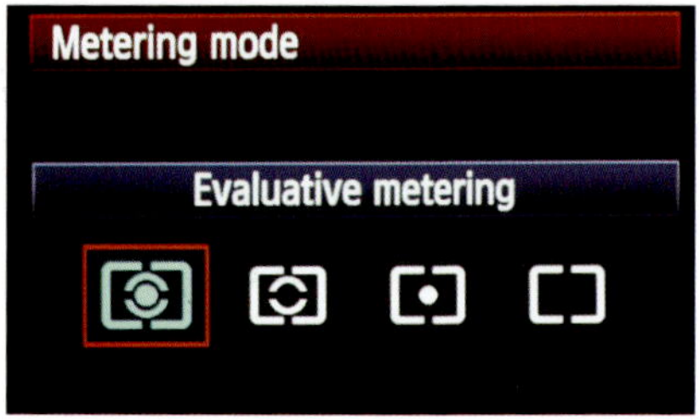

Center-weighted metering gives bias to the center of the frame and then averages out the remainder of the scene.

To select the metering mode, press **MENU**. Select Shooting menu 2, then **Metering mode**. Press **SET**. Use ◀ or ▶ to select the desired metering mode and press **SET**.

White balance

White balance is set via the **WB** button on the back of the camera, except in Basic Zone modes where AWB is mandatory.

In order for colors to be rendered accurately, it is necessary to ensure that white is represented exactly as desired. In most cases this means obtaining a pure white, without the color cast that comes with different artificial light sources, and from natural lighting at different times of the day, or in shade. These variations are measured according to what is known as color temperature, which is shown in degrees Kelvin, commonly abbreviated

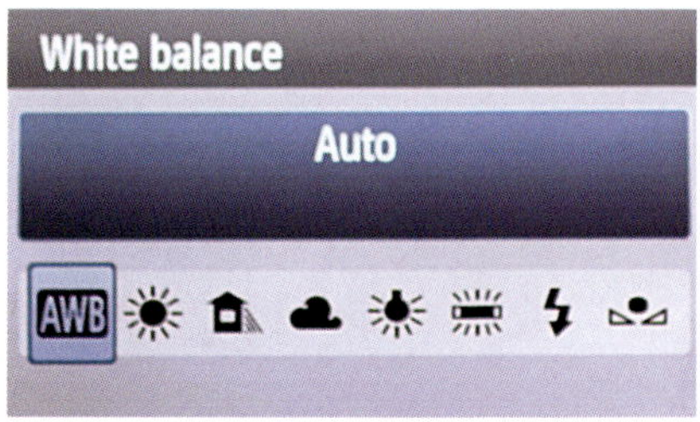

to °K. This figure is indicated above each preset WB setting accessed via the **WB** White balance button. To retain correct color rendition it is necessary to use these presets or to set a Custom white balance (see opposite page).

Setting Custom white balance

The White balance menu enables you to determine a Custom white balance setting to suit a particular shooting situation in which you are unable to gauge the precise color temperature.

1) To set Custom white balance, first photograph a white object using manual focus and the exposure indicated, without any compensation or bracketing. Make sure it fills the spot metering circle. Any white balance setting can be used at this stage.

2) Select Shooting menu 2, highlight **Custom WB** and press **SET**. The image you captured in step 1 will appear on the camera's LCD monitor.

3) A dialog box appears, reading **Use WB data from this image for Custom WB**. Select **OK**. The data will be imported, overwriting any previously set data.

Common errors

If the exposure obtained in step 1 above is significantly underexposed or overexposed, a correct white balance may not be obtained.

If the image you capture in step 1 is taken while the Picture Style is set to Monochrome, it cannot be imported in step 4.

4) You will be prompted to set the white balance to . Press **SET**. (Note that it is not actually necessary to set the white balance to until you need it.)

5) Exit the menu by pressing **MENU**.

6) Next time you wish to use your Custom white balance setting, press the **WB** button and select .

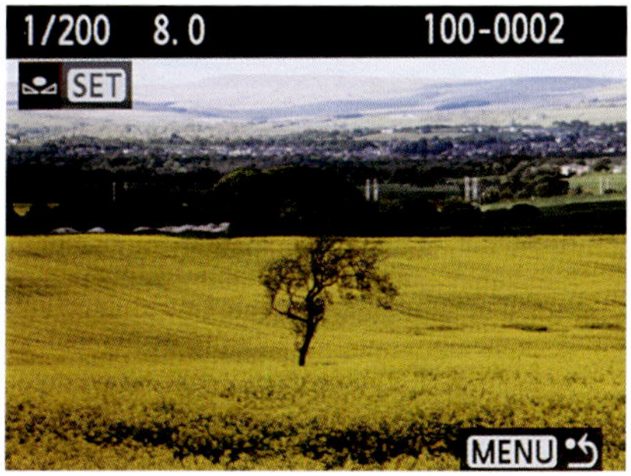

Tips

An 18% gray card can be used instead of a white object in step 1.

If you have registered a personal white balance setting using the software provided with the camera, it will be replaced by any new Custom white balance setting you create using this procedure.

White balance shift/bracketing

These two functions are incorporated into the same menu screen, which provides a simple graphic representation of a complex process. Adjusting the color settings is not unlike using color-correction filters, except that here, nine levels of correction are possible. Each increment is equivalent to a 5 mired shift.

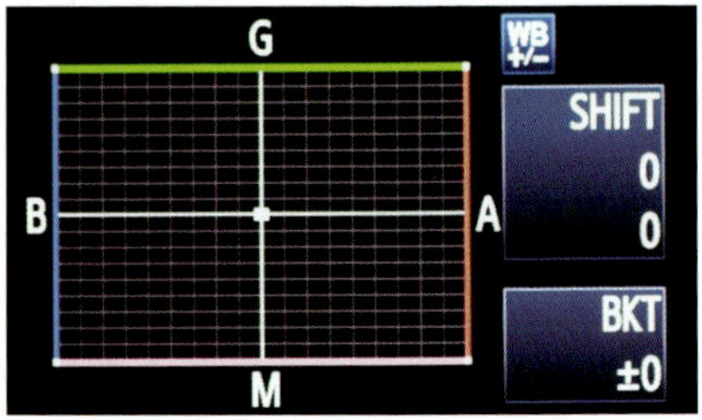

This facility can be applied to any white balance setting, including custom and preset white balance settings. It is only available in Creative Zone modes.

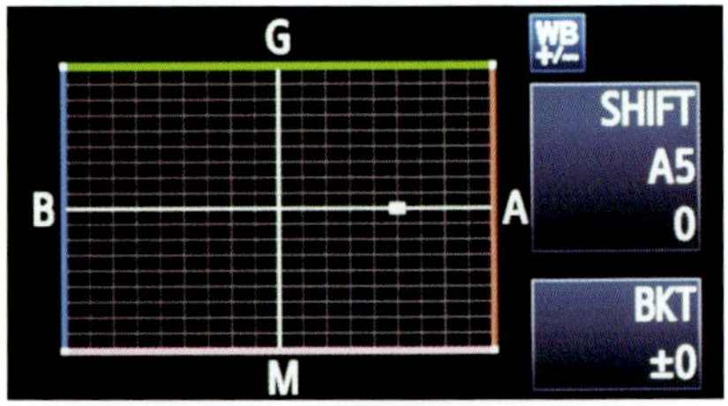

To set White balance shift:

1) In Shooting menu 2, highlight **WB SHIFT/BKT** and press **SET.**

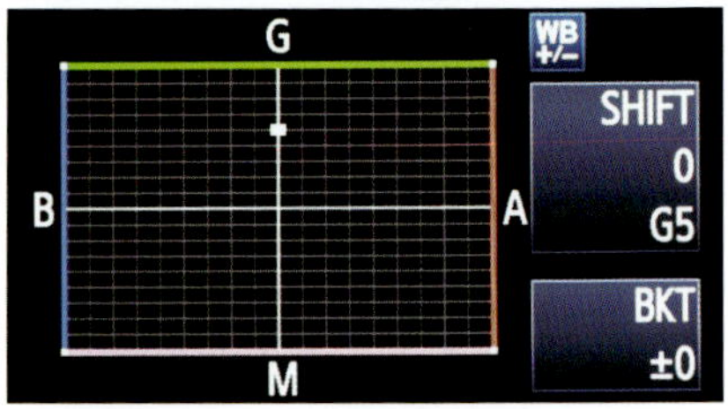

2) Use the ◀ ▶ ▲ ▼ buttons to move the white cursor ■ from its central position to the new setting. The bias can be toward Blue, Amber, Magenta, or Green and the blue panel at the top right displays the new coordinates using the initial letter of the color plus a number from 0–9.

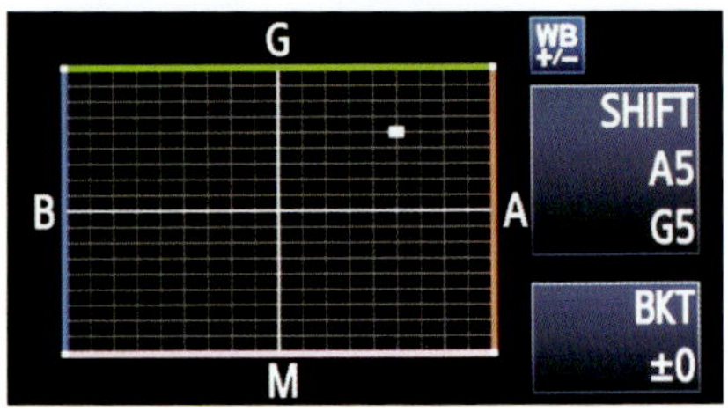

3) Press **DISP** at any time to reset the bias to 0,0.

4) Press **SET** to finalize your setting.

5) The **BW+/-** symbol will be shown in the viewfinder and on the LCD monitor.

White balance bracketing can be used in conjunction with White balance shift to capture three versions of the same image, each with a different color tone. The primary image will use the cursor location as set opposite. Either side of this, two further images will be captured with a difference of up to three levels in single-level increments, each increment being five mireds. You can bracket with either a Blue/Amber bias or a Magenta/Green bias.

Tip
It is only necessary to press the shutter release once with White balance bracketing selected in order to capture the three images. However, both the total number of shots available on the memory card and the number of burst images available will be reduced by three.

To set White balance bracketing:

1) In step 2 on page 96, rotate the Main Dial clockwise to set a Blue/Amber bias with one, two, or three levels difference. The increment chosen will be shown in the blue panel at the bottom right of the screen. Alternatively, rotate the Main Dial anticlockwise to set a Magenta/Green bias with one, two, or three levels difference.

2) Press **DISP** at any time to cancel bracketing (the cursor will be reset to 0,0).

3) When bracketing is selected (but before **SET** is pressed) it is still possible to move the cursor (now showing as ■ ■ ■) around the screen in order to adjust the color bias.

4) Press **SET** to finalize your settings and return to Shooting menu 2.

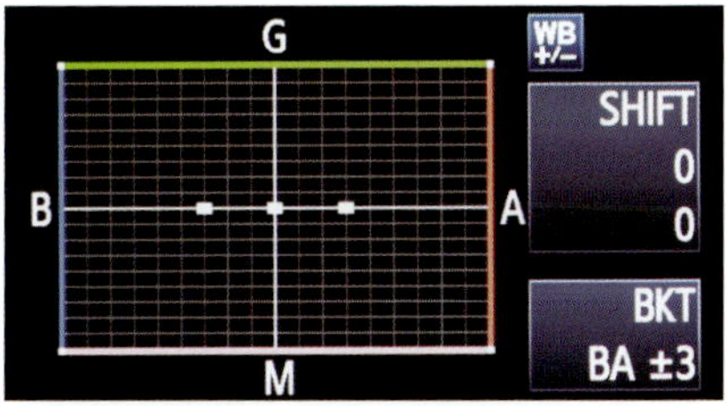

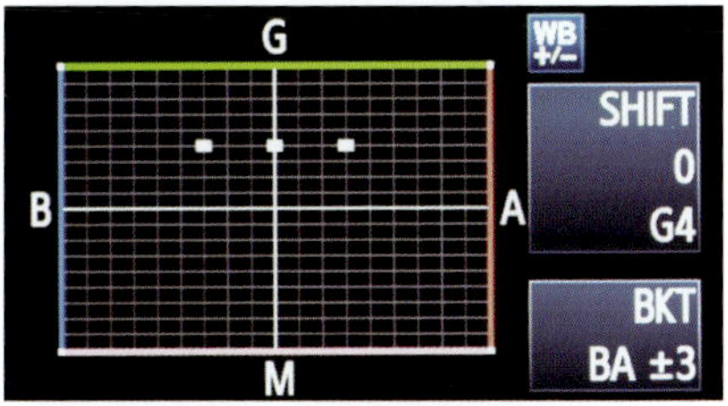

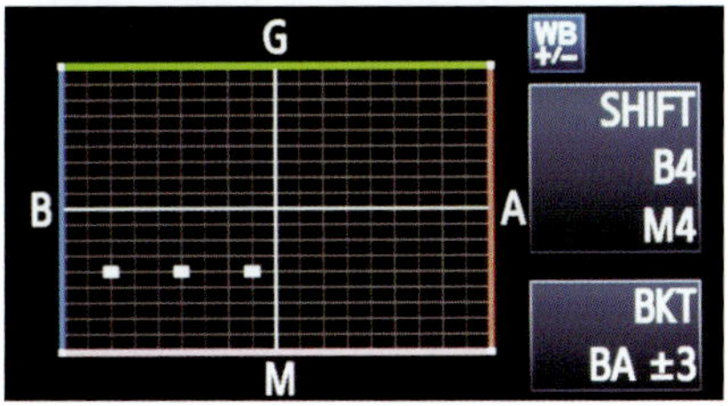

Color space

The term color space is used to describe the range of colors that can be reproduced within a given system. The Rebel T1i/EOS 500D provides two color spaces: sRGB and Adobe RGB. The latter offers a more extensive range and is likely to be used by those for whom the final image is to be converted to the CMYK color space for commercial printing in books, magazines, or catalogs. Canon recommend sRGB for what they classify as "normal use."

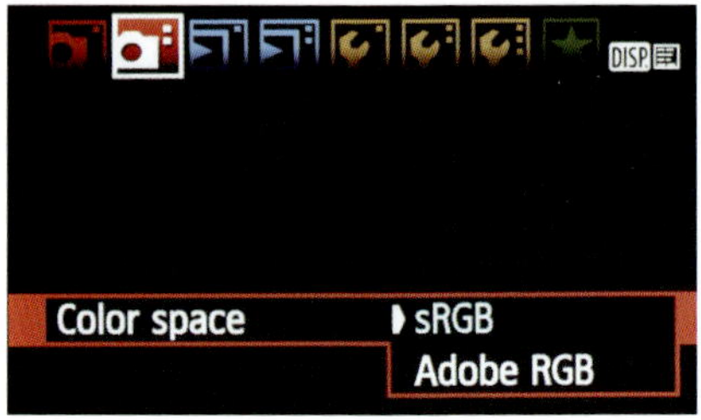

Picture Styles

In the Basic Zone modes, the appropriate Picture Style is selected automatically—for example, in Portrait mode the Portrait Picture Style is selected. In the Creative Zone, however, each Picture Style preset can also be adjusted according to your personal needs and preferences.

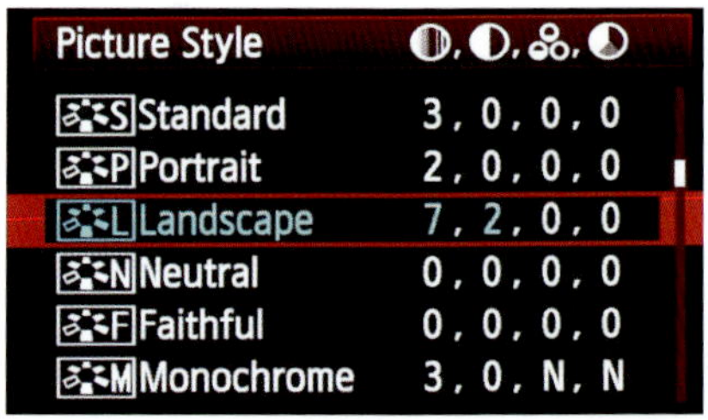

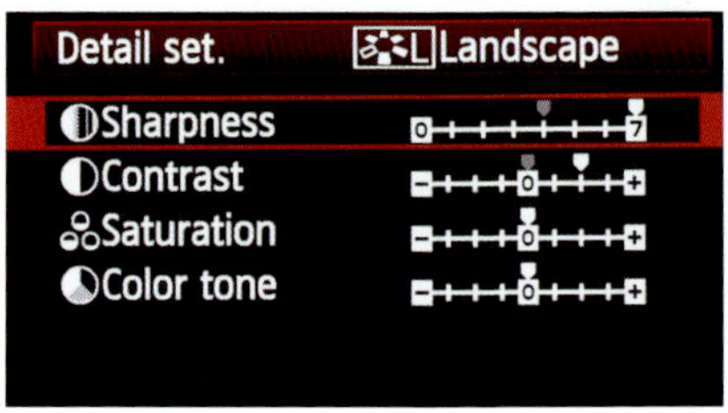

To change to a different Picture Style without changing parameters, a simple menu can be accessed by pressing the Picture Style selection button on the back of the camera. To change an individual Picture Style's parameters, you must access the Picture Style menu via the **MENU** button and Shooting menu 2.

All the Picture Style options discussed on pages 99–101 apply to both JPEG and RAW files, but if you shoot RAW you can reset or change Picture Style parameters on your computer after shooting, using dedicated Canon software.

Picture Style parameters

For each Picture Style there are four sets of parameters, as follows: Sharpness, Contrast, Saturation, and Color tone. With the exception of Sharpness, the settings for which range from 0 to +7, all the settings range from -4 to +4. Their effects are self-explanatory, with the exception of Color tone, in which a lower setting (-4, for example) produces a reddish skin tone, while a higher setting produces a yellower skin tone.

Tip

If you change a Picture Style parameter setting, the new setting is indicated by a white marker but the default setting remains in view as a gray marker. This makes it easy to revert to the factory settings.

Picture Style: Faithful

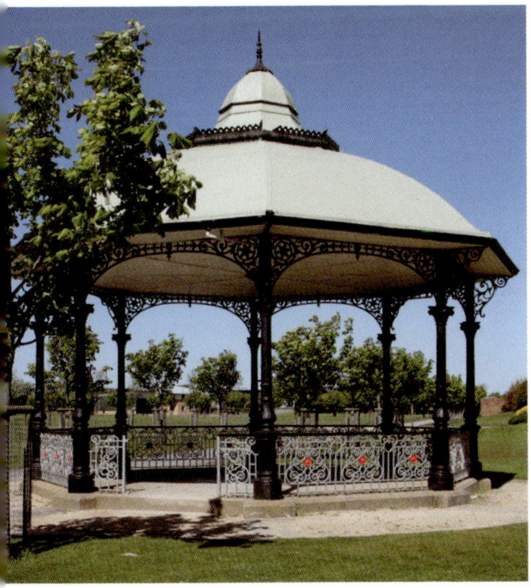

Picture Style: Landscape

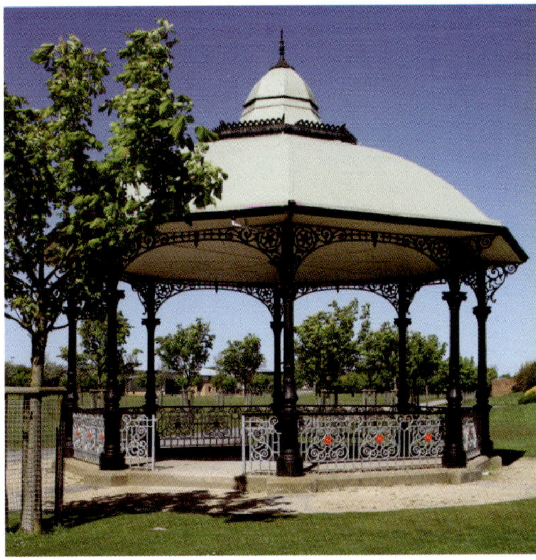

Changing Picture Style parameters

1) Press the **MENU** button. Select Shooting menu 2, then **Picture Style** and press **SET**.

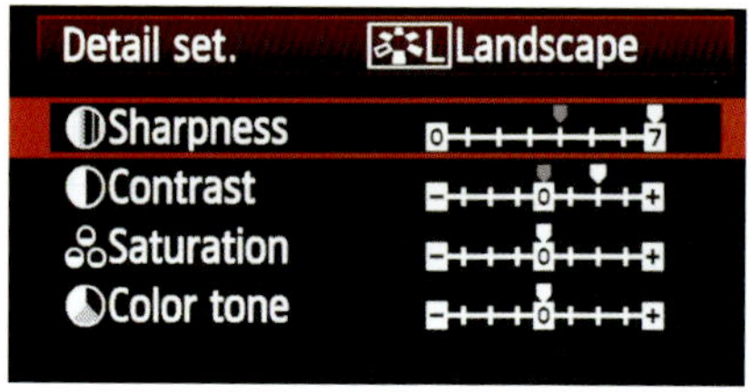

2) Use the ▼ button to scroll down to the desired Picture Style and press the **DISP** button to display the **Detail set.** screen for that Picture Style.

3) Use the ▲ ▼ buttons to highlight the parameter you wish to change. Press **SET**.

4) The chosen parameter will now appear on a screen on its own. Use the ◀ button to decrease the setting or ▶ to increase it. The white indicator will move along the scale accordingly, leaving a gray indicator showing the default setting.

5) Press **SET** to finalize the parameters. The **Detail set.** screen appears.

6) Repeat steps 3–5 as necessary.

7) Press **MENU** to return to the Picture Style screen, then press **SET** to finalize your choice of Picture Style and return to Shooting menu 2.

Setting a Monochrome Picture Style

The procedure for setting or adjusting the parameters for Sharpness and Contrast are exactly as outlined above. The procedure for setting Filter or Toning effects is the same up to the point where a single parameter is shown on screen. Instead you are presented with a menu from which to choose. The Filter effects menu offers a choice of yellow, orange, red, or green filter effects or none. The Toning effects menu offers a choice of sepia, blue, purple, green, or none.

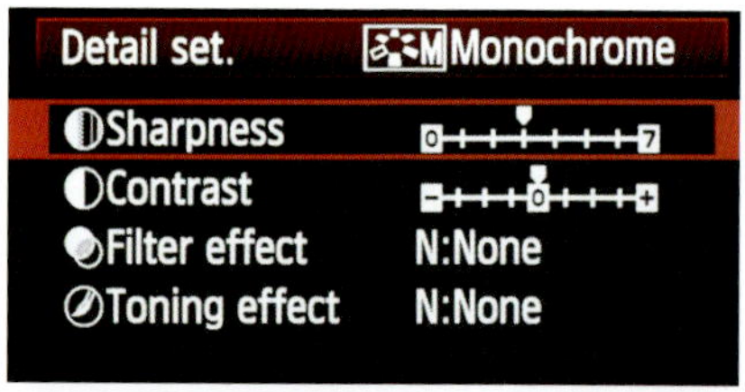

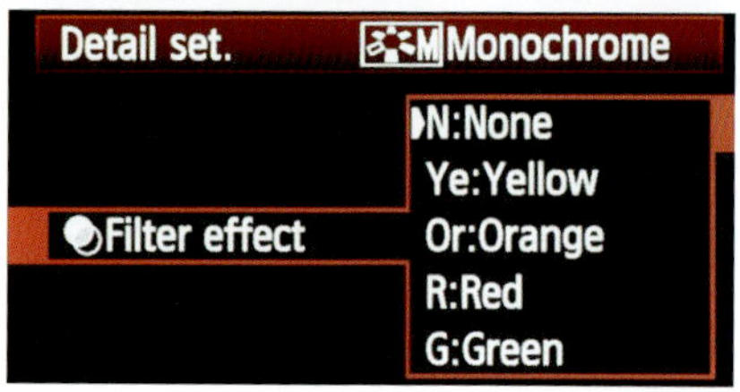

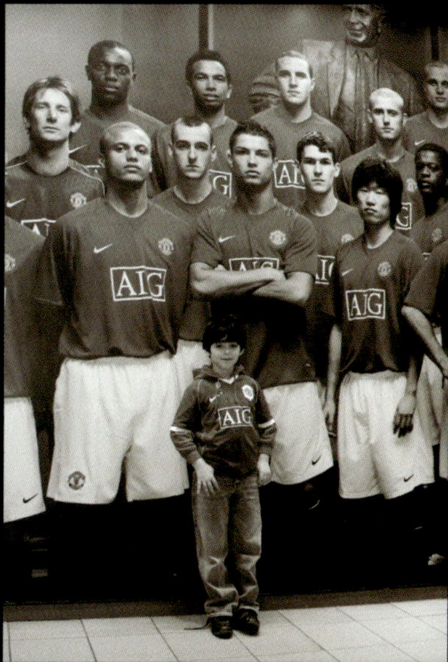

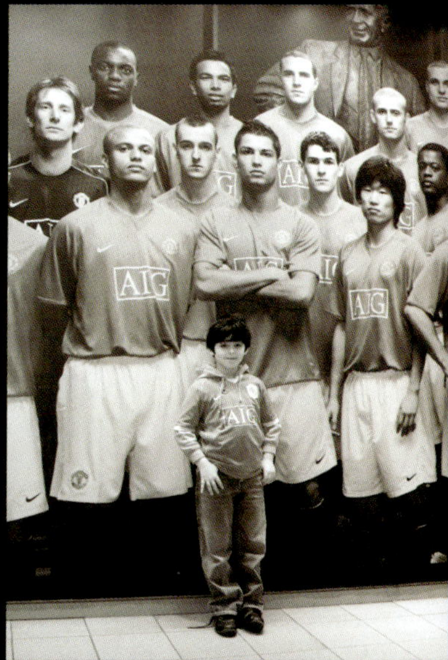

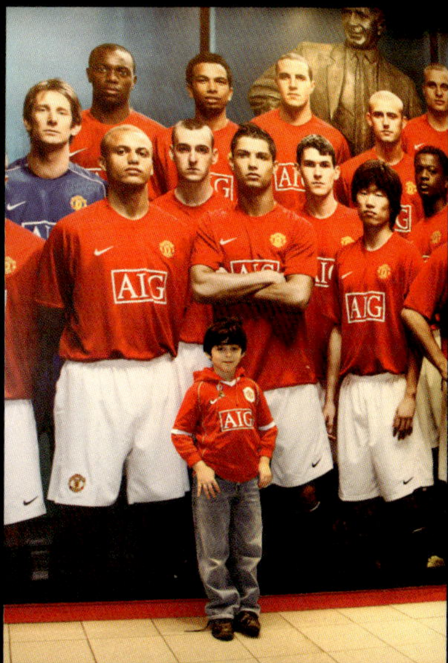

MONOCHROME FILTER EFFECTS

The Canon Rebel T1i/EOS 500D offers four monochrome filter effects. The Red filter lightens red tones considerably, as shown above, and produces a high-contrast effect. The Yellow filter is useful for making skies look less washed out, with better cloud definition. The Orange filter darkens blue skies and makes clouds more distinct. The Green filter is good for skin tones and makes foliage appear crisper.

(Left) Original image
(Above left) Mono conversion
(Above right) Red filter applied

Registering User-defined Picture Styles

Three User-defined Picture Styles can be created from the default settings for a base style.

1) Press the **MENU** button. Select 📷 Shooting menu 2 then **Picture Style** and press **SET**.

2) Use the ▼ button to scroll down to User Def 1, 2, or 3. Highlight one of these and press the **DISP** button to display the **Detail set.** screen for that Picture Style.

3) The top line of the menu will show the preset Picture Style currently used as the base style for the selected User-defined style. To amend this base style, press **SET** and use the ▲ and ▼ buttons to scroll through the preset styles. Select the desired preset and press **SET**.

4) Use the ▼ button to scroll down to the parameter you wish to amend and press **SET**. That parameter will now appear on a screen on its own. Use the ◀ button to lower the setting or ▶ to increase it. Press **SET** to finalize the selected parameter.

5) Repeat step 4 for other parameters.

6) Press **MENU** to return to the Picture Style screen, then press **SET** to finalize your choice of Picture Style and return to the Shooting menu.

Dust Delete Data

The camera's self-cleaning sensor unit will eliminate most of the dust that could show up on your images. But when visible traces remain, you can append the Dust Delete Data to your images to erase the dust spots automatically at a later stage in the Digital Photo Professional software provided. The data is appended to all the images (both RAW and JPEG) captured after this point but has no significant impact on file size.

1) To obtain the Dust Delete Data, find a solid-white subject and set the focal length of your lens to 50mm or longer. Set the lens to **MF** and rotate it to the infinity setting.

2) In 📷 Shooting menu 2 select **Dust Delete Data** and press **SET**. Select **OK** and press **SET**. The following message will appear: "Press the shutter button completely when ready for shooting."

3) Photograph the solid-white subject at a distance of 8–12in (20–30cm), making sure that the subject completely fills the frame. The image will be captured automatically in **Av** Aperture Priority mode at an aperture of f/22. This image will not be saved but the Dust Delete Data will be retained. A message appears reading "Data obtained." Press **OK**.

Playback menu 1

Playback menu 1 is identified by blue highlighting, and it covers the protection, deletion, and rotation of selected images. It also enables you to choose images for the purposes of printing or transferring to computer.

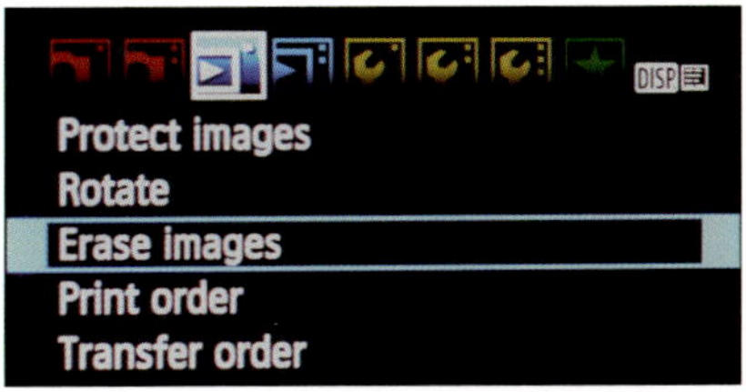

Protect images

In order to avoid accidental deletion, you can protect selected images. These, once protected, will display the key symbol.

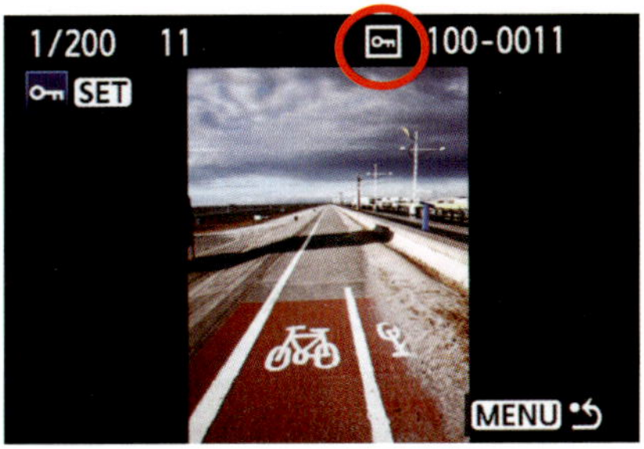

1) Press the **MENU** button and use the Main Dial or ▲▼ buttons to scroll through the menus until you reach ▶ Playback menu 1.

2) Select **Protect images** and press **SET**.

3) Using the ◀ or ▶ buttons, select the image to be protected and press **SET**. The key icon will appear above the protected image.

4) To cancel protection for an image, select it and press **SET**. The key icon will disappear.

5) To protect another image, repeat step 3.

6) To exit image protection, press the **MENU** button.

Warning!

Protected images will still be deleted when you format a memory card.

Tip

To delete protected images using the Erase function, image protection must be canceled individually for each image.

FUNCTIONS

Rotate images

The Rotate images facility enables you to rotate individual images—as opposed to the Auto Rotate function which, when selected, will automatically rotate all portrait-format images to the correct orientation. As the image area displayed is greater when a portrait-format image is rotated through 90 degrees, this function is useful for examining quality and focus.

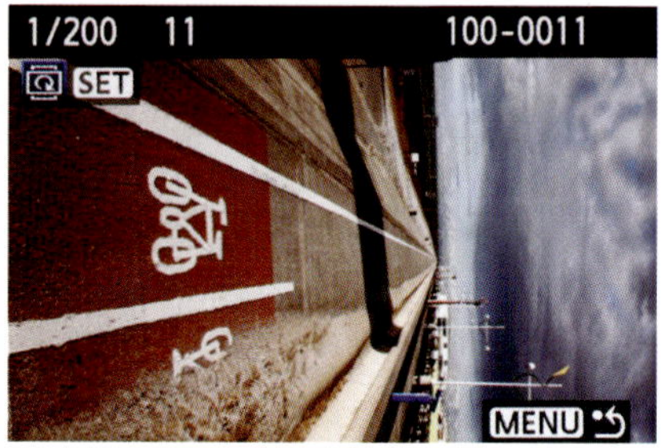

1) Press the **MENU** button and use the Main Dial or ◀ ▶ ▲ ▼ buttons to scroll through the menus until you reach ▶ Playback menu 1.

2) Select **Rotate** and press **SET**.

3) Using the ◀ and ▶ buttons, select the image to be rotated and press **SET** repeatedly until the desired orientation is obtained.

4) To rotate another image, repeat step 3. To exit, press the **MENU** button.

> **Tip**
> By using the ✱/▦•🔍 and ▦/🔍 buttons, you can toggle the monitor between a single image, four images, or nine images shown simultaneously.

Erase images

The Erase facility enables the deletion of either selected individual images or all the images on the memory card, with the exception of any protected images in both cases. There is a distinct advantage to erasing individual images via this menu as opposed to simply using the 🗑 button during review. This is that images are selected for deletion (marked with a tick) but not actually deleted until you press the 🗑 button to delete all selected images at once. As a result, you can scroll backward and forward through similar images to make comparisons and uncheck an image to retain it if necessary.

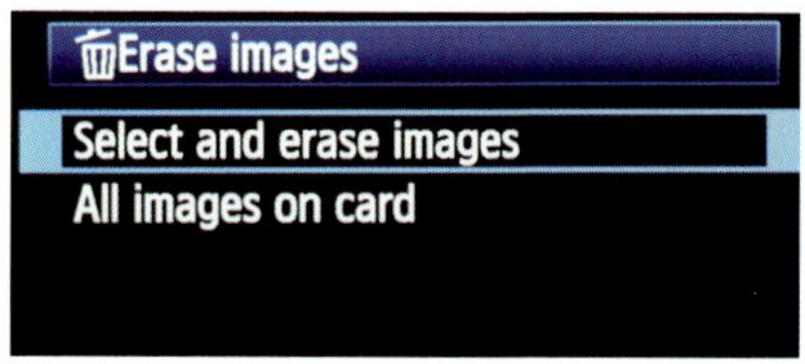

To erase selected images:

1) Press the **MENU** button and use the Main Dial or ▲ ▼ buttons to scroll through the menus until you reach ▶ Playback menu 1.

2) Select **Erase images** and press **SET**.

3) Choose **Select and erase images** and press **SET**.

4) Use the ◀ and ▶ buttons to scroll through the images.

5) Use the ▲ and ▼ buttons to select an image for deletion. A white tick will be displayed in a small box at the top left of the displayed image. Next to the delete symbol the total number of images selected for deletion will be displayed. To remove the tick, press ▼.

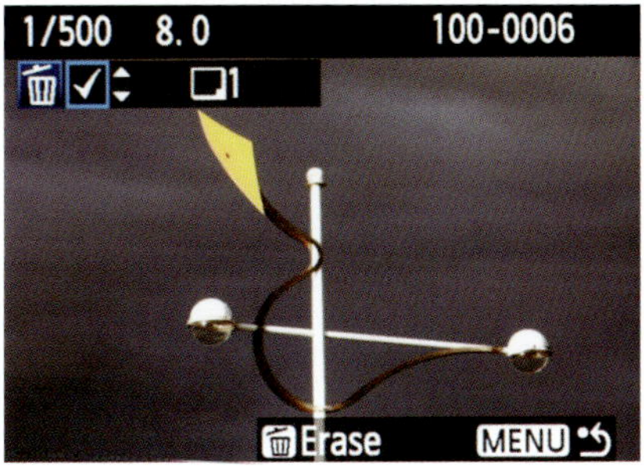

6) To select another image for deletion, repeat steps 4–5. To exit, press **MENU**.

Print order

The Print Order function allows you to select images for printing direct from the memory card. You can also specify which settings will be applied and the information to be printed with each image. Index printing enables you to print thumbnail images. This topic is explained fully in Chapter 9.

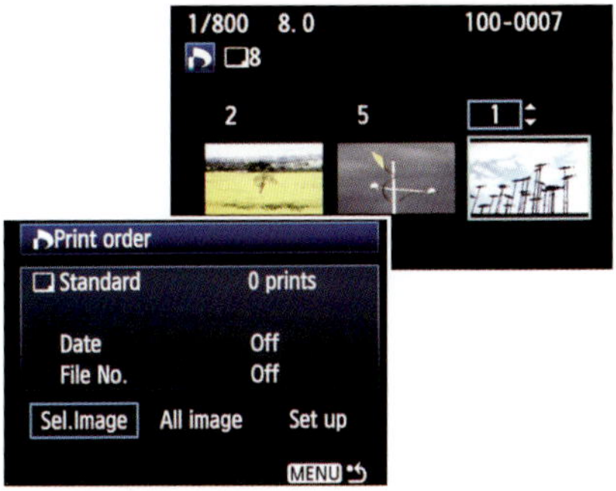

Transfer order

The Transfer Order function operates in a similar way to the Print Order function but relates to the transfer of images from the memory card to your computer. This topic is explained in more detail in Chapter 9.

FUNCTIONS

Playback menu 2

A very short menu, Playback menu 2 is primarily concerned with viewing and reviewing your images.

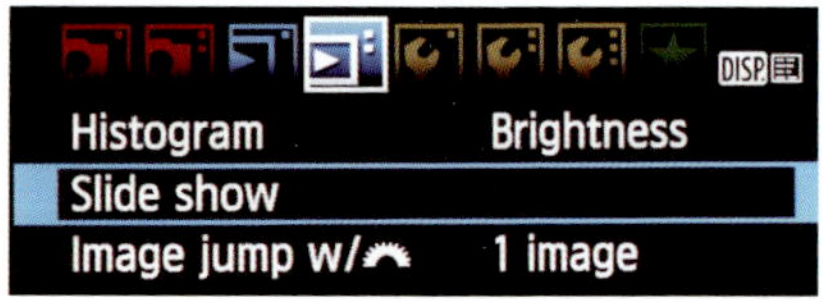

Histogram

During playback, pressing the **DISP** button brings up the Shooting Information display, which includes a histogram. This menu option allows you to choose whether a Brightness histogram or an RGB histogram is displayed. Pressing the **DISP** button a second time during playback will bring up a second display which incorporates both Brightness and RGB histograms, but with less shooting information.

Using the Brightness histogram

The Brightness histogram is a graph that shows the overall exposure level, the distribution of brightness, and the tonal gradation. It enables you to assess the exposure as a whole, to judge the richness of the overall tonal range, and ultimately to fine-tune the exposure that is required.

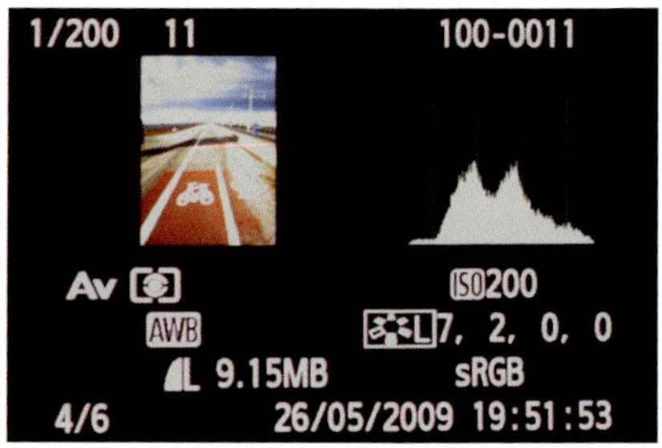

The histogram's horizontal axis shows the overall brightness level of the image. If the majority of the peaks appear on the left, it indicates that the image may be too dark. If the peaks are largely on the right, the image may be too bright. However, this all depends on the result you are seeking. You might actually want a very "heavy" result, or perhaps a high-key, soft-focus image which is bright and ethereal in quality.

The histogram's vertical axis shows how many pixels there are for each level of brightness. Too many pixels on the far left suggests that shadow detail will be lost. Too many pixels on the right suggests that highlight detail will be lost. The Highlight Alert function will cause these areas to blink on the image displayed.

In particularly contrasty situations, you may be in danger of losing both shadow and highlight detail in an image, in which case you may have to judge which you want to sacrifice in favor of the other (see page 65).

Using the RGB histogram

The RGB histogram is a graph showing the distribution of brightness in terms of each of the primary colors—red, green, and blue. The horizontal axis shows each color's brightness level (darker on the left and lighter on the right). The vertical axis shows how many pixels exist for each level of brightness in that particular color.

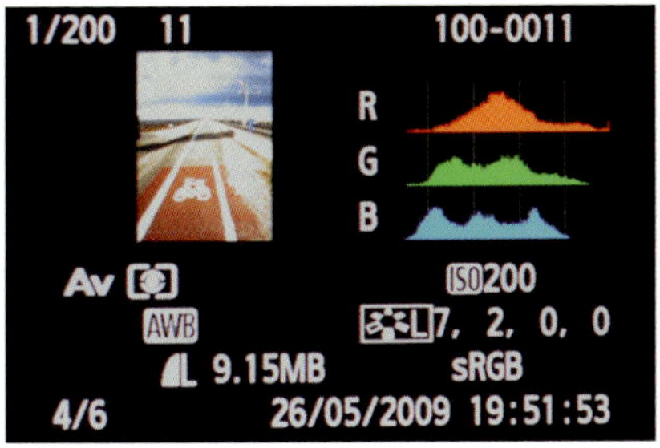

The greater the number of pixels on the left, the darker and less emphatic that particular color will appear. Conversely, the greater the number of pixels shown on the right, the brighter that color will be, possibly to such an extent that the color is far too saturated and won't hold detail.

Slide show

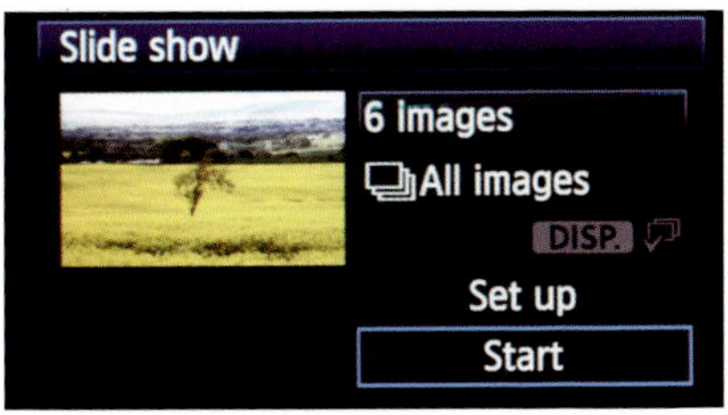

This initiates a slide show which works in conjunction with the Shooting Information display. Press **DISP** during the slide show to change the display from image-only to one of the three histogram display options. You can also pause and restart the slide show by pressing **SET**.

Image jump with

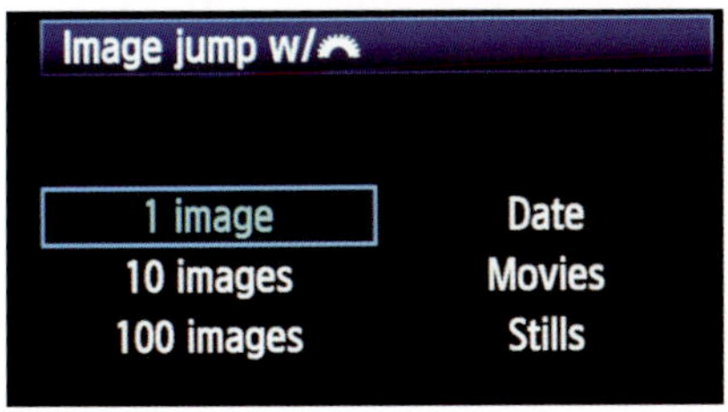

This function selects the criteria by which you toggle between groups of images—by stills or movies, by date, or by single image, 10 images, or 100 images. Toggling is achieved using the Main Dial.

Set-up menu 1

This is the first of three menus that cover settings which, in most cases, you will determine once and need not return to often, except in special circumstances. Highlighting for all Set-up menus is in yellow.

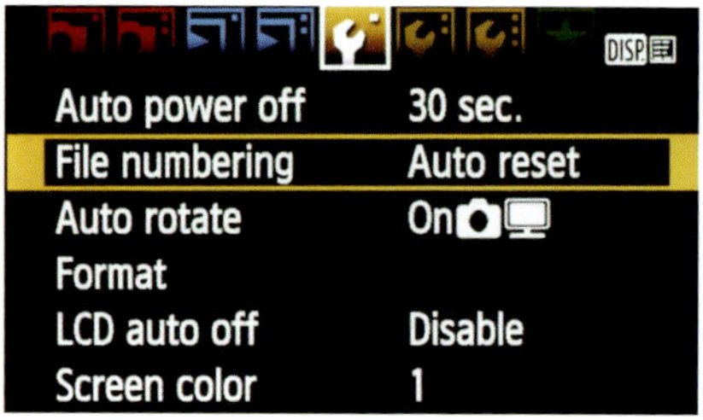

To set options in ⚙ Set-up menu 1:

1) Press the **MENU** button and use the Main Dial or ▲▼ buttons to scroll through the menus until you reach ⚙ Set-up menu 1.

2) To highlight a different item on the menu, use the ▲ and ▼ buttons.

3) To select an item once it is highlighted, press the **SET** button.

4) If secondary menus or confirmation dialog boxes are displayed, you may need to use the ◀▶▲▼ buttons, the **DISP** button, or **SET** in different ways.

5) Once a setting has been changed, press **SET** to save the new setting.

6) To exit at any stage, press the **MENU** button to go back one level at a time.

Auto power-off

With the Auto power-off setting, you can save battery power while keeping the camera ready for action. You can instruct the camera to turn itself off after a set interval ranging from 30 seconds to 15 minutes of inactivity, but power will be restored immediately when you partially depress the shutter-release button. If you wish the camera to remain switched on you should select the **Off** option.

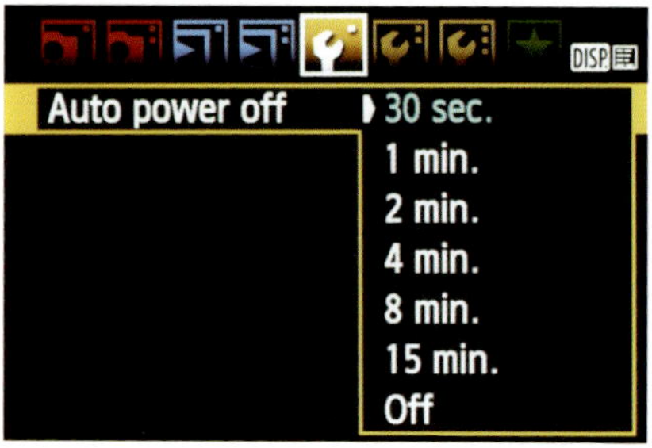

File numbering

Each time you record an image, the camera allocates a file number to it and places it in a folder. The file numbers and folder names can be changed when they are on your computer, but not in camera.

Images are assigned a sequential file number from 0001 to 9999 and are saved in one folder. The prefix IMG_ is used regardless of file type, but the suffix will be either .JPG or .CR2 for RAW files.

When a folder is full and contains 9999 images, the camera automatically creates a new folder. The first image in the new folder will always revert to 0001, even if **Continuous** is selected in the File numbering menu. The camera can create up to 999 folders. A new folder is also created for each new shooting date.

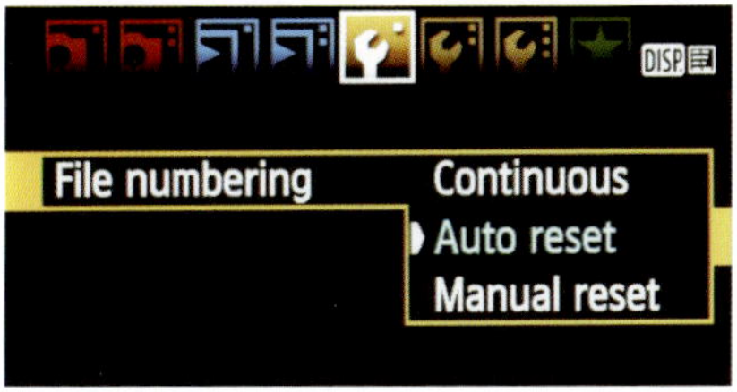

Continuous

If you select this option, when you change a memory card, the file number of the first image recorded on the new card will continue from the last image on the card you removed. So, if the last shot taken on a card was IMG_0673.JPG, the first shot on the new card will be IMG_0674.JPG. As soon as the file number reaches 9999, a new folder will still be created and the file number will revert to 0001.

Auto reset

Each time you replace a memory card, file numbering automatically starts from 0001.

Common problems

Continuous file numbering is sometimes assumed to be a mechanism for counting the number of shutter actuations, but in fact it relates only to the file-numbering sequence that continues when you replace the camera's memory card.

Even when Auto reset is selected, if you insert a memory card that contains previously captured images, the camera is likely to continue the sequential file numbering from the last image shot on that card. To avoid this you should format the card to delete all previous images—provided, of course, that you have already downloaded them to your computer or another storage device.

Manual reset

When you reset the file numbering manually, the camera creates a new folder immediately and starts the file numbering in that folder from 0001. This is convenient if you are shooting similar images in a variety of different locations or at different times and want to keep each set of images separate. This can be extremely helpful when renaming files or adding captions at a later date. After a manual reset, the file-numbering sequence will return to Continuous or Auto reset.

Auto rotate

If Auto rotate is enabled, all vertical images will be rotated automatically so that they are displayed with the correct orientation. This can be applied to either the camera monitor and computer or just the computer, or it can be disabled altogether.

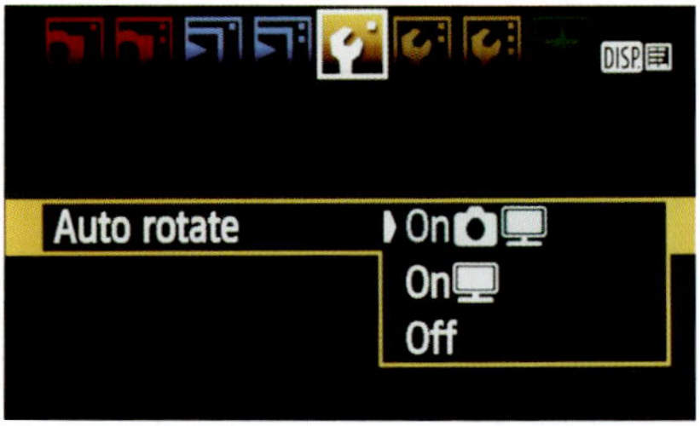

Format

If the memory card is new, or has been in use in a different camera, the Format function will initialize the card ready for use in the current camera. Formatting a card removes all images and data stored on that card, including images which have been protected through the **Protect images** function in the Playback menu (see page 103).

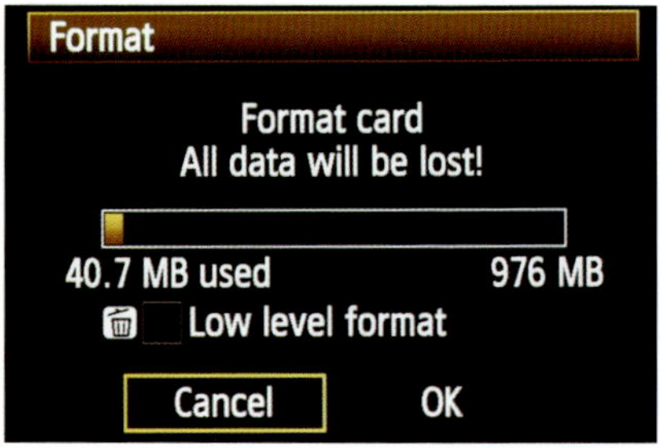

LCD auto off

The LCD monitor displays menus and secondary dialog boxes, images captured, and shooting information. The default setting is for the Shooting settings screen to be displayed when the camera is switched on. When you partially depress the shutter-release button, this display is temporarily turned off. The Shooting settings screen can also be turned off by pressing either the **DISP** or **SET** buttons. Other default settings include the display of menus when you press **MENU** or image playback when you press ▶. In each case the display is switched off again when you press the same button.

The **LCD on/off button** menu allows you to choose how the Shooting settings screen is activated or deactivated (menu and image playback displays are not affected).

Shutter btn. (default): Display turns off temporarily while the shutter-release button is depressed.

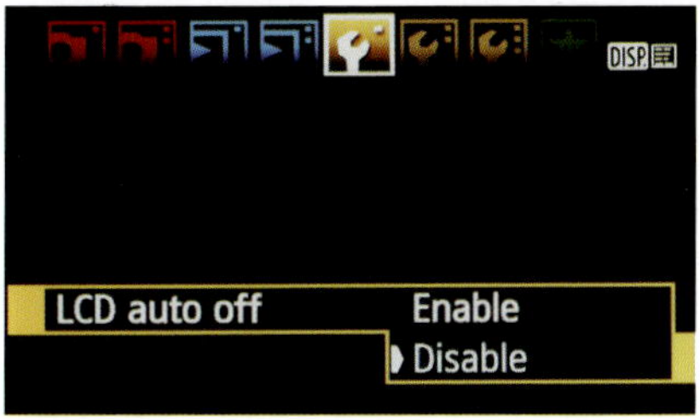

Shutter/DISP: Display turns off when the shutter-release button is depressed but then remains off. To switch the display on again, press **DISP** or **SET**.

Remains on: Display remains on, even when the shutter release is depressed. To switch it off, press **DISP** or **SET**.

> **Tip**
> Unnecessary use of the LCD monitor should be avoided to help conserve the battery.

Screen color

Four different color schemes can be selected for the Shooting settings display. Menu screens are not affected.

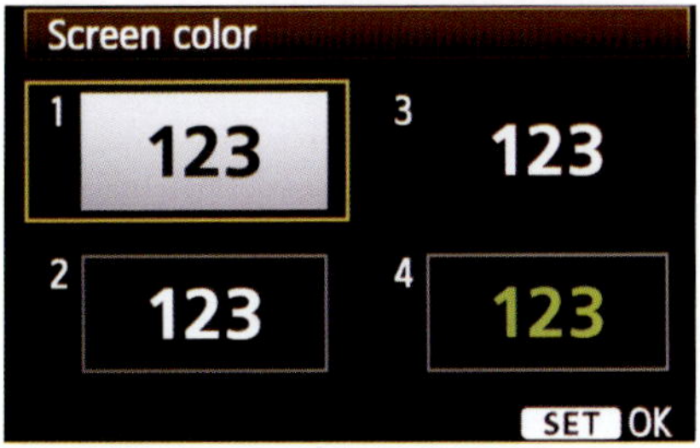

FUNCTIONS

Set-up menu 2

As with Set-up menu 1, you will visit most of the settings in Set-up menu 2 when you first acquire the camera, but rarely afterwards—with the possible exceptions of the Sensor cleaning and Live View functions.

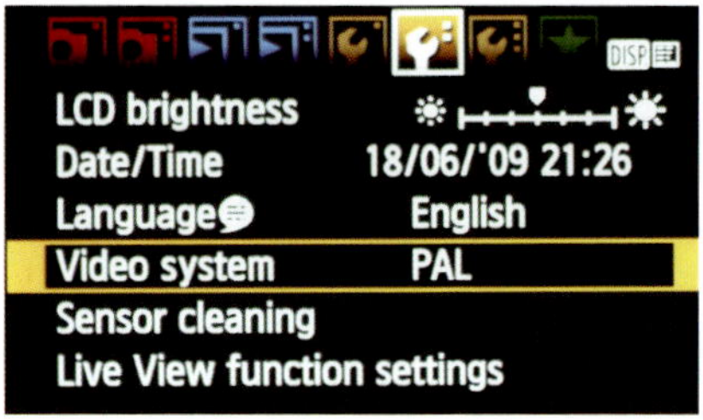

To set options in ƳƬ: Set-up menu 2:

1) Press the **MENU** button and use the Main Dial or ▲▼ buttons to scroll through the menus until you reach ƳƬ: Set-up menu 2.

2) To highlight a different item on the menu, use the ◀ and ▶ buttons.

3) To select an item once it is highlighted, press the **SET** button.

4) If secondary menus or confirmation dialog boxes are displayed, you may need to use the ◀▶▲▼ buttons, the **DISP** button, or **SET** in different ways.

5) When a setting has been changed, press **SET** to save the new setting.

6) To exit at any stage, press the **MENU** button to go back one level at a time.

LCD brightness

When this function is selected, three items are displayed on the monitor: the last image recorded, a grayscale on the right of the monitor, and a slider control at the bottom. If no images are stored on the memory card, only the grayscale and slider are displayed.

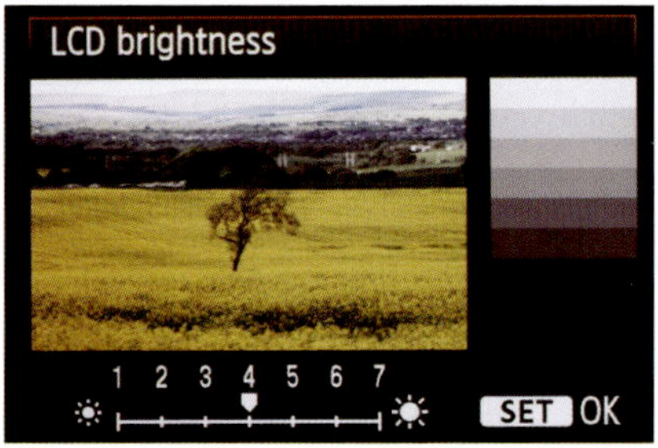

The ◀ and ▶ buttons are used to change the setting. When a change is made, the arrow on the slider will move along the seven-point scale and all the bands of the grayscale graphic will become darker or lighter, as will the displayed image.

Date/Time

To set or amend the Date/Time:

1) Use the ◀ and ▶ buttons to highlight the item to be changed.

2) To change a setting, highlight it and press **SET**. Press either ▲ or ▼ (repeatedly when necessary) to increase or decrease the setting.

3) Press **SET** to confirm the change.

4) Repeat steps 1–2 for each setting you wish to change.

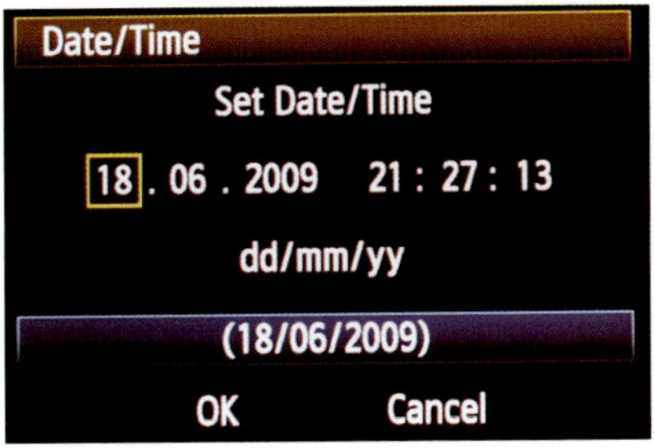

5) To save your changes, highlight **OK** and press **SET**.

Language

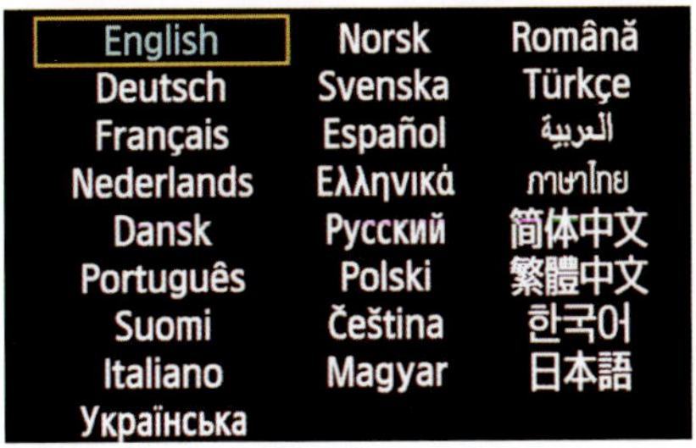

Twenty-five languages are programmed into the Canon Rebel T1i/EOS 500D.

Video system

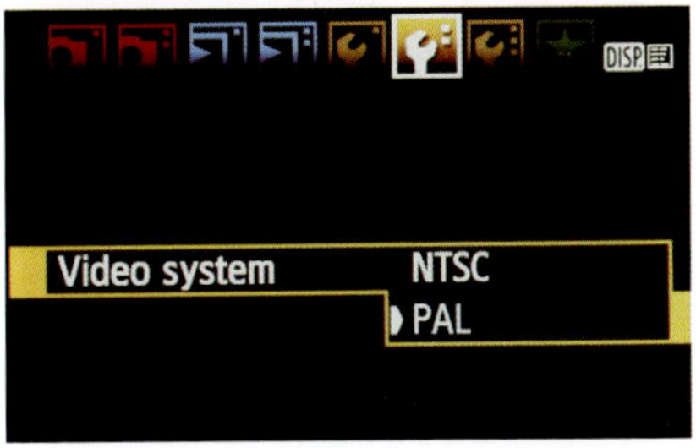

You can connect the camera to a TV set using the cable provided, making it easy to share your images with family and friends. This topic is covered in detail in Chapter 9. However, you must first use this menu to establish the correct video format. The choice is between **NTSC** (common in North America) and **PAL** (the format usually used in Europe).

Sensor cleaning

Dust specks on the camera sensor are one of digital photography's major irritations. They show up particularly in areas of plain color, such as expanses of blue sky, and when using narrow apertures. To minimize the problem, avoid changing lenses often, especially in dusty or windy environments, and don't use f/22 when f/8 will do!

The camera's Integrated Cleaning System is designed to shake off particles of dust, but it may still be necessary to have your sensor professionally cleaned occasionally by an authorized Canon service center.

If you enable **Auto cleaning** in the Sensor cleaning menu, the Self-cleaning sensor unit, which is attached to the sensor's front layer, will operate for approximately one second each time you turn the camera on and off, and the LCD monitor displays a message to this effect. Auto cleaning can also be disabled using the same menu.

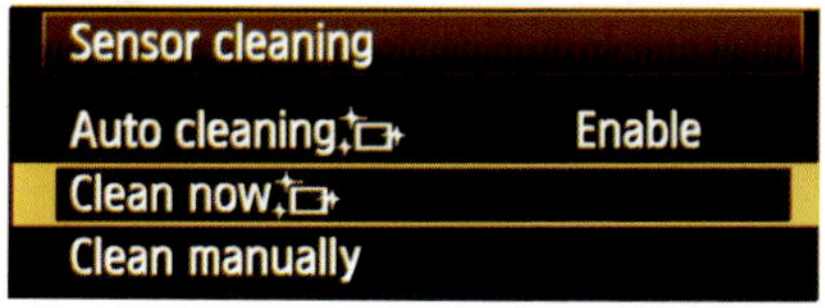

You can also operate the sensor cleaning operation immediately by selecting **Clean now**. This may take slightly longer than the automatic operation. The sound of a single shutter operation will be heard but no image is recorded.

Tips

The Auto cleaning process can be interrupted by partially depressing the shutter-release button as a prelude to shooting.

The **Clean manually** setting is for use only by service technicians.

Live View function settings

See Chapter 3 for full details of Live View and Movie mode.

Note

Live View is not available in Basic Zone modes.

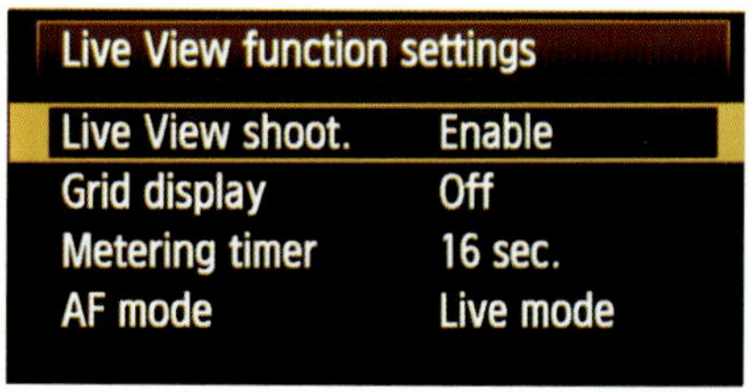

Set-up menu 3

This menu includes the 13 Custom Functions. It is also used to clear all camera settings and all Custom Functions back to their default values, so care needs to be taken not to do this accidentally. Set-up menu 3 also identifies the firmware installed on the camera.

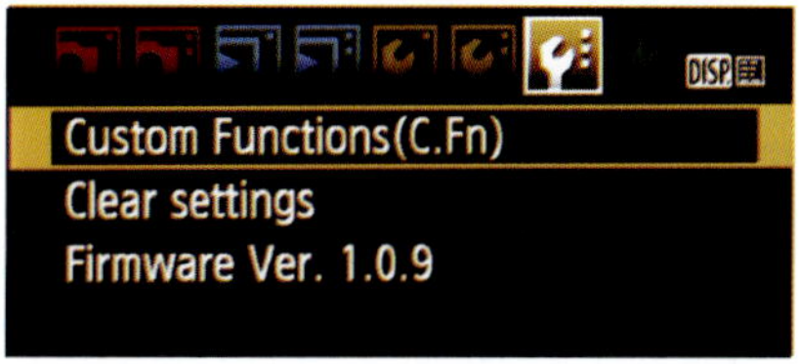

Custom Functions

Custom Functions are divided into groups primarily concerned with Exposure, Image, Autofocus, and Drive, with a final group called Operation/Others. These groups are abbreviated using Roman numerals to C.Fn I, C.Fn II, and so on. On the Rebel T1i/EOS 500D all Custom Functions are accessed from a single Custom Functions menu and are numbered from 1–13 consecutively, despite their subcategory.

The procedure for accessing each menu item is the same, as follows:

Note
This menu cannot be accessed in Basic Zone modes.

1) Press the **MENU** button and use the Main Dial or the ◀ and ▶ buttons to scroll through the menus until you reach Set-up menu 3.

2) Select **Custom Functions** from the menu and press **SET**.

3) Use the ◀ and ▶ buttons to scroll through the options until you reach the appropriate one. Press **SET**.

4) Use the ▲ and ▼ buttons to choose the desired setting and press **SET**. The current setting will be highlighted in blue.

5) Repeat steps 3–4 to change other Custom Function settings.

6) Press **MENU** to exit to the main menu.

C.Fn I: Exposure

C.Fn-1 Exposure level increments

This provides a choice between ⅓- or ½-stop increments for both normal and flash exposure settings.

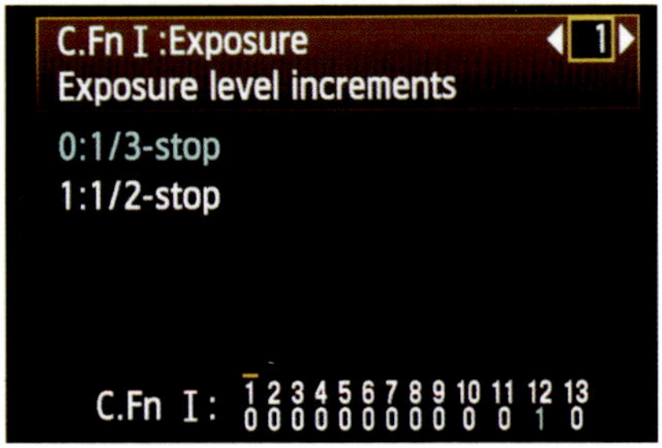

C.Fn-2 ISO expansion

This function enables the maximum ISO to be increased from 3200 to either 6400 or H (12800). The lowest setting remains 100. An increase in image noise may be noticeable at high ISO settings.

If Highlight tone priority is enabled, the ISO range will remain 200–3200.

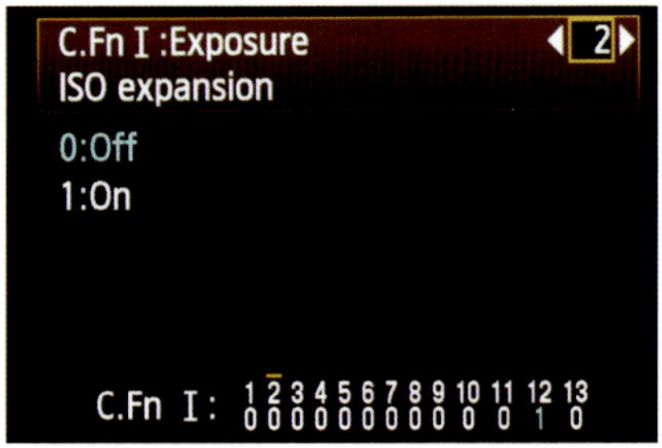

C.Fn-3 Flash sync speed in Av mode

This applies solely to Aperture Priority (Av) mode and the use of flash. The flash sync speed can fixed at 1/200 sec or set to **Auto**, when it will set a speed to match the ambient light, up to a maximum of 1/200 sec. An intermediate auto setting of 1/200–1/60 sec can also be selected. Note that high-speed flash synchronization is also possible with compatible Speedlites.

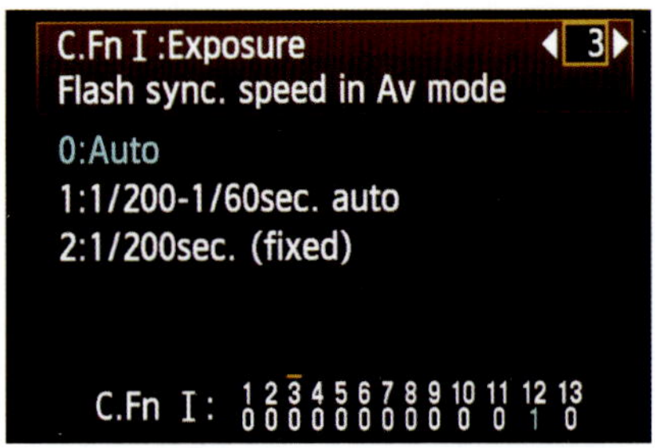

C.Fn II: Image

C.Fn-4 Long exposure noise reduction

The default setting for this function is **OFF**. When changed to **Auto**, the camera will automatically apply noise reduction to exposures of 1 sec or longer provided it detects noise in the image just captured. When switched to **On**, this function will apply noise reduction to all exposures of 1 sec or longer.

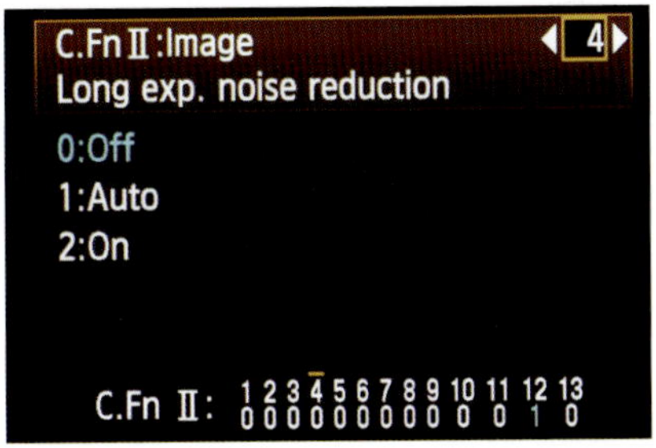

Tips

The noise-reduction process is applied after the image is captured and will effectively double the time taken to record the image.

If set to **On** and shooting with Live View, the LCD monitor will be disabled while noise reduction is applied.

The size of the maximum burst for continuous shooting will be drastically reduced when noise reduction is applied.

C.Fn-5 High ISO speed noise reduction

This function will reduce noise at all ISO settings, not just high ISO speeds as the name seems to suggest. When used with lower ISO speeds, a reduction in shadow noise may be obtained.

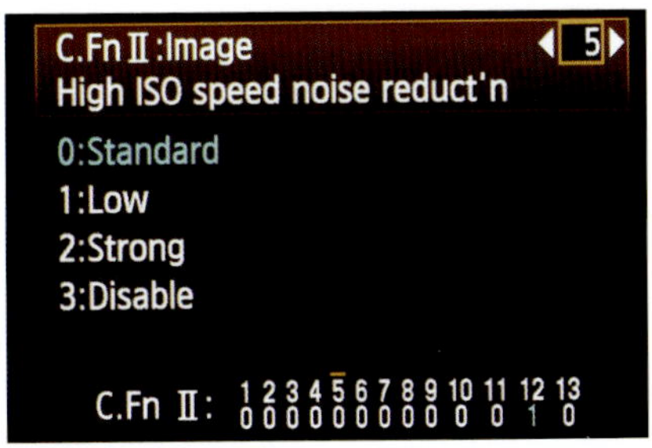

C.Fn-6 Highlight tone priority

This function improves the recording of highlight detail by increasing the dynamic range and rendering smoother gradation between tones at the lighter end of the scale. However, this may result in increased noise in the shadow areas. When it is selected, the **D+** icon will be displayed with the ISO setting on the LCD and in the viewfinder. The maximum ISO range will remain 200–3200 regardless of any other settings.

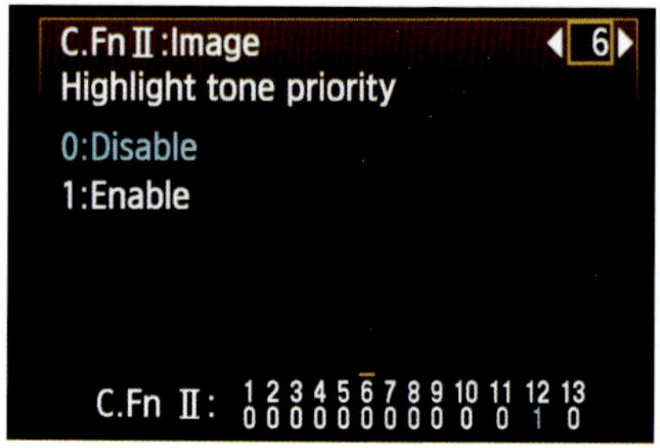

C.Fn-7 Auto Lighting Optimizer

This feature enables dark or low-contrast images to be corrected automatically, though in some situations there can be an increase in noise. The feature is applied automatically in all Basic Zone modes at Standard strength and cannot be disabled. In Creative Zone modes, Auto Lighting Optimizer can be disabled or set to one of three strengths—Standard, Low, or Strong—but it will not work in either Manual or Bulb modes. It will be applied to RAW images if they are processed using the Digital Photo Professional software provided with the camera.

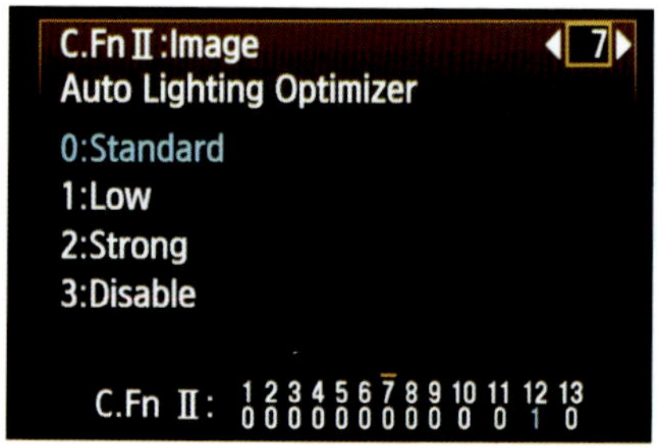

C.Fn III: Autofocus/Drive

C.Fn-8 AF-assist beam firing

Both the built-in flash and EX Speedlites can assist with focusing in low-light situations using this facility. If **Enable** is selected, both the built-in flash and an EX Speedlite, whichever is being employed, will use the AF-assist beam. If **Disable** is selected, neither will be able to use it. Finally, it is possible to enable only an external flash's AF-assist beam, as long as this function is not disabled on the Speedlite, the settings of which will override the settings on the camera.

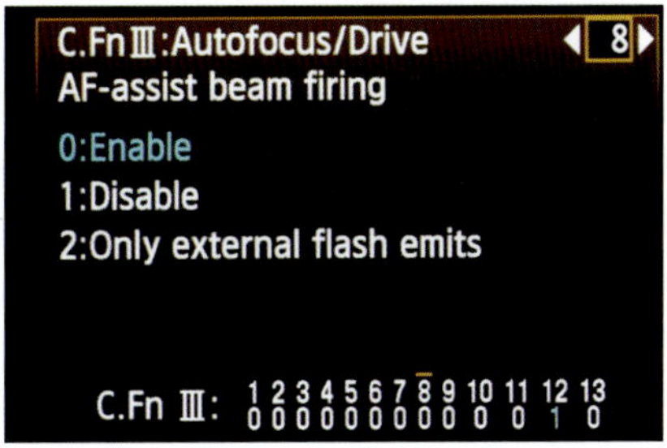

C.Fn-9 Mirror lock-up

To prevent the slight vibration that can be caused by the reflex mirror operation, the mirror can be locked up as soon as your focusing, framing, and exposure-setting procedures have been completed. When the Mirror lock-up function is enabled, fully depressing the shutter-release button once swings the mirror up and locks it in place. This operation sounds like shutter actuation but is not. The shutter-release button is then pressed a second time to take the exposure and release the mirror. The remote release RS-60 E3 should be used to further reduce the risk of vibration.

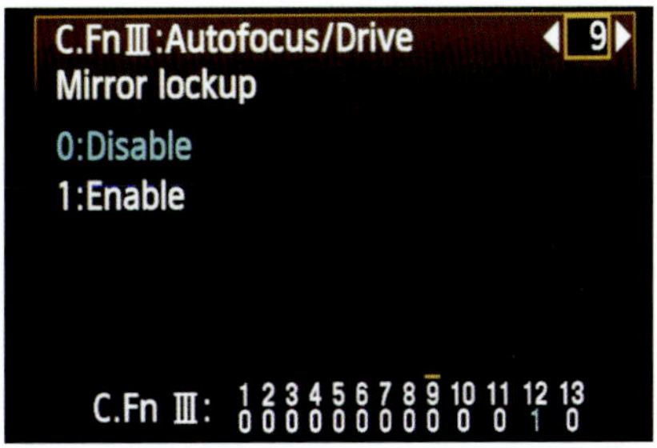

C.Fn IV: Operation/Other functions

C.Fn-10 Shutter/AE lock button

This menu offers several combinations for the shutter release and ✱/⊞•Q AE lock button, all of which involve auto exposure lock and autofocus. There are handling implications for each combination and any reprogramming should be thought through very carefully.

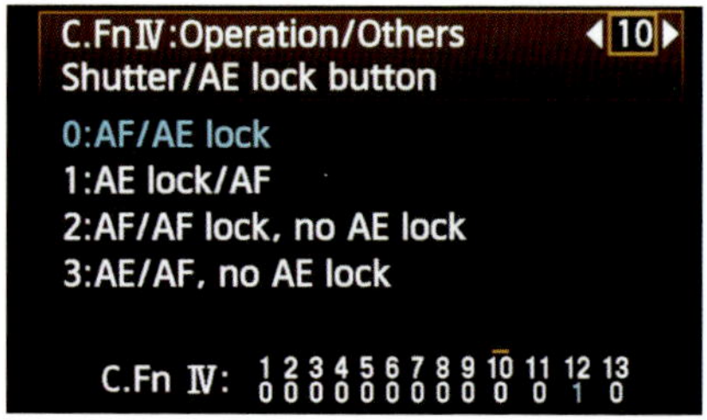

C.Fn-11 Assign SET button

The **SET** button can be programmed to perform various functions, any of which you may like to access quickly. It can be used to control the LCD monitor display, bring up the image-quality screen, set flash exposure compensation, or access the Menu system. It can also be used in conjunction with My Menu (see page 84) to access frequently used functions.

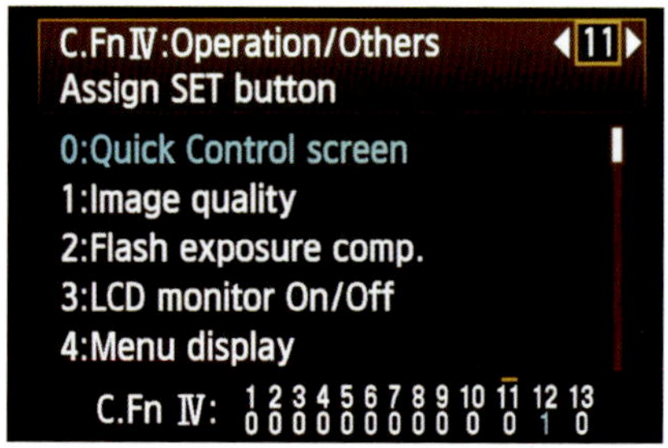

C.Fn-12 LCD display when power ON

When **Display** is enabled, the Shooting settings screen will be displayed when the camera is switched on. If **Retain power OFF status** is enabled, the Shooting settings screen will not be displayed when the camera is turned on, as long as the display was switched off using the **DISP** button before the camera was last turned off.

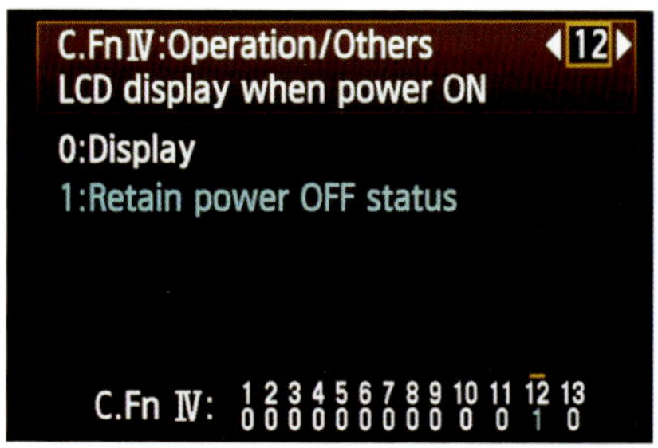

C.Fn-13 Add original decision data

When this function is **On**, data is added to all subsequently captured images to confirm their originality. For anyone to verify originality they must purchase the Original Data Security Kit OSK-E3.

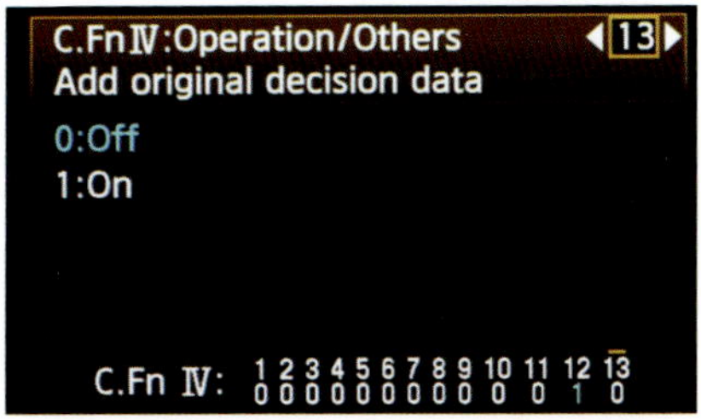

Clear settings

The **Clear all camera settings** function changes all shooting functions back to their default settings. Note that this will also delete both Custom WB information and Dust Delete Data. Custom Function settings are not affected.

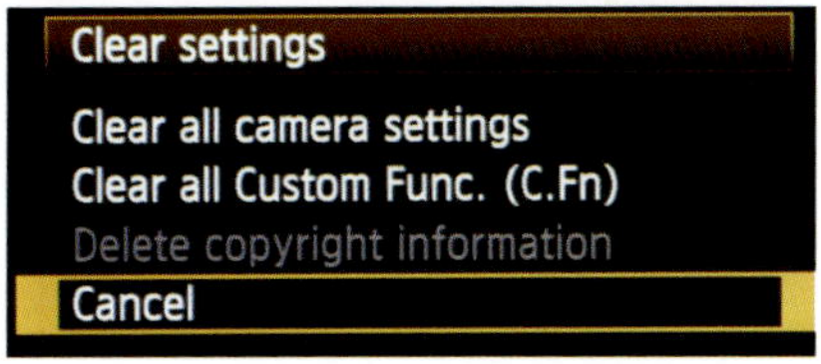

Clear all Custom Func. restores just the Custom Function settings to default values.

Firmware version

Set-up menu 3 displays the firmware version currently installed on the camera, provided one of the Creative Zone modes is selected on the Mode Dial. Canon periodically update the camera's firmware; check their website for new versions and installation instructions. The usual method is to copy the required data to a memory card and then use the card to update the camera itself. Full instructions are provided on the Canon website.

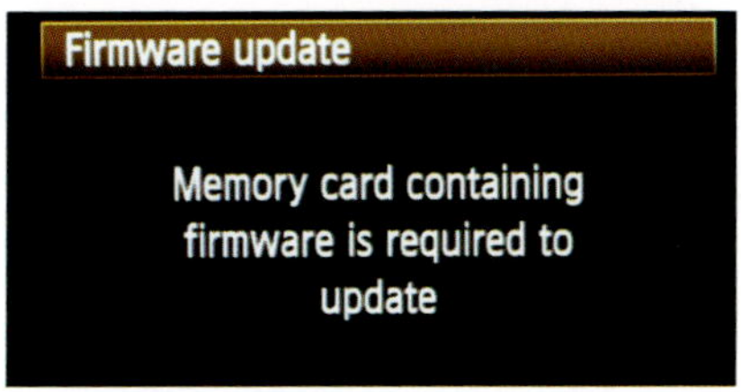

Alternatively, you can have the updated firmware installed for you at a Canon service center.

Chapter 3

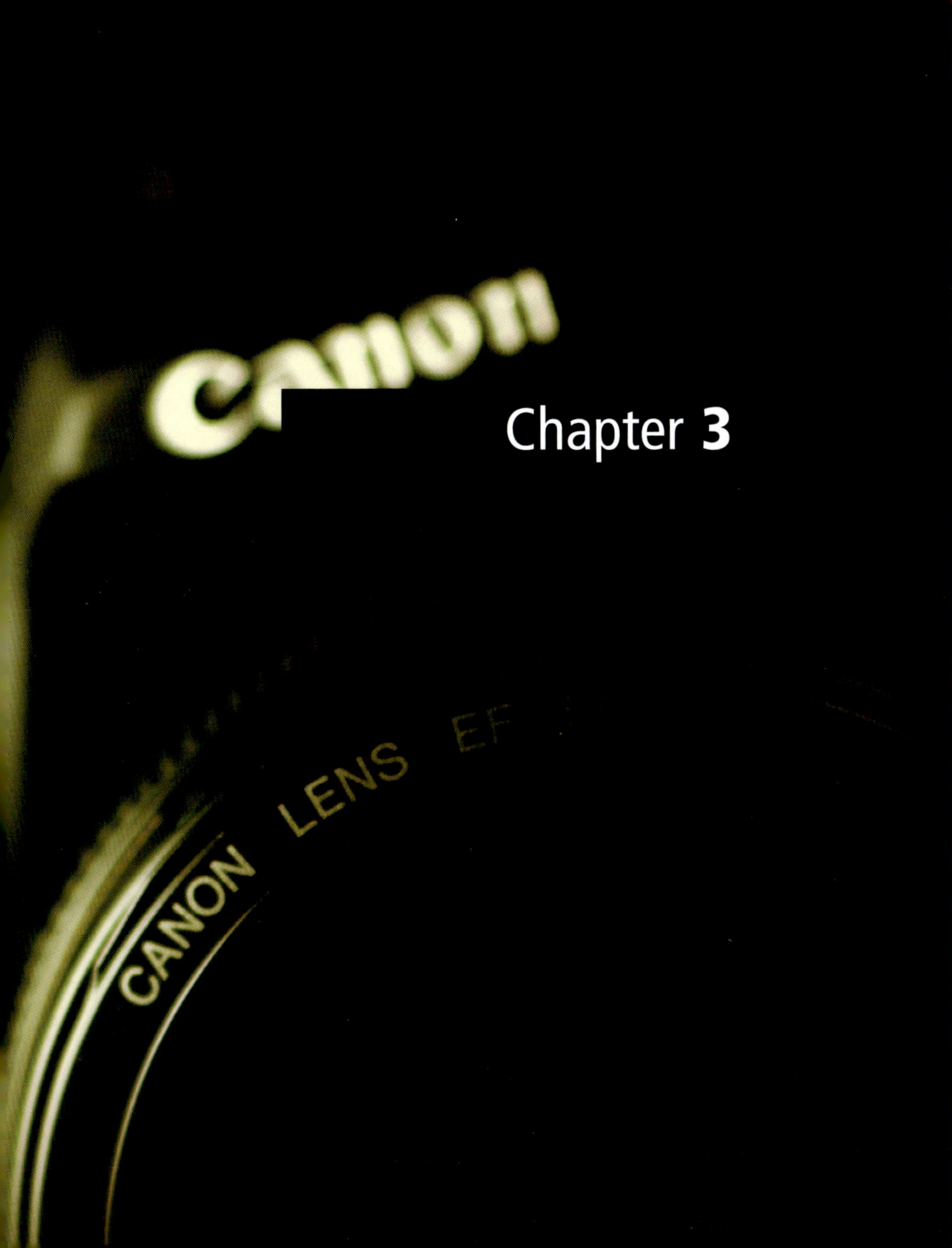

Live View & Movie mode

On the Rebel T1i/EOS 500D the Live View facility and the ability to shoot movies are treated as two separate shooting modes, though they have a number of features in common.

Designed some time before movie mode was added to DSLRs, Live View was devised to view the subject on the camera's LCD monitor rather than through the viewfinder, but without the time-lag associated with compact cameras. However, the Rebel T1i/EOS 500D is not suitable for being held at arm's length like a compact and Live View is easiest to use when the camera is mounted on a tripod, in situations where the subject remains still and the camera-to-subject distance remains constant.

Live View will only function in Creative Zone modes and shooting can also take place with the image displayed on a computer screen and the camera operated remotely using EOS Utility (see page 225). Refer to the software instruction manual provided on CD-ROM with the camera for full details.

The option to shoot movies on a DSLR is a recent phenomenon but it is an innovation which is quickly finding its way onto many new DSLR models and is clearly here to stay. The Rebel T1i/EOS 500D is capable of shooting High Definition movies with 1080 vertical pixels, requiring an SD card of at least Class 6. Full details of Movie mode can be found on pages 131–5.

Live View functions

Preparation

Warning!
Do not point the camera directly into any light source, especially the sun, when in Live View mode.

Do not use extension tubes or TS-E lenses with Live View.

1) Set up your subject, tripod, lighting, and camera using only the viewfinder at this stage. This will conserve battery power and prevent unnecessary heat build-up in the camera.

2) Select a Creative Zone shooting mode.

3) Select Set-up menu 2 and highlight **Live View function settings**. Press **SET**.

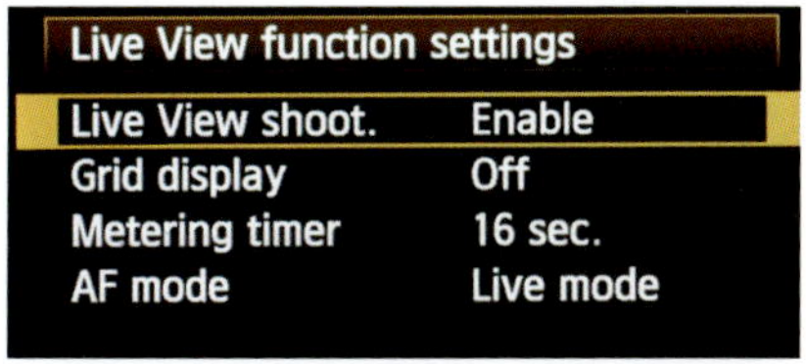

4) Select **Live View shoot.** and press **SET**.

5) Select **Enable** and press **SET**.

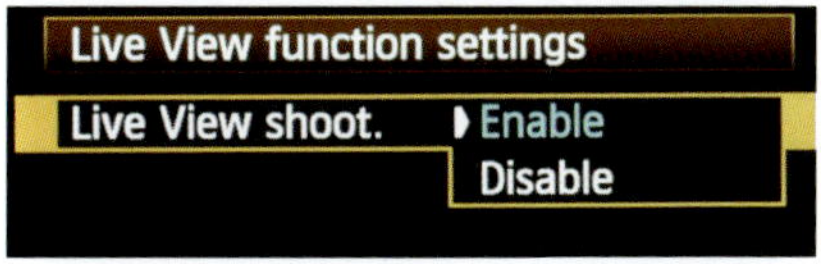

6) Select and enable **Grid display** if desired (see page 132).

7) Adjust the Metering timer as desired. Six settings ranging from 4 sec to 30 min are available.

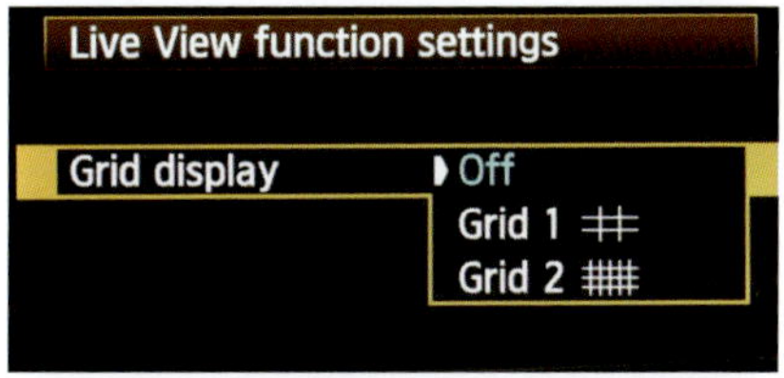

8) Select the AF mode: Live Mode, Live Face Detection Mode or Quick Mode (see pages 127–8).

9) Press **MENU** to exit to the main menu and press it again to exit all menus.

Your camera is now ready to shoot in Live View mode. Go to step 10 on page 127.

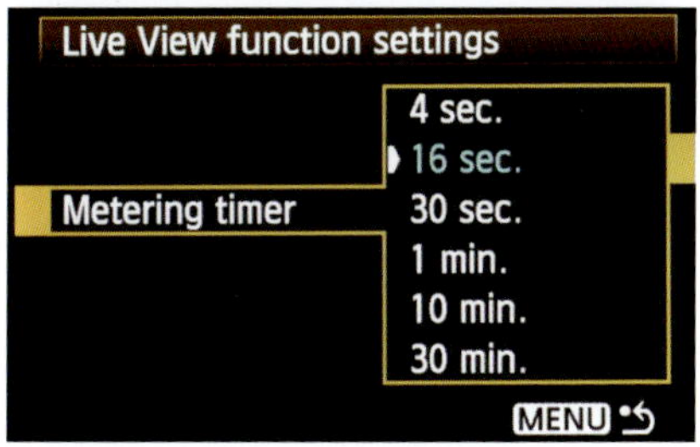

Warning!

Prolonged use of Live View may lead to high internal camera temperature which may ultimately cause damage to internal components. If the high temperature warning icon is displayed during shooting you should cease using Live View immediately to allow the internal camera temperature to drop. If the internal temperature is sufficiently high, the camera will automatically disable Live View shooting temporarily.

Warning!
High temperatures increase image noise significantly, especially when combined with long exposures and/or high ISO settings. Allow the camera to cool periodically under these circumstances to improve results.

General hints on using Live View

Evaluative metering will be applied regardless of current metering setting.

Flash exposure lock will not function with either the built-in flash or an EX Speedlite.

Auto Lighting Optimizer may make the image too bright. It can be disabled in C.Fn-7 (see page 118).

Do not take the picture while a magnified view is displayed (see page 129).

Bright light sources may appear black on the LCD monitor but will appear normal in the recorded image.

If subject lighting changes suddenly and significantly, the image on the monitor may be destabilized for a moment. Wait until the image is stable before shooting.

Using **A-DEP** mode will give exactly the same results as using **P** mode.

If the LCD monitor's brightness is set to a higher setting, some chrominance noise may be visible in the displayed image but will not be apparent in the recorded image.

Autofocus is not possible with Remote Switch RS-60E3.

Battery life when using Live View will be reduced significantly, providing approximately one-third the number of exposures compared with regular camera use.

Most menu functions can be accessed normally via the **MENU** button during Live View shooting. However, selecting Dust Delete Data, Sensor cleaning, Clear settings, or Firmware version will cause Live View to terminate.

Display image

10) Press to enter Live View mode. The mirror will be raised and the subject displayed on the LCD monitor.

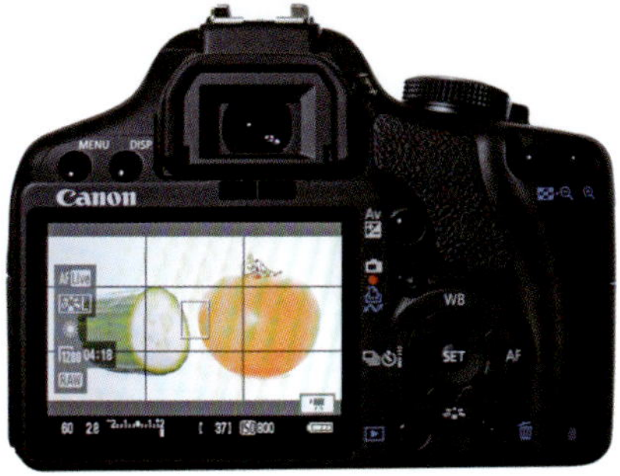

11) The brightness of the image displayed will be indicative of the brightness of the recorded image. (In Manual mode, the image will appear darker or lighter when you adjust the shutter speed or aperture. Rotate the Main Dial to adjust the shutter speed. Adjust the aperture by holding down the **Av+/-** button while rotating the Main Dial.)

12) Press **SET** to display the shooting functions: AF mode, Picture Style, White balance, Drive mode, and File quality setting. Use the ◀ ▶ ▲ ▼ buttons to choose the function (highlighted in blue) to be changed and rotate the Main Dial to adjust the setting. Press **SET**.

Quick mode AF AF Quick

Note: For Live Mode AF, go to step 16.

Quick mode displays a white rectangle and selected AF point(s) on the screen. The white rectangle indicates the area to be magnified using the / button (see page 129). Use the following procedure to focus in Quick mode AF:

13) Press **SET** to bring up the Shooting functions display, which will also display the AF points array. Press ▶ to display the currently selected AF point(s), which will be highlighted in blue. Rotate the Main Dial to select a different AF point, or to choose automatic AF point selection.

14) To focus, press */ • and hold it down until focus is achieved. When focus is acquired, the beep will sound and the selected AF point(s) will turn red briefly. Because Quick mode AF uses the same AF system as the viewfinder, the Live View operation is briefly interrupted by the mirror operation. It sounds as if the shutter has been activated but it has not.

15) Press the shutter-release button to take the picture.

Live mode AF AF Live

In Live mode, the white rectangle displayed on the screen serves both as an enlarged focusing point and as the magnifying frame. Conventional AF points are not displayed.

16) Use the ◀ ▶ ▲ ▼ buttons to move the focusing frame (the white rectangle) around the image to the area of the subject you wish to focus on. (It is not possible to move the focusing frame right to the edge of the picture.) To return the focusing frame to the center, press 🗑.

17) Press the ✱/⊞•🔍 button to achieve focus, holding it down until the white rectangle turns green and the beep sounds (unless the latter has been disabled—📷 Shooting menu 1 can be accessed via the **MENU** button as normal

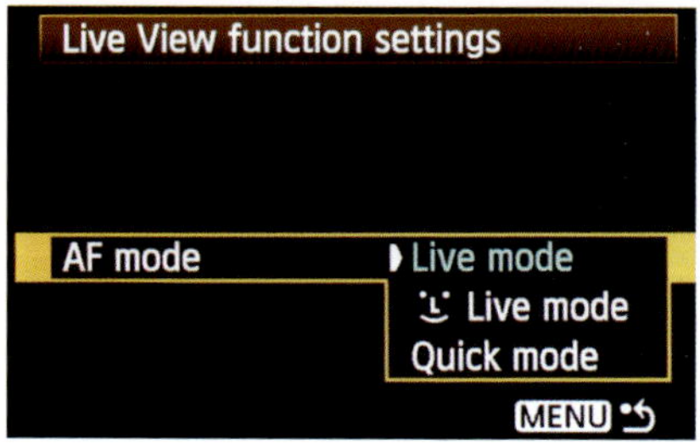

during Live Mode to enable or disable the beep). If focus is not achieved, the focusing frame will turn red.

18) Press the shutter-release button to take the picture.

19) To end Live View shooting, press 📷.

Face Detection mode AF ☺

Face Detection mode is basically the same as Live mode except that the camera is programmed to recognize a forward-facing human face and to focus on this instead of the nearest part of the subject. This clearly depends upon the extent to which the whole face is visible and its relative prominence in the frame.

To use Face Detection mode, point the camera at the subject. When a single face is detected the ⸢ ⸣ focusing frame will center on the subject's face. The size of the ⸢ ⸣ focusing frame will vary according to the area occupied by the subject. If more than one face is detected, the ‹ › focusing frame will be displayed. Use the ◀ or ▶ buttons to move the ‹ › focusing frame over the face of the desired subject.

Press ✱/⊞•🔍 to focus on the face covered by the frame. The frame will turn green and the beep will sound when focus is achieved. If focus is not achieved, the focusing frame will turn red. Press the shutter-release button to take the picture.

Tips

The camera may sometimes interpret another subject as a face if certain characteristics are present.

Face detection may be adversely affected by the face being either very large or very small within the frame as a whole, by excessive or poor light levels, or by tilting the camera. Pressing the [-⁝-]/⊕ button in Live ☺ mode will not magnify the image.

Autofocus is not possible if the face is close to the edge of the frame, in which case the [ ] will be grayed out.

Manual focus

It is still possible to use manual focus with Live View. Simply switch the lens over to **MF** then use the focusing/magnifying frame as you would in Live mode AF while manually focusing the lens.

Magnifying the image

1) Use the ◀▶▲▼ buttons to move the magnifying frame (the white rectangle) around the image to the area of subject you wish to focus on.

2) Press the [-⁝-]/⊕ button once for ×5 magnification and press it again for ×10. Press [-⁝-]/⊕ a third time to return to an unmagnified display (the ✱/⊞•⊖ reduce button initiates focus and will not reduce the magnification).

3) You can also use the depth of field preview function to check focus while an image is magnified.

4) While the magnified view is active, the shutter speed and aperture will be displayed in red.

Note

Image magnification is available in Live mode and Quick mode only.

Live View information display

Pressing **DISP** during Live View operation will display the main shooting functions plus the Brightness or RGB histogram (depending on which has been set in ▶: Playback menu 2). When **ExpSIM** is displayed in white, it indicates that the brightness of the Live View image closely resembles that of the image that will be captured. If **ExpSIM** blinks, the Live View image displayed on the screen is not representative of the image that will be captured by the camera, but the captured image will still match the exposure settings you have selected. This discrepancy is due to excessively dark or bright shooting conditions.

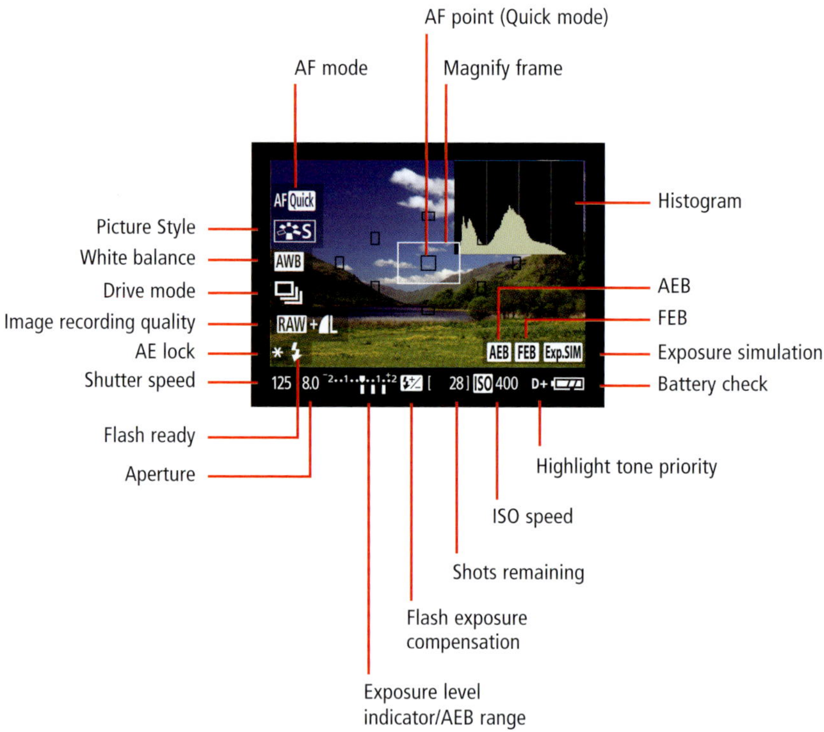

Movie mode

As well as shooting movie clips, it is possible to shoot still images either while shooting movies or while playing them back. Movies can also be played back on a TV. You should use an SD Class 6 or higher memory card with a capacity of at least 4GB, which will give you 12 minutes of recording time at the highest movie definition setting of 1920 × 1080. A single fully charged battery should provide at least an hour of recording.

Shooting movies

Shooting movies using the camera's default settings is simplicity itself.

1) Set the Mode Dial to 🎥. You will hear the reflex mirror as it is raised and the image seen through the lens will be displayed on the LCD monitor.

Tips

The ISO setting, shutter speed, and aperture are set automatically. These settings will also be used if you shoot a still photograph while recording a movie.

AE lock is possible by pressing the **ISO** button. To cancel AE lock, press the ⊞/🔍 button.

2) Point the camera at the subject and press ✱/⊞•🔍 to focus. Hold the camera steady while it achieves focus, which will be indicated by a beep. (See also AF modes on page 133.)

3) Press the 📷 button to start recording. While recording is taking place a red dot will be displayed top right on the monitor. A continuous movie clip will be recorded as a single file.

4) To stop recording, press 📷 again.

5) To play back the recording, press ▶. Press **SET**, then—with the 🎞 symbol highlighted in blue—press **SET** again. To stop playback and exit, press ▶.

Movie functions

With 🎥 selected on the Mode Dial, press **MENU** to display the menu screen. If it is not already selected, choose the 🎥 Movie functions menu. The table below shows the menu options available.

Movie functions menu 🎥 (Red)	
Grid display	Off / Grid 1 / Grid 2
Metering timer	4 sec / 16 sec / 30 sec / 1 min / 10 min / 30 min
Movie recording size	1920 × 1080 / 1280 × 720 / 640 × 480
AF mode	Live mode / Live Face Detection mode / Quick mode
Sound recording	On / Off
Remote control	Disable / Enable

Grid display

Two different grid patterns are available to make it easier to line up your subject in relation to the frame. The grid will not appear in the recorded movie.

Metering timer

Six settings are available, ranging from 4 sec to 30 min. This setting determines how long AE lock is to be maintained when set using the **ISO** button.

Movie recording size

Three different quality settings are available: Full High Definition, High Definition, and Standard.

Note that when **Standard** recording quality is selected, the screen format will change to 4:3.

Quality	Recording size	File size	Frame rate	4GB card	16GB card
Full HD	1920 × 1080	330 MB/min	20 fps	12 min	49 min
HD	1280 × 720	222 MB/min	30 fps	18 min	73 min
Standard	640 × 480	165 MB/min	30 fps	24 min	99 min

AF mode

The focusing operation takes place as a separate function before you start to record your movie. Three AF modes are possible: Quick mode AF Quick, Live mode AF Live and Live Face Detection mode ☺. These function in exactly the same way as they do in Live View (see pages 127–8).

Note
Continuous focus adjustment is not possible in Movie mode.

Sound recording

When sound recording is enabled, monaural sound will be added to the movie using the built-in microphone. Note that the camera's microphone will pick up camera and lens sounds. An external microphone can reduce or eliminate such noises. Sound recording level will be adjusted automatically.

Remote control

The RC-1 or RC-5 Remote Control (both sold separately) can be used for shooting movies. The RC-1 should be set to its two-second delay setting; if it is set to ● for immediate shooting, only a still photograph will be recorded.

Tips
In Movie mode, some functions can be adjusted without entering the menu system. With the image displayed on the monitor, press **SET** to display the following adjustable settings: AF mode, Picture Style, White balance and Movie recording size. The current adjustable function will be highlighted in blue. Use the ◀ ▶ ▲ ▼ buttons to select the function you wish to change and rotate the Main Dial to make the necessary adjustment.

Exposure compensation can be set by holding down the **Av+/-** button while rotating the Main Dial. Note that the adjusted exposure compensation will also be applied to all Creative Zone modes except Manual. Similarly, any compensation not canceled in any Creative Zone mode (except Manual) will also be applied to Movie mode.

Shooting stills in Movie mode

You can take a still photo at any time while shooting movies by pressing the shutter-release button. Shutter speed and aperture are set automatically. Movie recording will resume as soon as the captured still image is recorded to the memory card as a separate file. Only single-frame shooting is possible and flash will not function. When the movie is played back, it will incorporate the still image, lasting approximately one second. The still image will occupy the full monitor area, irrespective of the semi-transparent mask which may be displayed for movie mode.

Shooting settings display

When the **DISP** button is pressed, the Shooting settings screen is displayed. Repeatedly pressing the **DISP** button toggles between three screens showing shooting information on the left and below the image, reduced shooting information only below the image, and no information at all.

Movie mode information display

During movie recording the remaining-time display will change to elapsed-time.

The icon (bottom right) replaces the **ExpSIM** (Exposure Simulation) icon used on the Live View information display, but performs the same function (see page 130).

If there is insufficient capacity on the memory card, the remaining-time display and recording size are displayed in red.

A slow writing speed may cause a five-bar graphic to be displayed on the right of the LCD monitor, indicating the amount of data stored in the buffer which is yet to be written to the memory card. If all five bars are indicated, the buffer is full and movie shooting will stop automatically.

Lenses with Image Stabilization (IS) will make use of this function if it is switched on. It will operate at all times and will be an additional drain on the battery, so it should be switched off if not required.

When a single continuous movie reaches 4GB in size, movie recording will stop automatically. You can start recording again by pressing the button.

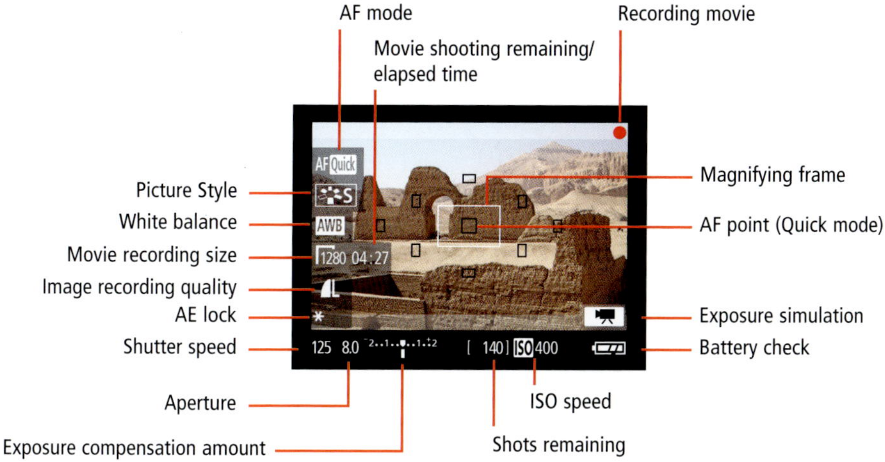

Movie playback

To play back movie clips, press the ▶ button and then press **SET**. The menu options shown below will be displayed, with the symbols shown in the left column displayed along the bottom of the LCD monitor.

Function	Playback Description
↶ Exit	Returns to the single-image display
▶ Play	Pressing **SET** toggles between play and pause
I▶ Slow motion	Adjust the slow-motion speed by pressing the ◀▶ key
⏮ First frame	Displays the movie's first frame
◀II Previous frame	Each time you press **SET**, a single previous frame is displayed. If you hold down **SET**, it will rewind the movie
II▶ Next frame	Each time you press **SET**, the movie will play frame by frame. If you hold down **SET**, it will fast forward the movie
⏭ Last frame	Displays the movie's last frame
▬▬▬	Playback position
volume icon Volume	Adjust the built-in speaker's volume by turning the dial icon dial

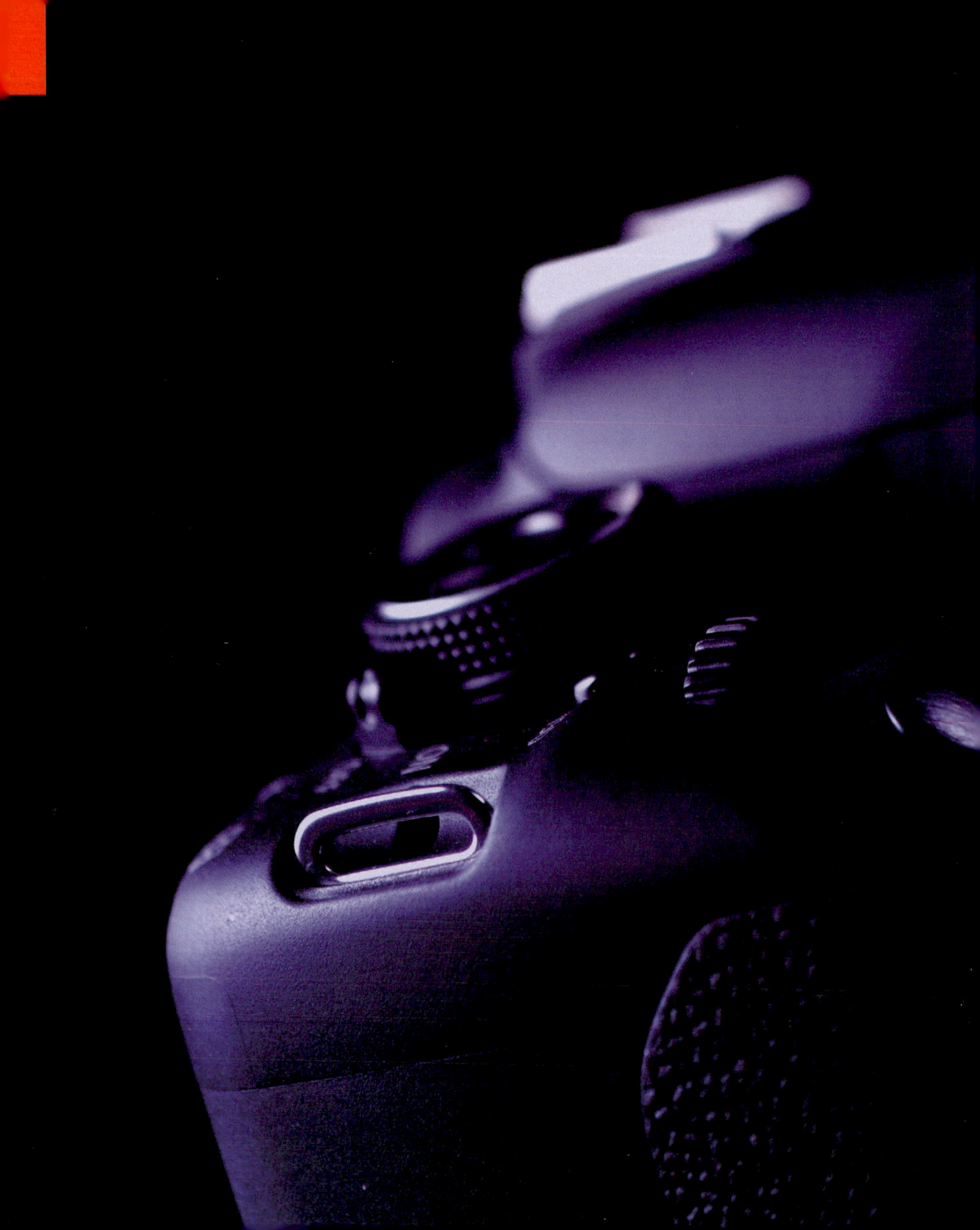

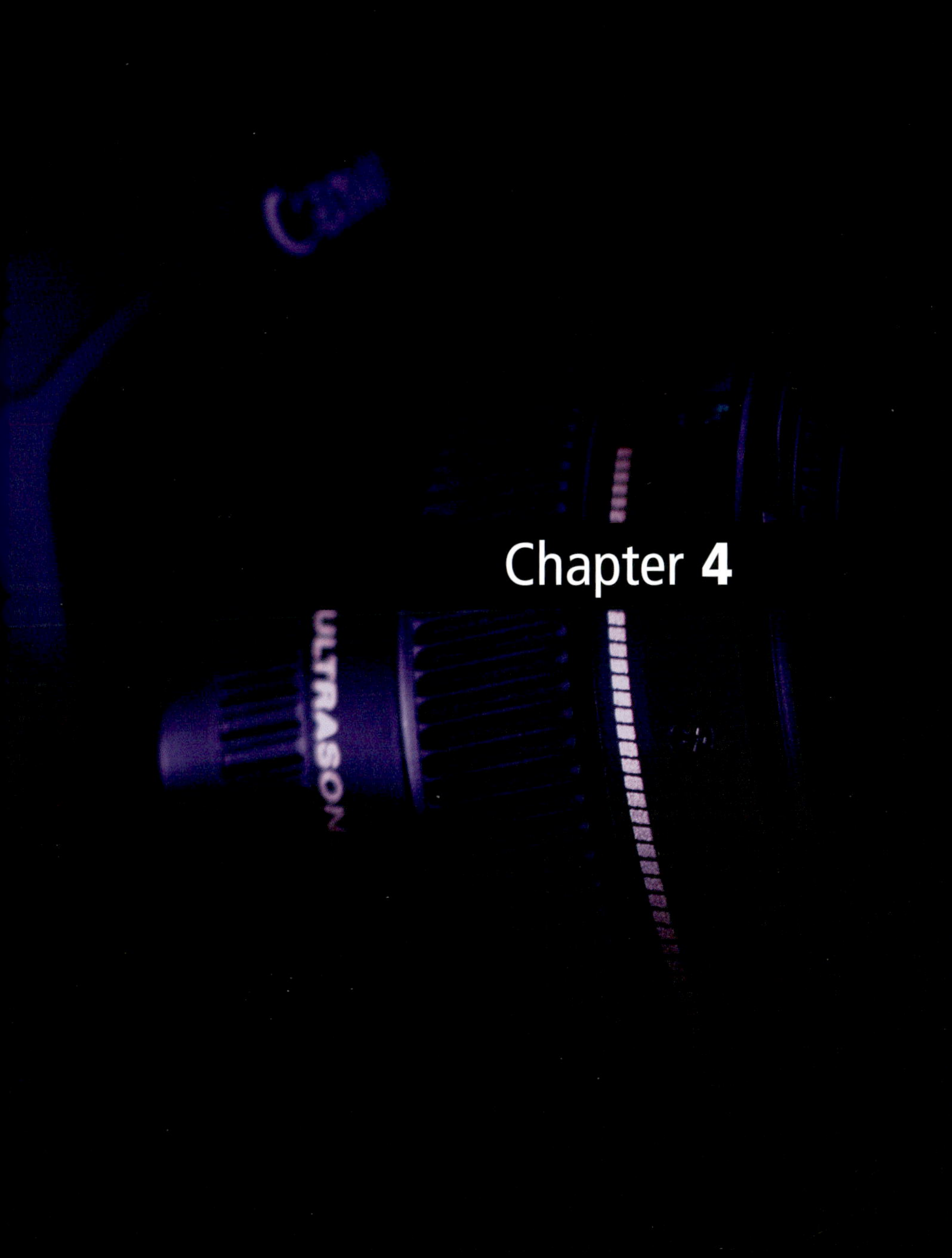

Chapter 4

In the field

Every photograph is a snapshot in so far as it records a moment in time, usually measured in hundredths, if not thousandths, of a second. But not every photograph is worth a thousand words, as the old adage goes. So what is it that makes the difference?

Leaving technical competence aside for a moment, the four most important factors are, firstly, the intentions of the photographer, and finally, the impact the image has on the viewer. In between those two factors lie the content of the image and its treatment, both of which have to be considered in the light of what doesn't take place within the frame as much as what does.

The simplest approach for the aspiring photographer is to visualize what you want to achieve before even picking up the camera. When the end result is envisaged, the other considerations can fall into place quite quickly when one has a degree of experience. But this is an equally valid approach for the novice: how can you judge your degree of success if you don't know what you were setting out to achieve? Anything else is just a happy accident.

The reference to what doesn't take place is also an aspect of photography that professionals deal with instinctively but beginners rarely consider. It's important to step back from the scene in front of you and look for distracting elements, whether it's a discarded crisp packet in the foreground or someone with a bright red jacket in the background.

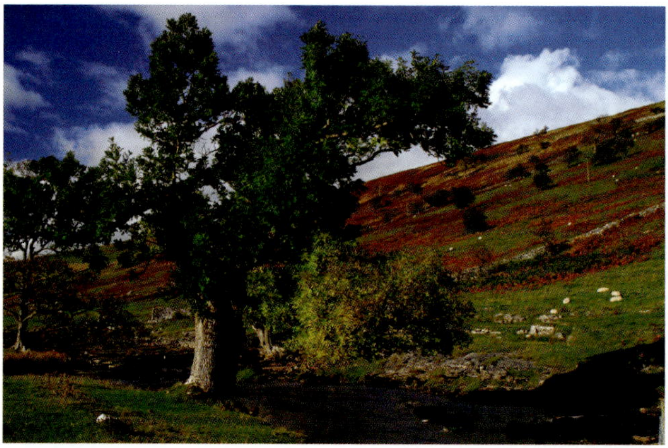

YORKSHIRE DALES, UK
After capturing an image like this, it would be a shame to return home and then discover some distracting element you didn't notice at the time. Check the area carefully (and not just through the viewfinder) for any unwanted intrusions.

Depth of field

No lens has two clearly defined zones—in focus and out of focus. What it does have is a single plane of sharp focus with a gradual transition, both in front of and behind that plane, toward being out of focus. There comes a point in that transition where relative sharpness ceases to be acceptable. This point will occur twice: both in front of and behind the plane of sharp focus—unless the far point is deemed to be so far away that it reaches infinity. The term "depth of field" is used to identify this zone within the image which is deemed to be in acceptable apparent focus.

Circle of confusion

The term "acceptable apparent focus" sounds subjective, rather than absolute, and that is indeed true. While a lens on a test bench can have all sorts of tests performed to determine absolute measurements, depth of field is not one of them. Depth of field depends in particular on the intended magnification of the image and on the chosen size of the circle of confusion, the latter being the size of an area of the image at which a point ceases to be a point and becomes a small circle. For 35mm cameras and their digital counterparts, this is generally in the order of 0.001in (0.035mm) and assumes an average magnification of ×5, resulting in a 5 × 7in (13 × 18cm) print. With these factors in mind, lens manufacturers mark their lenses with a depth-of-field scale that indicates this zone of acceptable sharpness.

However, both professional and keen amateur photographers are likely to want enlargements greater than 5 × 7in. Many professionals choose to use an aperture at least one stop smaller than the depth-of-field scale on the lens indicates for the distances required (i.e. the closest and furthest points in focus)

Many lens manufacturers have reduced the depth of field scales (or omitted them entirely) on their lenses

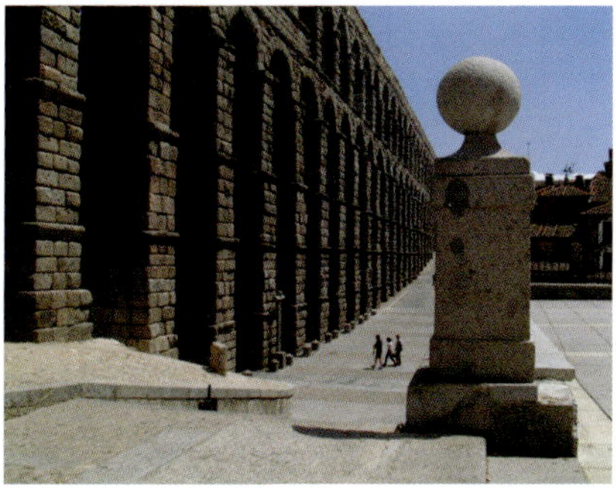

ROMAN AQUEDUCT, SEGOVIA, SPAIN
A scene like this calls for the greatest possible depth of field and consequently a narrow aperture but a slower shutter speed.

until they are so cramped or lacking in aperture markings as to be almost meaningless. The reason for this seems to be the reduced arc through which the lens travels in order to achieve focus, so that autofocus speeds can be faster and faster.

It could be argued that autofocus systems are now so sophisticated, especially with the A-DEP mode, that there isn't the need to be so concerned about depth of field. Serious landscape photographers, however, will always see depth of field as a matter of prime importance and it is they who plead for the retention of decent depth-of-field scales on lenses—mainly as a result of their frequent use of the hyperfocal distance focusing technique.

DEPTH OF FIELD SCALE
The depth of field scale on older lenses like this EF 28mm f/2.8 is much easier to use than those featured on more recent designs.

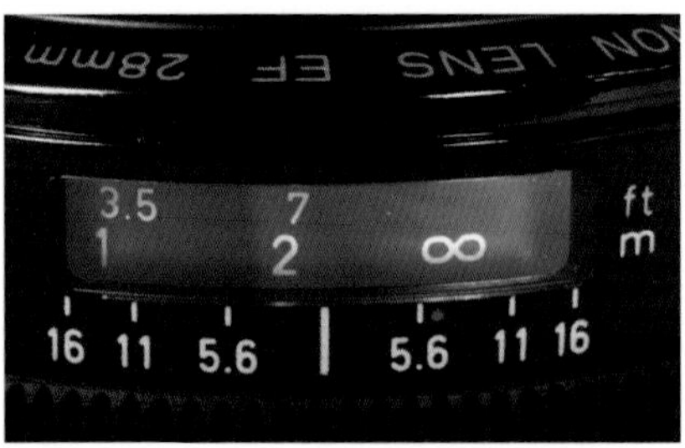

> **Tip**
> With any lens, narrow depth of field is achieved by using wide apertures. Wider depth of field is achieved by using narrower apertures.

Using hyperfocal distance
The hyperfocal distance at a given aperture is the closest point of focus at which infinity falls within the depth of field. The hyperfocal distance varies according to aperture.

This is the point on which you would focus the lens to ensure that everything from that point to infinity is in focus, along with a significant zone in front of it. You do not even need to look through the viewfinder to do it: simply switch the lens to manual focus and manually turn the focus ring so that the infinity mark is just inside the mark for the selected aperture on the depth-of-field scale. The equivalent mark at the other end of the scale shows the closest point that will be in focus.

Sensor confusion
There is a need to comment here on cameras which use a less than full-frame sensor—like the Rebel T1i/EOS 500D, which has a 1.6× crop factor. In effect, this means that if you placed a Rebel T1i/EOS 500D side by side with a full-frame camera

and fitted them both with identical lenses, the field of view of the full-frame camera would be 1.6× greater.

The image projected by the lens onto the film or sensor is circular rather than rectangular. In the first illustration below, you can see that a full-frame sensor (left) is large enough to accommodate the maximum amount of the projected image circle. However, the smaller APS-C sensor (center) covers a smaller proportion of the image circle projected by a lens designed for 35mm or a full-frame sensor. Finally, an EF-S lens, designed solely for use with an APS-C sensor, has a smaller image circle, once again maximizing the sensor area (right).

In the second illustration, the triangles represent a main subject within the image as a whole, assuming an identical camera-to-subject distance and the same focal-length lens. Note that the main subject as projected onto the sensor is identical in terms of absolute size in both cases, but the smaller sensor has cropped away a lot of the area around the main subject.

There is a great deal of confusion about the implications of this as regards lenses. Some people insist on making comparisons such as saying that a 50mm lens on a camera with the smaller APS-C sensor is equivalent to an 80mm lens (i.e. 50mm × 1.6) with a full-frame sensor. Not true. A 50mm lens behaves like a 50mm lens no matter what camera it is on, and the size of the projected image will always be the same, assuming identical camera-to-subject distance. The only thing that changes is the field of view.

In summary, assuming that the four key factors of focal length, circle of confusion size, aperture, and camera-to-subject distance are identical, there is no difference in depth of field between full-frame and less than full-frame sensor cameras. Any claim to the contrary is not comparing like with like.

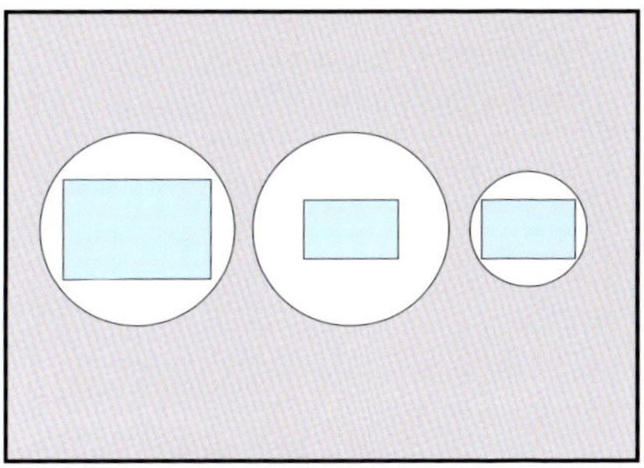

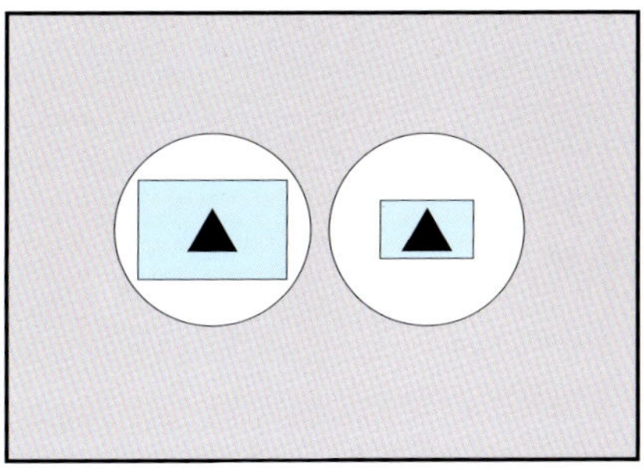

Subjects in motion

Capturing movement is one of the more difficult skills to master. It demands quick reflexes, a good grounding in basic photographic techniques, and an ability to predict the best vantage point from which to capture the action.

Capture the action

In order to capture a pin-sharp image of a fast-moving subject, three factors must be considered: a fast shutter speed, a firmly held or supported camera position, and an understanding of the nature of what I call "apparent speed."

Ignore the actual speed of travel at this point: what really matters is the speed of movement across the frame. A moving subject that passes at right angles to the camera has the highest apparent speed. A subject that is approaching head-on seems to move much more slowly. Very often the best compromise is a vantage point which has the subject moving toward you at an angle of around 45 degrees. Compared with a subject crossing at right angles, you will probably need less than half the shutter speed and can more easily control just the right amount of blur.

Tips

Avoid shooting subjects that are moving away from you. Subjects photographed from the rear are usually far less interesting.

Camera support is a matter of personal choice, but the single most useful tool for action shots is the monopod, which provides support while allowing mobility.

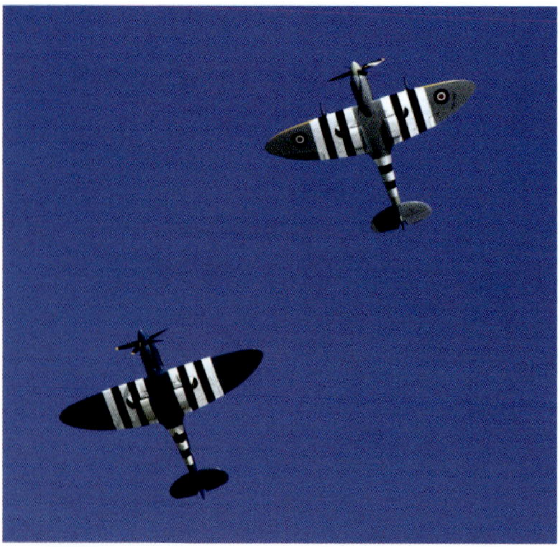

SPITFIRES
Freezing the subject isn't always the best approach. Some blur in the propellers would increase the sense of movement.

1954 MV AGUSTA 500/4
The faster the subject, the greater the need to find the perfect spot to capture the action. When panning, make sure that there is a consistent and uncluttered background and that the sweep of your lens is not hindered by anything between you and the subject.

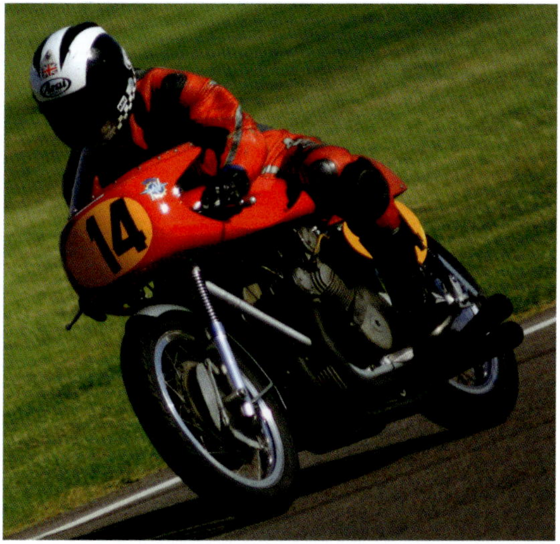

Panning

If you stand perfectly still and photograph a fast-moving subject, the likely result is that the subject will be blurred and all the stationary elements of the image will be sharp. Panning the camera (i.e. moving the camera through a single plane, usually horizontal, while keeping the subject in the viewfinder) can produce the opposite result: the moving object is sharp and the stationary elements are blurred.

The result depends largely on the selected shutter speed. An extremely fast shutter speed may even freeze the background if panning slowly. Conversely, a slow shutter speed may create a blurred background and a blurred subject—this can be quite effective if the degree of blur differs between the subject and the background. The use of flash, especially second-curtain flash, in conjunction with the latter technique can produce very good results.

Tip

Filling the frame with a well-exposed moving subject is one of the hardest aspects of recording motion. If you are just starting out, try using a focal length and camera-to-subject distance that will leave the subject a little smaller in the frame, and crop the result later on the computer.

Blurring for effect

The most popular subject for this technique is undoubtedly water. As with fast-moving subjects, the scale and speed of travel across the frame are the key issues. It is helpful if the water's direction of travel is across the frame—the opposite of fast-moving subjects. To obtain a slow shutter speed under bright conditions, a slow ISO and small aperture will be required. In very bright conditions a neutral density filter or polarizing filter can also be useful in reducing shutter speed by two stops or more. The precise shutter speeds needed to blur water vary with the situation, but at least half a second is a good rule of thumb.

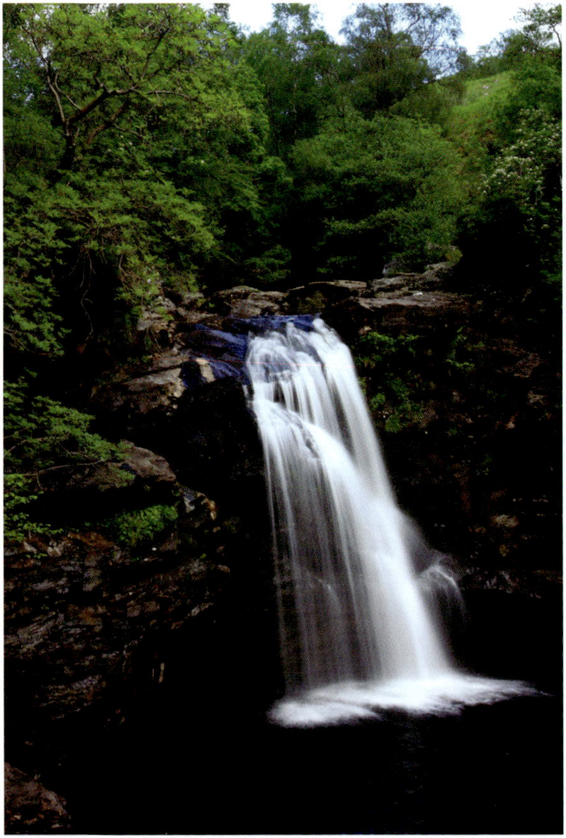

WATERFALL
Water is a popular subject for motion-blur photographs. A shutter speed of at least half a second will usually produce the best results.

Composition

Personal preferences and intuition are all-important in relation to composition, but it is always worth learning from other photographers. It is also worthwhile experimenting with different approaches to cropping using your own work.

Balance

Every photograph includes a number of elements and they all contribute to its overall impact. Balance must be considered in terms of not just shape but color, density, activity, mood, light, and perspective. Once again, this is a matter of personal preference, but it also has a great deal to do with the dimensions of the final photograph as well as the subject matter and its treatment.

To achieve balance, you must think in terms of the essence of the image. If the shot is highly dynamic, you will want it to have a "busy" feel, which can be achieved with striking angles, vivid color, blurred motion, and lots of detail. If you want a restful image, all of its components should be in harmony: keep it as simple as possible and avoid "hard" shapes, straight lines, and vibrant colors like red and yellow.

When it comes down to simple composition, one might say that a symmetrical photo is one which has absolute balance, but symmetry can make a composition seem far too anchored, so use it sparingly. Trust your instincts, don't try to follow set rules and shoot from a variety of viewpoints. The great thing about digital photography is that it will cost you nothing to experiment.

Often the photographer has little or no control over the positioning of the subject and its component parts. To circumvent this problem, it is often possible to adjust your own position in relation to the subject.

Inexperienced photographers tend to place the principal subject centrally in the frame, allowing it to dominate without regard for its context. This is not always the best approach, as demonstrated in the series of images on page 146.

Directing the eye

It is generally accepted that an image will first have an immediate impact as a whole on the viewer. After that, there are a number of processes that can be harnessed to direct the viewer's eye to specific points in the image and also to lead the viewer through the image in the way you would like. The eye will naturally be drawn toward colors that stand out, especially reds and yellows, and along strong lines.

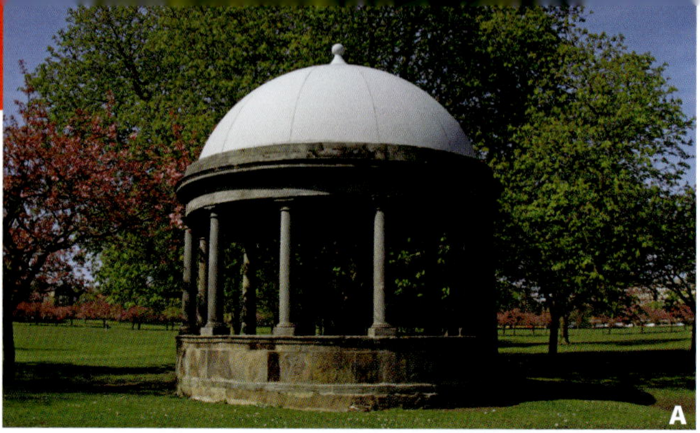

A

TEWIT WELL, HARROGATE, UK
The first shot (A) in this sequence places the principal subject in the center of the frame. However, by reducing the relative size of the main subject (B and C), more can shown of its situation. In addition, it could just as easily be placed off-center (D). In fact, arguably the best shot of all (E) doesn't even show the whole of the subject.

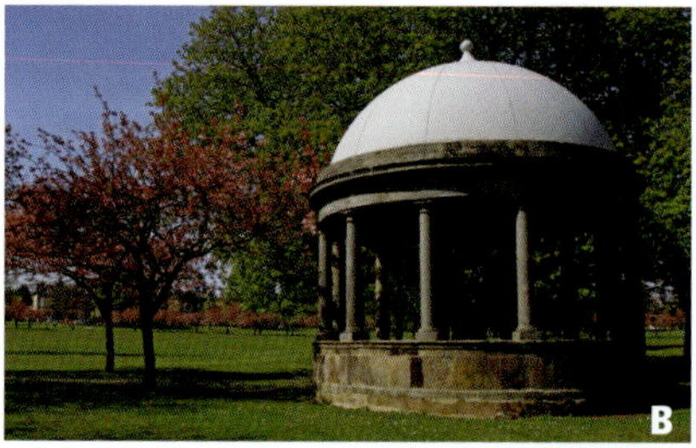

B

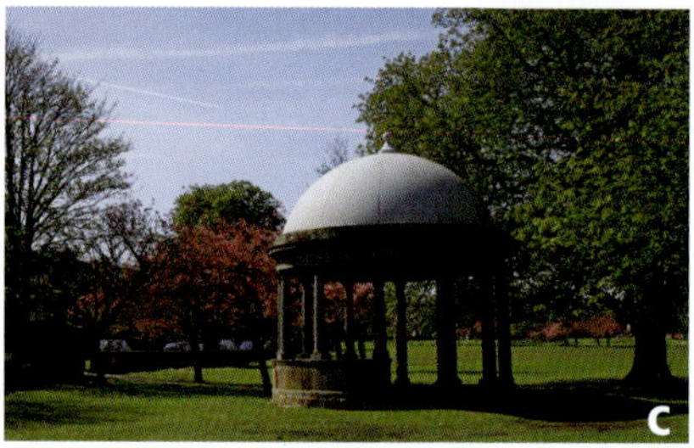

C

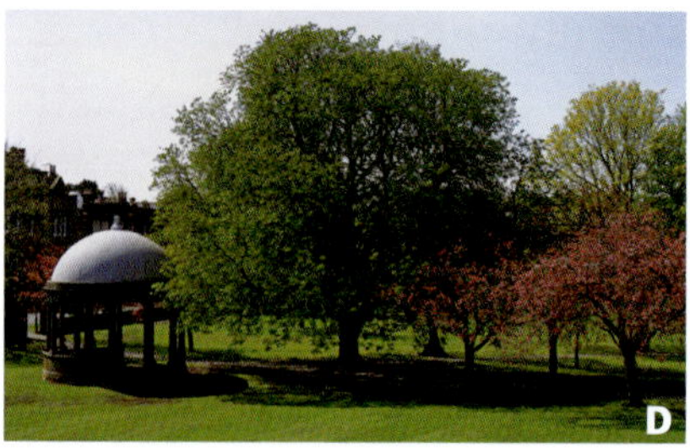

D

Converging lines are of particular importance. These tend to create triangles which act as arrows and, as we have noted, a great deal of dynamism is derived from diagonal lines in a composition. These points of convergence also act as "stoppers" that temporarily arrest the viewer's eye movement while they linger on a specific area of the image.

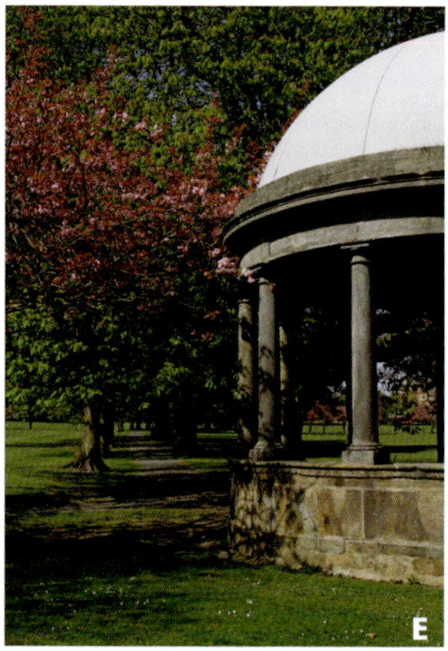

E

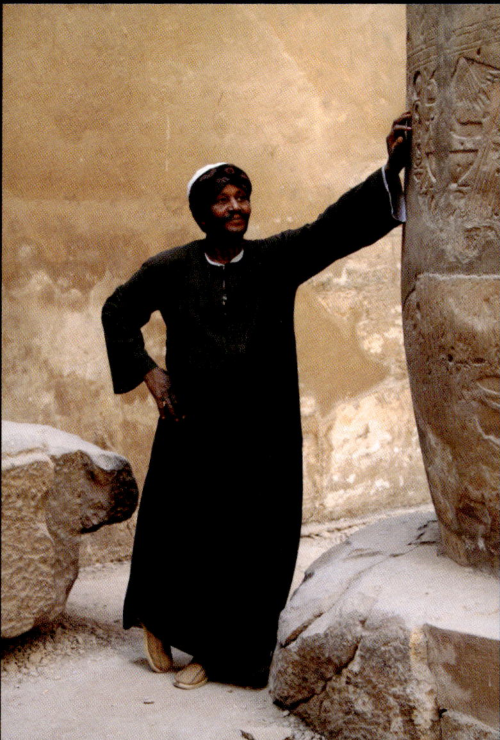

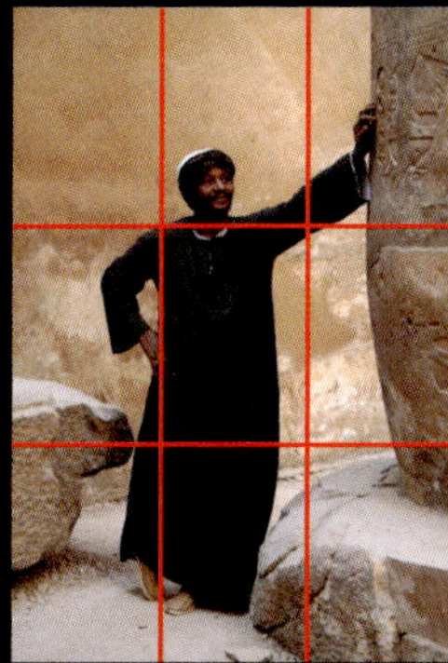

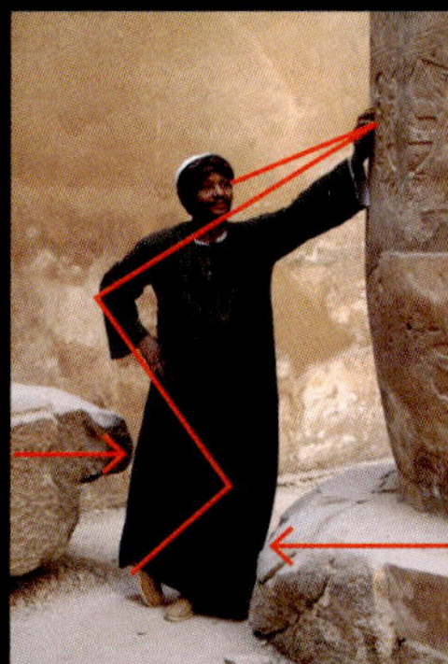

LUXOR TEMPLE, EGYPT

The main subject in this image is obviously the man, but the column with its hieroglyphs is also of secondary importance. The first inset image (top right) shows how this subject occupies the frame when it is divided into thirds. Of more importance, in terms of dynamics, are the lines shown in the second inset image. Note how the blocks of stone at the bottom of the image act as "stoppers" which help to concentrate the eye on the central figure. (The block on the left also lies on a "third.") The diagonal lines also help to keep the eye centered on the main subject, with a strong diagonal formed by the arms traveling almost through the face to meet his line of sight, where his hand rests on the pillar and its strongest hieroglyph.

Settings

Aperture priority
ISO 200
1/30 sec at f/4
Evaluative metering
White balance: Daylight
Picture Style: Landscape
One Shot AF

Lighting

Light, or sometimes the absence of it, is crucial to effective photography; the word "photography," derived from Greek, means "drawing with light." But light possesses qualities above and beyond its mere presence and it is the manipulation of these qualities that sets a good photograph apart from a mediocre one. True, there are occasions when the subject is powerful enough to stand alone, as with reportage photography, but even then a dramatic picture can be further enhanced by the use of color, light direction, or contrast. These are the attributes of light which most frequently concern photographers.

Light sources

Photography commonly makes use of two types of light source: direct and reflected. The most commonly used direct source is the sun. That doesn't mean that it has to be visible: even on a dull winter's day thick with cloud, any available light is still coming from that orb in the sky. The second source commonly used is flash, with artificial light sources such as domestic lighting, street lighting, and studio lighting following behind. Each of these has particular qualities that can be harnessed to good effect, notably its inherent color, which is known as its color temperature.

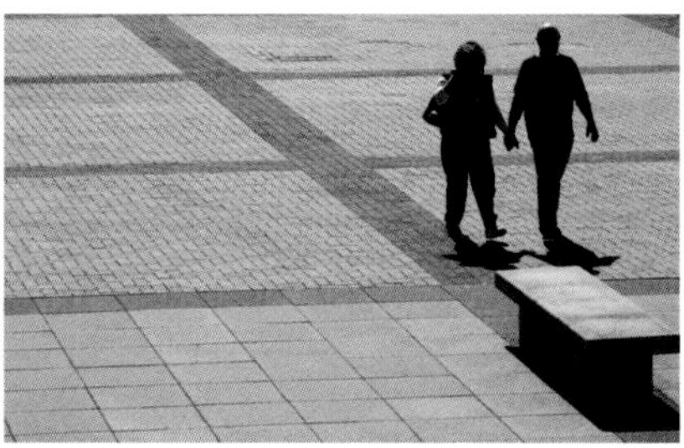

Color

Photography makes use of three types of color. There is the color which a subject appears to have in its own right (but which is actually just a function of reflected light). Then there is the color of the light falling on the subject, and finally the colors used for printing or displaying the image. The last two, in particular, are ones which we can exercise a lot of control over, even removing color from an image to render it as a set of gray tones. It could be argued that there is also a fourth category of color, taking into account the way that specialized films such as infrared record color. The Rebel T1i/ EOS 500D has the ability to select white balance options in order to

CONTRE JOUR

This is the French expression often used for shooting against the light. A higher viewpoint avoids shooting straight into the sun and therefore prevents any risk of flare.

SIDE LIGHTING
Strong graphic subjects like these ripples on a beach often benefit from side lighting—it brings out the texture.

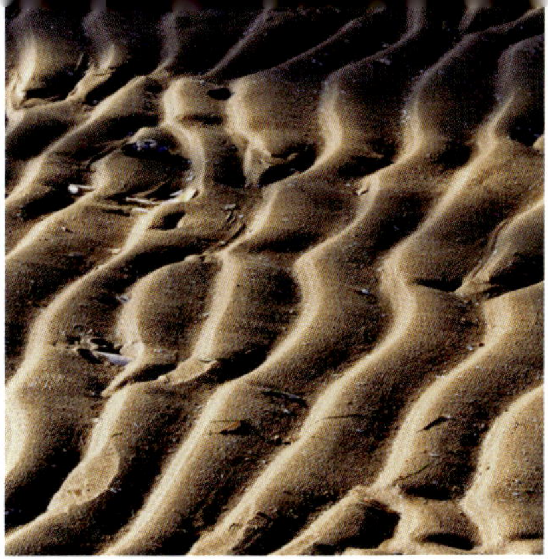

correct the color temperature of the light emanating from various sources under many different circumstances.

Direction

This plays a much more important role than most people realize and it affects far more than just the direction in which the shadows fall. It affects the overall appearance of the subject: frontal lighting produces little shadow and a more colorful appearance; side lighting can increase shadow, which can mean less color but more interesting shapes; backlit subjects may appear as silhouettes or possess an ethereal, translucent quality.

There is always a temptation to shoot with the sun behind us on a sunny day, but it is always worth exploring additional options. Take the time to "stalk" a subject, exploring it for different possibilities and from different angles. If you have control over the direction of light—when using flash, for example —try out different setups with direct, diffused, and reflected light. Similarly, if you can't control the direction of the light but have the option of moving the subject in relation to it, you can position the subject in different situations to achieve varying results.

> **Tip**
> Bracket your exposures in difficult situations as even ⅓ stop can make a significant difference.

Contrast

Contrast is the term given to the difference between light and dark areas in an image. Ideally, we manage to render some detail in both of these, but it is possible to have too much of a good thing and strong lighting is one such example.

Extensive highlight areas require a methodical approach to metering and exposure, combined with a decision-making process regarding which areas of the image are most important in terms of recording detail. Thankfully, contrast is also one of the easiest qualities to adjust in post-processing.

Image properties

One aspect of digital photography that perplexes newcomers and recent converts from film is the fact that digital images can suddenly appear to take on a life of their own, displaying some rather strange effects which the photographer definitely hadn't intended.

Noise

Noise occurs in digital images due to missing information at pixel level. Images are composed of millions of pixels, some of which may function poorly or even fail to function at all, in which case they may appear white or lacking the correct color. These pixels blend into the image creating undesirable flecks of random color, especially noticeable in darker areas of smooth color such as shadows.

The appearance of noise can be exacerbated by a number of factors, including ambient temperature, long exposures and a high ISO setting. When two or more factors are present, noise is more likely.

Flare

This is a phenomenon that will be familiar to former film users. Flare occurs due to the scattering of light waves within the lens and manifests itself in the form of diffuse rays emanating from a pronounced highlight, with odd colored shapes along their path. While image-manipulation software can remedy many problems, flare isn't generally one of them, though if it is only minor it may be possible to copy sections of the image and paste

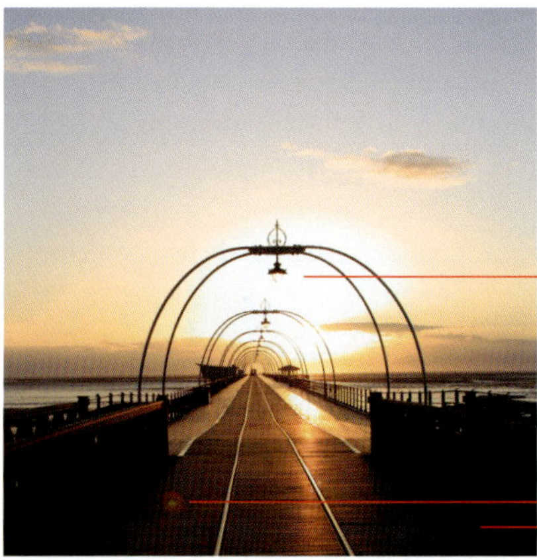

IMAGE ISSUES
This image exhibits three common problems: flare, shadow clipping, and highlight clipping.

them over the offending signs of flare. The best solution is to avoid the flare in the first place by using an appropriate lens hood and not shooting directly into a light source.

Clipping

Dynamic range is the term given to the spread of tones, from the darkest to the lightest, that can be recorded in an image. If the tones in the scene exceed this range, detail will be lost, whether it is in the highlights, the shadows, or both. This loss of detail is referred to as "clipping."

The top of the dynamic range is reached when a pixel records the brightest tone possible without being pure white. At the opposite end of the scale the reverse is true, with a pixel recording detail just short of being black. The extent of this range is determined by the ISO setting, with lower ISO settings providing the greatest range. Lower ISO settings will also give a smoother transition between tones. Camera manufacturers are rumored to be working on a way of applying different ISO settings to different parts of a single image, which would help to eliminate clipping entirely.

Aliasing

This is the term used to describe the process by which individual pixels start to become visible in the image at normal levels of magnification. Aliasing tends to be more apparent in low-resolution images and in particular those that feature diagonal or curved lines—telephone lines running diagonally across an image are a common example. Part of the answer lies in prevention rather than cure: as often as possible, shoot in RAW or Large/Fine JPEG format. It is far easier to create a good-quality small image from a larger one than the other way round.

A common cause of aliasing is the overzealous use of sharpening, especially in images with smaller file sizes. If you are shooting JPEGs and know that your images are only going to be used as thumbnails or low-resolution images for use on screen, you can use the Picture Style options to reduce the setting for the sharpening parameter. You will only be able to do this if you work in one of the Creative Zone modes. If you use a Basic Zone exposure mode, you lose control over sharpening and other parameters.

Sharpening images

One issue which film users find it hard to get used to is the need to sharpen digital images—not because they are out of focus or blurred, but because all digital images are inherently unsharp to a degree.

Most casual amateur photographers remain blissfully unaware of this because they shoot JPEGs, which are sharpened in-camera long before the results are printed or displayed on screen. However, anyone who shoots RAW files will quickly realize that most images need some degree of sharpening, certainly if they are to be enlarged or used commercially.

Generally speaking, sharpening images works fine as long as the image is to be used at its original size or larger. However, sharpening images and then reducing them in size significantly can result in an over-sharpened appearance, which is true relative to the image size. If you want to produce thumbnails or other small images for any reason, it is better to do this before sharpening takes place. Sharpening JPEGs can always be carried out later on the computer. However, once sharpening has been performed, either in-camera or on the computer, it cannot be undone unless you are working with RAW files.

With RAW files the original data is always retained. If you make changes to the original files in post-processing, those changes can be reversed. If you make changes and then convert the RAW file to a different file format, you will not be able to undo those changes in the new file format. But you can go back to the original RAW file, undo the changes or make corrections, and then convert the file again.

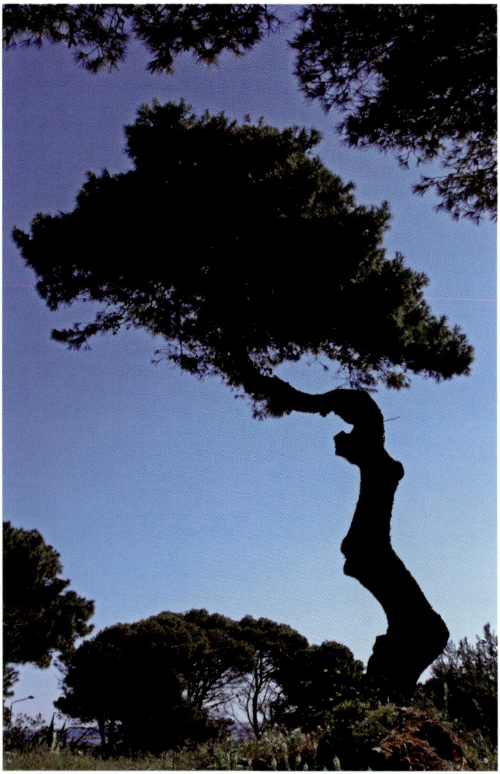

TWISTED TREE
The tones in this image have been compressed using the Levels tool in Photoshop, creating a near-silhouette while retaining just enough midtone to register some color in the foliage.

Any sharpening which has been programmed in-camera using the Picture Style parameters when shooting RAW files can also be undone later using the Digital Photo Professional software. However, it is important to remember that the scales used in-camera and by Digital Photo Professional are not the same. The in-camera sharpening parameter uses a scale of 0–7, while the scale used in Digital Photo Professional runs from 0–10.

While this seems strange, it does offer an advantage. If the Picture Style sharpening parameter is set in-camera to its maximum setting of 7, when you open the captured image in Digital Photo Professional the sharpness will still indicate a setting of 7. This means that not only can you undo or reduce the sharpening in post-processing, you can also increase it beyond the maximum level that was possible at the time of shooting.

Dynamic range

As we have seen, this is the range over which detail can be recorded from the lightest highlights through to the deepest shadows, from almost white to almost black. While digital images can record a far wider range of tones than, say, transparency (slide) film, they still fall some way short of the range that the human eye can distinguish.

As a result, the photographer usually has three options when faced with the widest possible range of tones: favoring the highlights and allowing the deepest shadow tones to merge; favoring the shadows and allowing the highlights to burn out; or aiming somewhere between the two and allowing some clipping at both ends of the range.

The choice is usually determined by the intended end product. For instance, when producing images for magazine or book use, the quality of the paper to be used by the intended publisher can play a part, whereas photos for screen display are far less demanding and depend more on the end user's screen calibration than dynamic range.

Sometimes it is desirable to compress the tones in an image rather than attempt to extend them. The Levels tool in Photoshop can be used to compress just the darker tones or just the highlights, or to shift the balance of the whole image.

Using exposure compensation

All light meters work the same way: they average what they see and give a reading based on the assumption that you are looking at an 18% gray card.

Subjects such as the one below will fool a meter into giving a reading that won't actually give you the best result. The large expanse of white porcelain against a pale background suggested a reading two stops less than was actually required. As it happens, this image was shot using flash, but the same principle applies and flash exposure compensation works in exactly the same way.

Precisely how much exposure compensation is needed is a matter of experience, trial and error, educated guesswork, or bracketing. Using increments of either ½ or ⅓ stop, three exposures can be taken with or without additional exposure compensation in situations such as this. The large LCD monitor of the Rebel T1i/EOS 500D is ideal for reviewing the results.

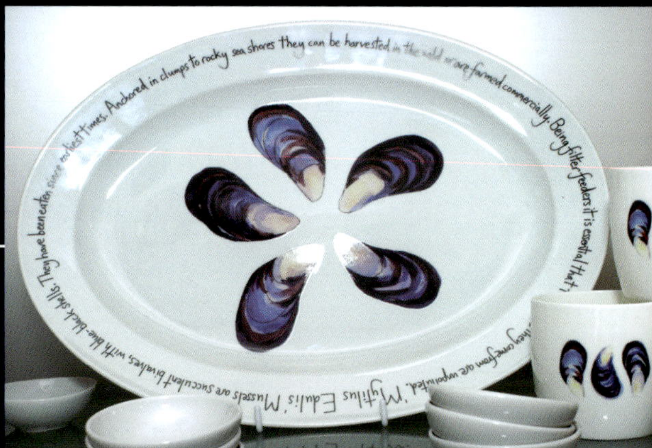

Settings
Aperture priority (Av) mode
Evaluative metering
ISO 100
1/200 sec at f/8
Flash exposure compensation: +2 stops

MUSSELS
This display of porcelain at a pottery is an attractive subject but throws meter readings out by a large margin.

Sunsets

One of the most popular subjects for photography, sunsets are also a frequent source of disappointment. The simplest approach is look for an interesting silhouette, because that limits the picture to two elements: the silhouette itself and the background sky. The first has line and shape, but no tonal detail to worry about, and the latter is simply a matter of color. By taking a reading from the sky (but not including the sun itself) you will obtain a reading that will give the sky some body, leaving the foreground in silhouette. To avoid disappointment later, don't include the setting sun in every shot: your lens may be prone to flare, and the sun will bleach out in the image.

People tend to get tunnel vision when viewing sunsets and don't consider the full image area—they put too much emphasis on the sky and not enough on the silhouette in the foreground.

Also, pay attention to all the subtle changes that the scene goes through, taking regular meter readings from the sky as the light can change rapidly. In some cases, as in the image below, evaluative metering will suffice.

NILE SUNSET
This combination of ambient light at sunset and the color reflected by the water makes for a stunning image.

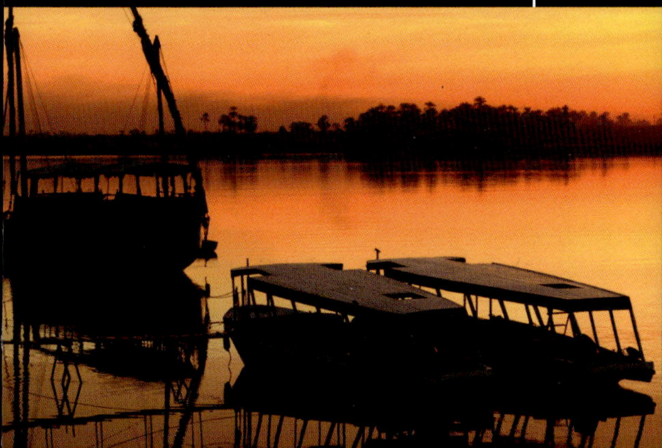

Settings
Aperture Priority (Av)
ISO 200
1/50 sec at f/8
Evaluative metering
White balance: 6200°K
Picture Style: Landscape
One shot AF

Photo essays

The great thing about digital photography is that you can fire off as many shots as you like at no extra cost. This makes it ideal for what I refer to as "stalking the subject" when I am compiling a group of images on a single theme. When a number of images are used together, whether framed as a group on a wall in your home or published in a magazine, they are described as a photo essay.

When I come across a favorable photographic situation, I always want to make the most of it and produce a variety of usable images. But I also find that stalking the subject gradually hones my ideas and the shots obtained usually get better as I go along. However, it is usually still necessary to obtain a straightforward "establishing shot" which acts as an introduction—just like the first paragraph in an essay. This image may be no more than a technically competent record of the subject. The vital factor is that it should contain each of the elements which are explored in greater detail later on.

Surprisingly few photographers crop their images in order to achieve what can be either a subtle change in emphasis or a completely different image. In the example opposite, the foreground of one image has been cropped to produce a panoramic image in its own right.

I often shoot as many portrait format (vertical) frames as I do landscape format, especially for

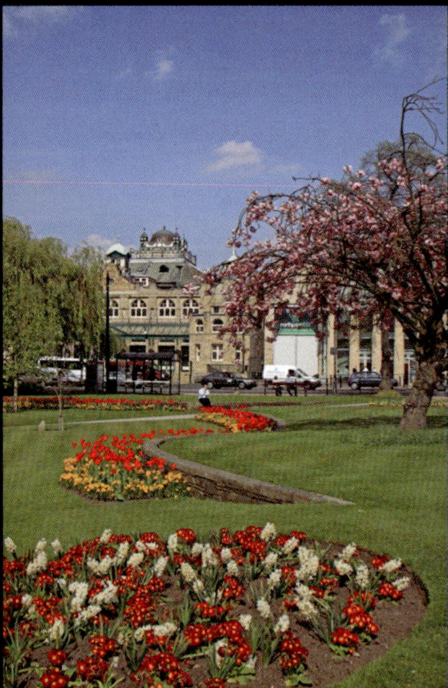

MUNICIPAL PLANTING
The establishing shot encompasses the whole subject and places it in context.

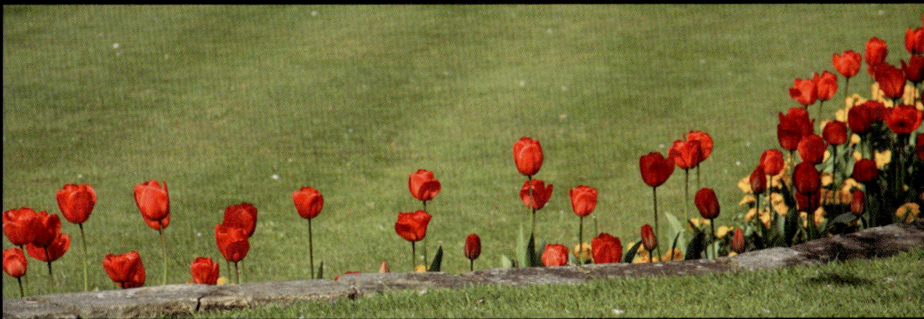

CROPPING AND FRAMING
The panoramic picture above was cropped from the foreground of another image. Portrait-format frames (below) are particularly useful if your images are destined for publication.

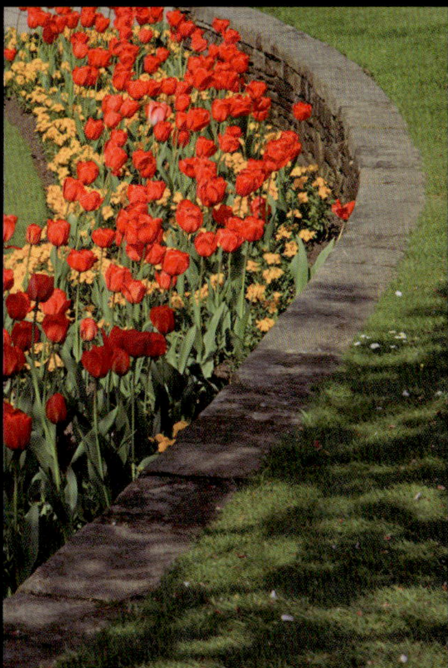

magazine use. This is also a useful way of dealing with finer detail. For the budding professional, a vertical image stands a better chance of being used full-page—which means twice the money! In such cases editors will also want to be able to drop text over part of the image—the lower right side of the picture shown here would be ideal for this purpose.

General settings
Aperture priority (Av) mode
ISO 100
1/250 sec at f/8
Evaluative metering
Color temperature: 5200°K
Focus mode: One Shot AF

A sense of depth

A popular technique in landscape photography is to use a physical feature—such as a river, road, or other strong line which winds its way from the foreground into the distance—to lead the eye into the picture. Features such as gates and arches also offer an "invitation" to the viewer to proceed farther into the image.

Another, more subtle, way of creating depth is to make use of foreground and middle-distance features which are on different planes. Although planes running parallel across a photograph can sometimes act as "stoppers," they can also successfully convey the impression of three dimensions.

To illustrate this as clearly as possible, a very simple example has been selected. The photograph below is of a ruined temple in the Egyptian desert, with just three planes: the foreground, the middle distance, and the mountains in the background.

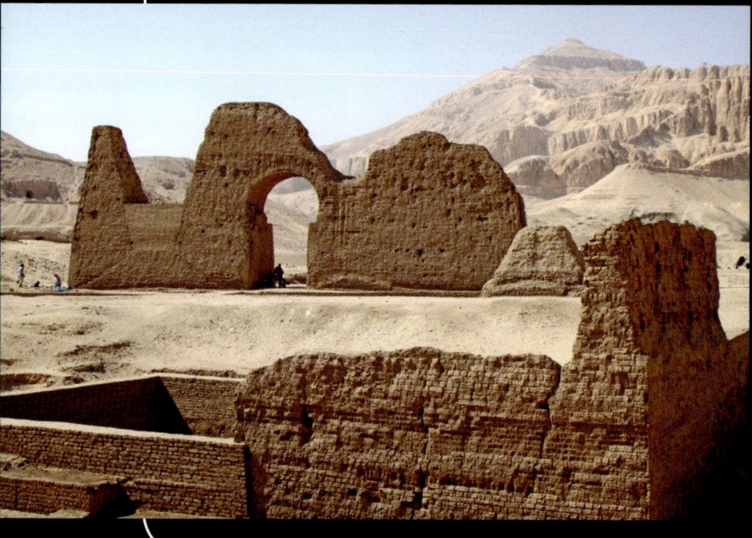

Settings

Aperture priority (Av)
ISO 200
1/500 at f/8
Evaluative metering
White balance: 5200°K
Picture Style: Landscape
One-shot AF

TEMPLE RUINS
Strong foreground, middle distance, and background create a great sense of depth.

Caring for your camera

The Rebel T1i/EOS 500D performs reliably under most circumstances, but it is not indestructible and the manufacturer's cautions regarding use and operating conditions should always be adhered to. The greatest enemies of digital cameras are dust, moisture, excessive heat, and sharp knocks, all of which can be avoided with a little forethought.

Basic camera care

Caring for your camera, like charity, begins at home. Keep it in a dry, dust-free environment—preferably your camera bag, which will also protect it from occasional knocks.

Out in the field, dust and sand can be a real problem and more so if it is windy. Part of the solution is to keep the camera in your camera bag except when it is needed and to take extra care when changing lenses. Keeping dust from entering the camera via the lens mounting is the priority, but you also need to keep dust and sand off the lens elements. Sand will scour the glass if you try to wipe it off, so careful use of a blower or blower-brush is recommended. You may wish to use a UV filter on the lens as this can be replaced quickly and cheaply.

Never leave the camera close to a magnetic field or radio waves that may affect the electronics or damage data. Finally, avoid dropping the camera, or having it knocked out of your hand in a crowd, by using the camera strap at all times.

In cold temperatures

The Rebel T1i/EOS 500D is designed to operate in temperatures from 32–104°F (0–40°C) at a maximum of 85% humidity. However, you should pay heed to the effective temperature, allowing for wind chill, rather than the still air temperature. At 32°F (0°C) a wind speed of just 25mph (40km/h) will make it feel like 18°F (-8°C). When temperatures drop below freezing and wind speed increases, the effective temperature drops very quickly.

Signs that the camera is becoming too cold, apart from reduced battery performance, are the darkening of the LCD monitor and sluggishness in moving parts, especially those which are lubricated. Does this mean

Warning!

The Canon Rebel T1i/EOS 500D does not provide the same level of protection from moisture and dust as Canon's EOS 1 series bodies, which are designed for use by press photographers in all weathers.

that you should put the camera away until better weather arrives? No, but it does mean that you need to work in a different way.

Camera batteries are notorious for their fall-off in performance when the temperature approaches freezing so always keep these inside your clothing when they are not needed. The camera, too, should be kept as warm as possible while not in use: if you need to keep it in a camera bag then you can always wrap it in something that will act as an extra layer of insulation. The author favors a spare woolly hat that can also double up as a beanbag for extra support when the camera needs to be rested on a rough surface.

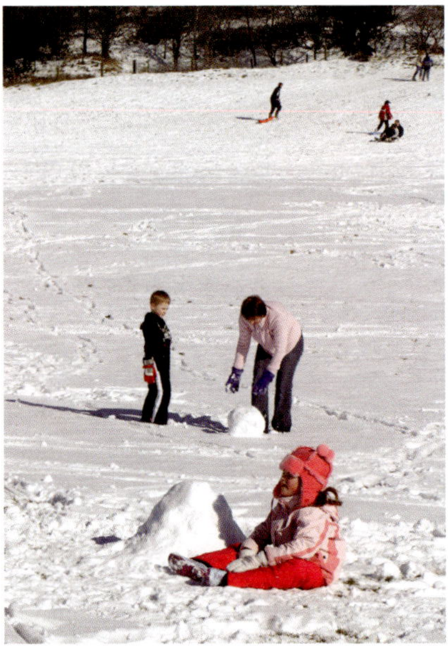

In heat and humidity

Short of dropping your camera into the sea, the only thing worse is excessive heat. The recommended maximum working temperature of 104°F (40°C) may seem to cover most situations in which you might find yourself. However, if you've ever had to climb into a car which has been parked in the hot sun for some time, you'll know that 104°F (40°C) is easily surpassed. Consequently, you should never leave an uninsulated camera in your car on a very hot day. You can leave the camera in an insulated coolbox such as those used for picnics or camping, but don't use the freezer packs that would normally aid the cooling process.

The other issue which heat raises is the expansion of non-metal parts. This can be a very real issue with lenses, particularly some of the newer, lightweight ones which make more extensive use of plastics. You may have noticed on some lenses that the infinity mark (∞) has

WINTER SCENE
A bright spell after a snowfall is a great time to take pictures, but follow a few simple rules to ensure that your camera performs in the cold.

changed from absolute infinity to ∟∞, which is a variable position to allow for heat expansion.

Protecting against humidity requires wrapping the camera in an airtight plastic bag or container, ideally with a small bag of silica gel. Silica gel absorbs moisture and a small bag of it usually comes in the box when you buy a new camera or lens – store it somewhere dry for occasions like this. In order to reduce condensation, allow your equipment and the bag or container in which it is stored to reach the ambient temperature before taking the equipment out.

Water protection

Prevention is better, and usually a whole lot cheaper, than cure—this saying could have been invented with a digital SLR camera and a wet environment in mind. The simplest advice is not to take any risks whatsoever.

However, there are times when we get caught out by unexpected events, and especially by the weather. It is worth investing in a camera bag which will prove good protection against the elements, such as Lowepro's AW (All Weather) models which have a rain cover that tucks away discreetly when not needed. Some models, such as the Stealth Reporter series, actually have two rain covers. The first is a thin showerproof cover that covers the lid of the camera bag, while the main rain cover is more substantial and wraps around the whole camera bag; it is stored on the underside of the bag, which also stops moisture getting through when you put the bag down on wet ground.

Finally, be extra cautious when working in a marine environment, as spray can be carried huge distances on a windy day. The air can also be laden with salt for a considerable distance away from the shore.

Tip

An excellent solution to the problem of changing lenses in a dusty environment is to use a changing bag. Remember those? For the uninitiated, it is a lightproof bag about 2ft (60cm) square with a zipped access for inserting equipment and two elasticated arm holes to put your hands through. Originally designed for loading extremely light-sensitive film in the camera or to load exposed film into a developing tank, it now serves a new purpose in the digital era.

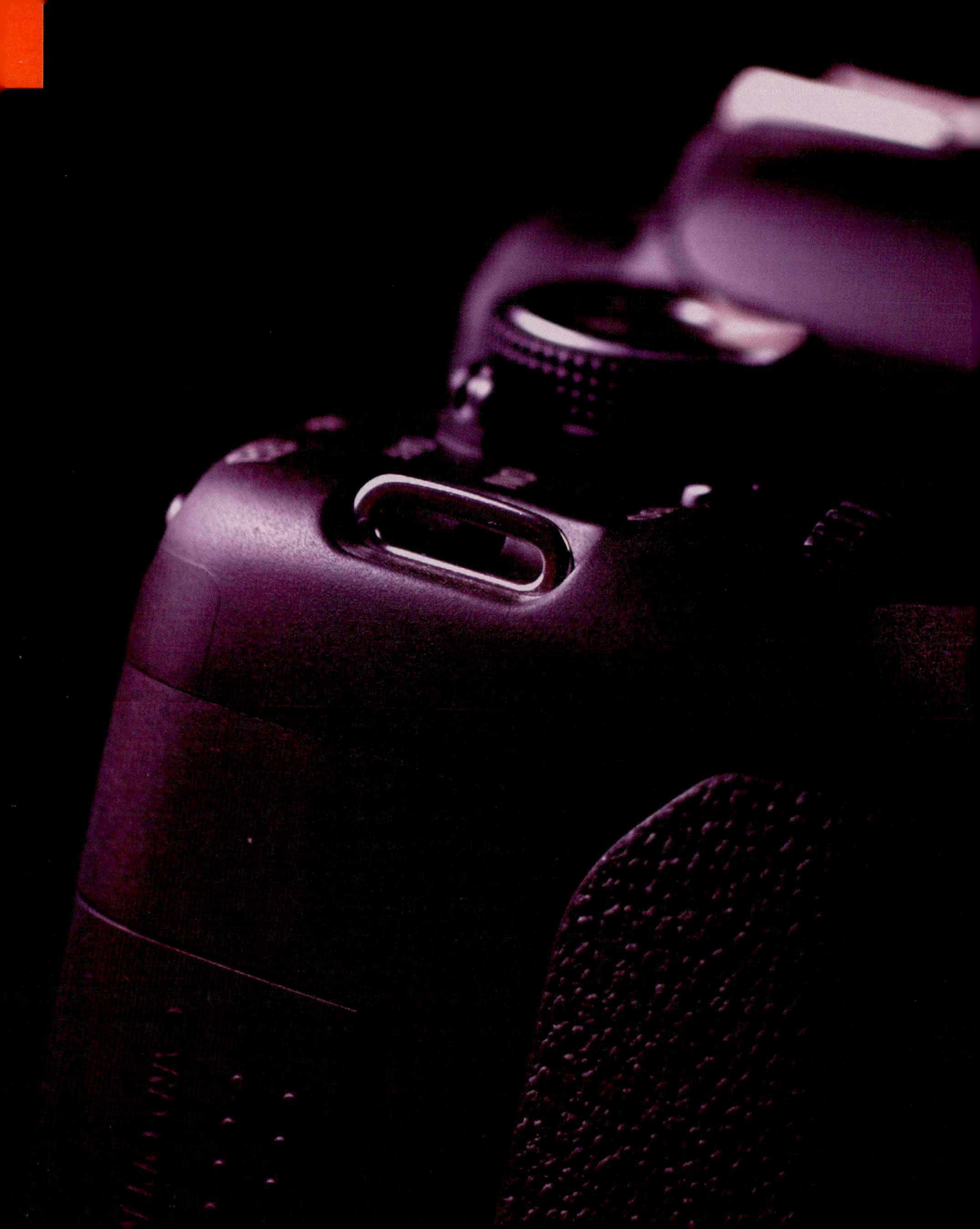

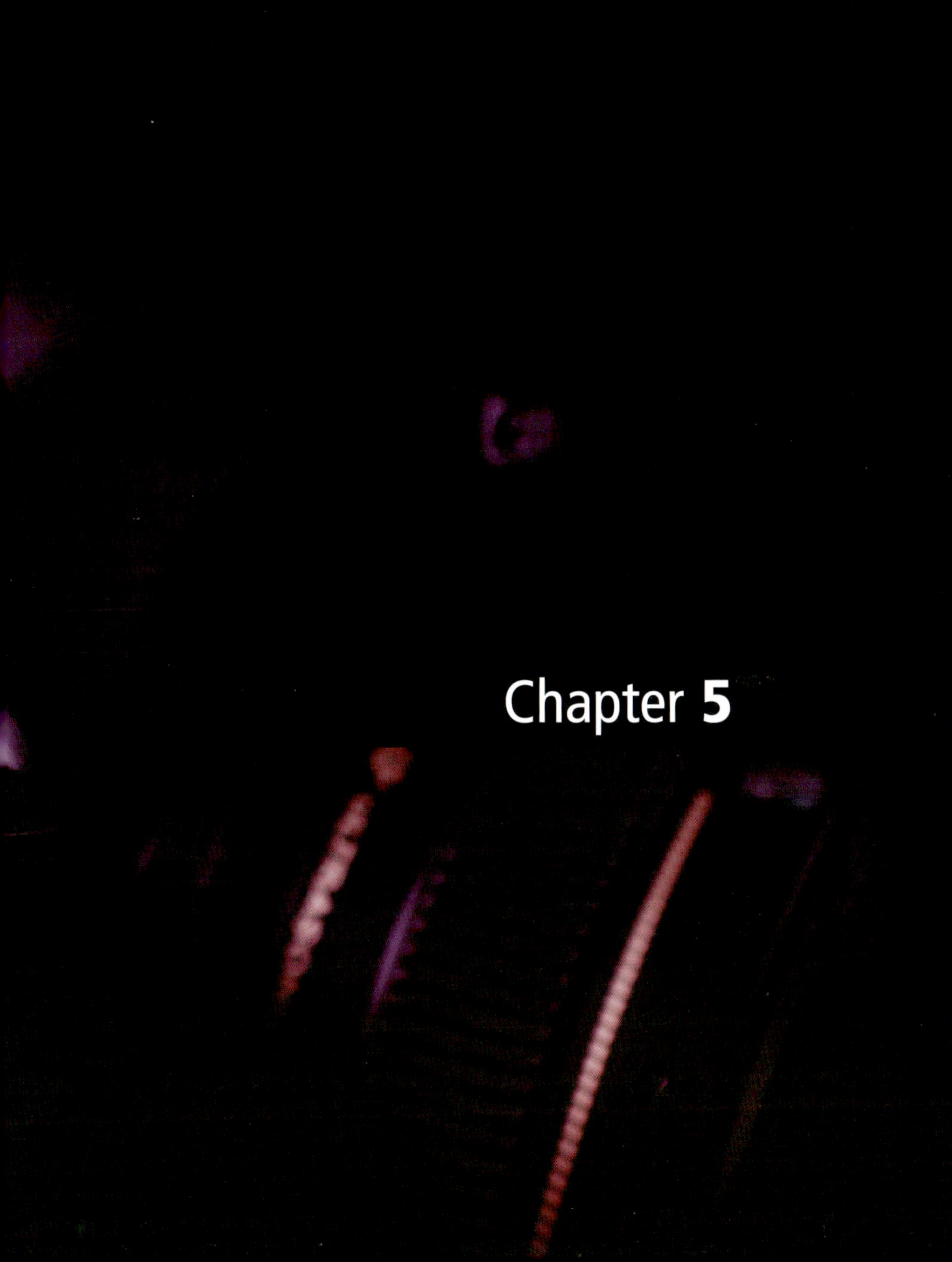

Chapter 5

Flash

Flash photography has developed to such an extent that it is often imbued with almost magical properties. Magic, say some, is simply the science that other people know but we don't: the following pages should help to dispel some of the mystery.

The Rebel T1i/EOS 500D is equipped with a built-in flash that provides a wide enough beam to be used with a 17mm lens and sufficient power to adequately light a subject 10ft (3m) away, assuming ISO 100 at f/4. In other words, it is a very useful tool in compact situations. The coverage is very even, not as harsh as earlier models such as the EOS 10D, and blends well with ambient light. It can be used as the main source of lighting or simply be used as fill-in to relieve some of the dark shadows on a sunny day. In Basic Zone modes built-in flash is automatic.

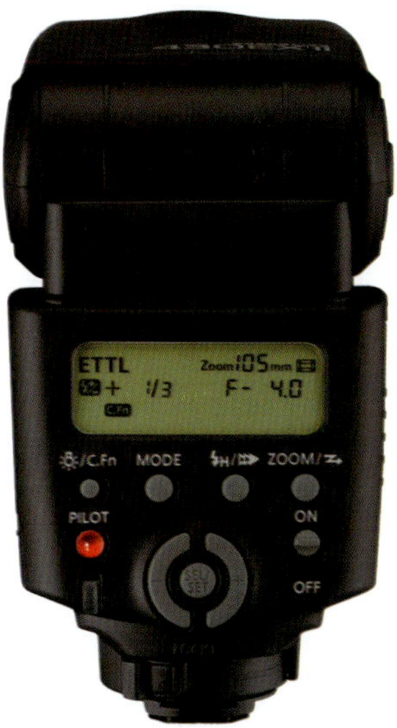

The advantages of using the built-in flash compared with using an EX Speedlite come down to weight and convenience. None of the Speedlites is exceptionally heavy, but it still means extra weight plus an extra set of batteries or a power pack, and possibly extra recharging at the end of the day. Both make use of E-TTL II metering, AF-assist beam, red-eye reduction, flash exposure bracketing, flash exposure lock and first- or second-curtain synchronization. All this means that the main advantages of using a Speedlite are its added power, off-camera capability, and variable output. Knowing these pros and cons means you can decide whether carrying the extra weight of a Speedlite is worthwhile for you.

E-TTL II flash exposure system

The third generation of Canon's auto flash exposure system provides almost seamless integration of flash and camera in most situations where

SIR JACKIE STEWART OBE
The built-in flash does a fine job of filling in shadows in the contrasty light of a sunny day.

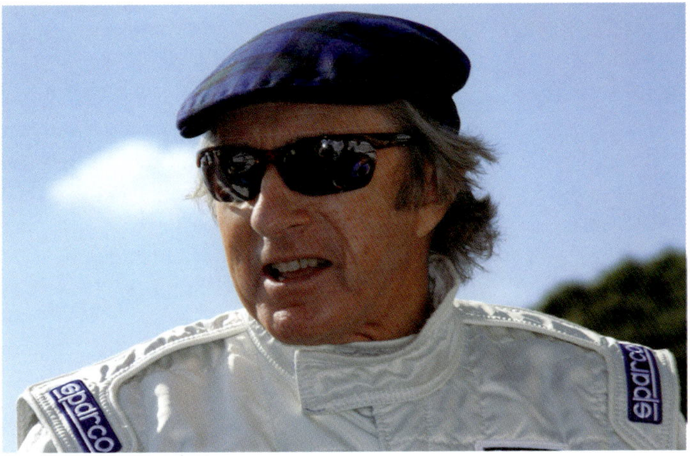

flash would be either helpful or mandatory. The E-TTL designation stands for "evaluative through-the-lens" metering, as opposed to measuring the flash exposure from a sensor within the flash gun. The fact that the exposure is based on what is seen through the lens means that you can position the flash off-camera, at a different angle to the subject than that of the camera, and still achieve accurate exposure with EX Speedlites.

When the shutter-release button is fully depressed, it signals the Speedlite, assuming it is a recent E-TTL II model, to fire a pre-exposure metering burst in order to ascertain the correct exposure. The data gathered on the brightness levels of the subject during this initial burst of flash is compared with the data for the same areas of the image under ambient light. From these two sets of data the correct flash output and exposure are calculated. With many EF lenses this burst will also assess the distance to the subject. The shutter activation and the main flash burst (assuming first-curtain sync is set) will follow so quickly on the back of the metering burst that the two will be inseparable to the naked eye.

Note
For E-TTL II-compatible lenses that deliver distance information to help calculate flash exposure more accurately, see individual lens specifications on Canon's website.

Guide numbers

There is an easy way to compare the performance of different models of flashgun and that is to look at their guide numbers (GN). This is a measurement of power that can be applied equally to any flash unit, and measures the maximum distance over which the flash will provide effective coverage. As this distance is dependent upon the sensitivity of the film or sensor, the measurement is qualified by the addition of an ISO setting. The guide number for Canon's 580EX II Speedlite is 190/58 (ft/m) at ISO 100.

Calculating flash exposure

Aperture also affects flash coverage, but the equations involved in calculating flash exposure are simple enough for us to calculate the third factor involved as long as we have the other two. (In the following examples, the term "flash-to-subject distance" is used because the flash could be used off-camera.)

The basic equation is as follows: *Guide Number / Flash-to-subject distance = Aperture.* This could also be written as *Guide Number / Aperture = Flash-to-subject distance or Flash-to-subject distance × Aperture = Guide Number.*

Take the 580EX II as an example using the maximum flash-to-subject distance: *190 (GN) / 190 ft = Aperture.* We would therefore need an aperture of f/1 to achieve flash coverage. As this is unrealistic, let's take another example using a flash-to-subject distance of 50ft: *190 (GN) / 50ft = f/3.8* (f/4 for practical purposes).

If we know the guide number and we know the aperture we want to use, f/16 for example, but aren't sure of the flash-to-subject distance limitations we can still calculate this easily: *190 (GN) / f/16 = Flash to subject distance.* This would give us an answer of 11.9ft (3.6m) as the maximum distance over which the flash would perform adequately with f/16 as our working aperture.

To make life easier, Canon provide zoom heads on some flashguns. These sense the focal length in use and harness the power of the flash more effectively by narrowing (or widening) the flash beam to suit the lens. For this reason the full Guide Number also refers to the maximum focal length that the zoom head will accommodate automatically. Consequently, the full Guide Number for our example of the 580EX II Speedlite is 190/58 (ft/m) ISO 100 at 105mm. EX Speedlites also display a useful graphic indicating the distance over which flash can be used at current settings.

Flash exposure lock

When part of the subject is critical in terms of exposure, you can take a flash exposure reading of that area of the image using the same metering circle as the Partial metering mode, and lock it into the camera/flash combination.

1) Adjust all the appropriate settings and switch on the external flash or raise the built-in flash. Aim the camera at the critical part of the subject.

2) Partially depress the shutter release and check that the ϟ symbol is lit.

3) Focus with the center of the viewfinder over the important part of the subject and press the ✱/⚄• 🔍 FE lock button.

4) The flash head will emit a metering pre-flash and the camera will calculate the correct exposure.

5) The ϟ* Flash exposure lock symbol is displayed in the viewfinder.

6) Recompose the shot and press the shutter-release button.

7) The flash will fire, the picture will be taken, and the ϟ* symbol will be replaced by the ϟ Flash Ready symbol, indicating that no exposure settings are retained.

Flash exposure bracketing

Flash exposure bracketing is not built into the Rebel T1i/EOS 500D but can be found on EX Speedlites from the 550EX upward. A less convenient but equally effective alternative with the Rebel T1i/EOS 500D is to adjust the flash exposure compensation settings for each of three shots, matching the bracketing process.

Common errors

Any flash exposure compensation settings are retained after switching the camera off. When you enter a new shooting situation, pay attention to the viewfinder symbol as a reminder that an adjustment has been made.

Tips

Flash exposure compensation can be set at any time. The built-in flash does not need to be in its active position, nor does an external flash need to be switched on.

When the flash-to-subject distance is too great and correct exposure cannot be achieved, the ϟ Flash ready symbol blinks in the viewfinder.

Flash exposure compensation

It is possible to select flash exposure compensation when using either the built-in flash or a compatible external flash, providing you are using one of the Creative Zone modes. This works in exactly the same way as normal exposure compensation, taking three different pictures up to +/-2 stops, and permits you to control the end result so that the subject has a more natural appearance.

1) Press the **MENU** button.

2) Select Shooting menu 1 > **Flash control.** > **Built-in flash func. setting** > **Flash exp. comp**.

3) Press **SET** and use the ◀ button to decrease the exposure or the ▶ button to increase it. Press **SET**.

4) When you partially depress the shutter-release button, the Flash exposure compensation symbol appears in the viewfinder at bottom left. The Quick Control Screen shows the same symbol plus the amount of compensation.

5) Take the picture and review the result, adjusting compensation and repeating the shot if necessary.

The Inverse Square Law

As you double the flash-to-subject distance, four times the illumination is required. This is known as the Inverse Square Law.

A one-stop increase in aperture doubles the exposure, so two stops will give four times the exposure.

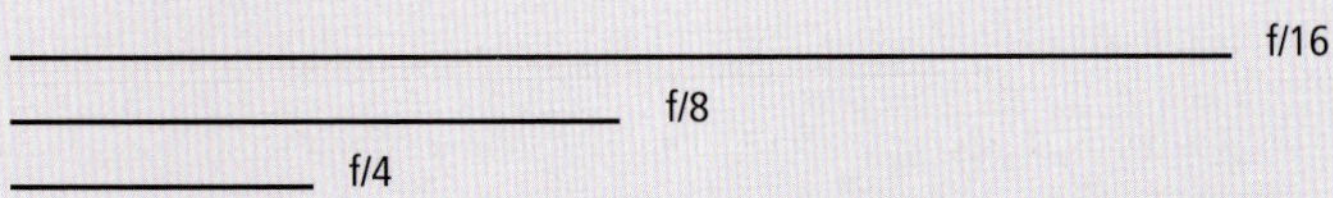

Flash coverage requires an increase of two stops when the camera-to-subject distance doubles.

Bounce and direct flash

The two most popular techniques for reducing the impact of direct flash are the use of a diffuser and bouncing the flash off a suitable reflective surface. While there is a small diffuser on the market that will fit the built-in flash, bounce flash remains the sole preserve of those using EX Speedlites and other compatible flashguns mounted on the hotshoe or used off-camera with the Off-camera shoe cord.

Depending on the model, if the flashgun is mounted on the camera's hotshoe, bounce flash can be achieved by rotating and tilting the flash head to point at the reflecting surface—which, ideally, should normally be a little above and to one side of the subject. Bounce flash, especially when used with the flash gun off-camera, is a good way of both softening shadows and controlling where they fall.

LOCOMOTIVE WHEEL
Controlling the glare from direct flash when it is used with reflective surfaces can be a problem. In this image, the brushed finish of the metals helped to reduce the glare.

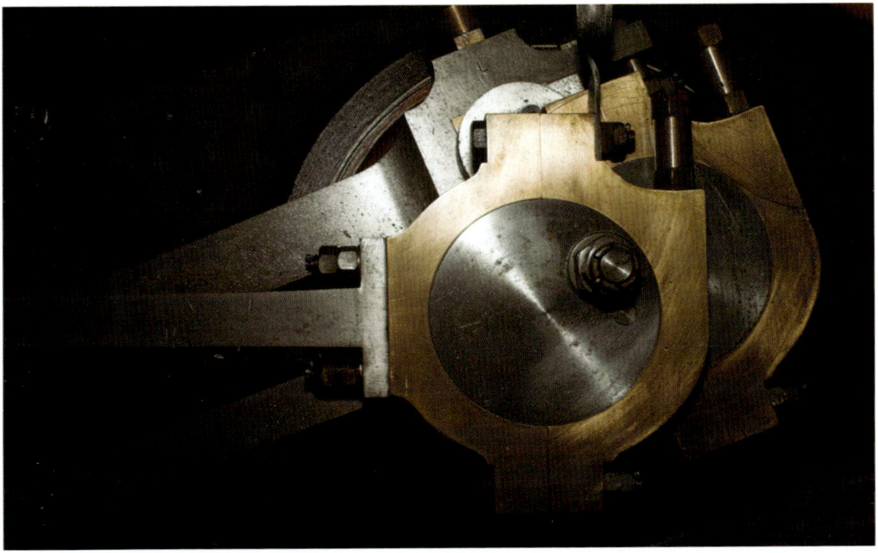

Bounce flash

The concept of bounce flash is that the surface(s) being used to reflect the flash will provide, in effect, a larger and therefore more diffuse light source. This also assumes that it is light enough in tone to perform this purpose and that it won't imbue the subject with a color cast. If the reflecting surface has a matte finish or is darker in tone, it will be less effective because it will absorb some of the light and will require a much wider aperture or shorter flash-to-subject distance to work.

With the bounce flash technique, the flash-to-subject distance includes the distance to the reflecting surface and from that surface to the subject. In addition, about two stops of light are likely to be lost when using this technique, so the flash-to-subject distance will be considerably shorter than would normally be the case for any given aperture.

> **Tip**
> When the flash is at the same height as the subject, an otherwise pleasing shot can be ruined by hard shadows against the background. To avoid this, try to put some distance between the subject and background. With a wide aperture the background will also be more out of focus and less distracting.

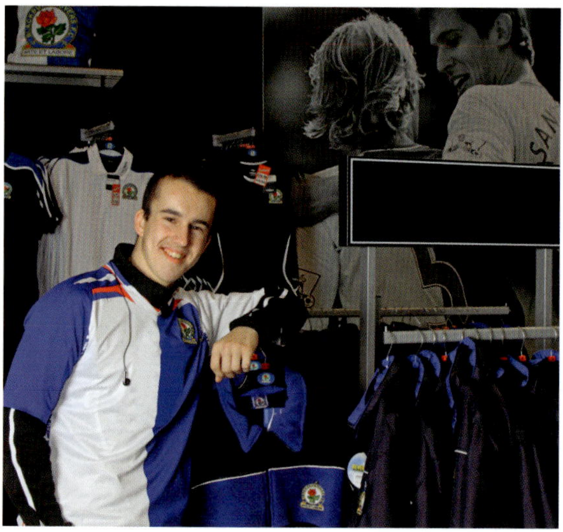

SOCCER FAN
Direct flash would have been too harsh at such a close distance, so the camera-mounted Speedlite was bounced off a large white pillar immediately to the left. The greater the size of the reflective area, the softer the light will be.

Direct flash

One of the common problems with direct flash (i.e. not diffused or bounced) is red-eye, when light from the flash is picked up by the blood vessels at the back of the eye. It is particularly noticeable when the flash gun is mounted on top of the camera. At one time, the only technique for dealing with this was to use diffused lighting or to move the flash gun away from the lens axis, or both.

The Rebel T1i/EOS 500D's red-eye reduction function, enabled in 📷 Shooting menu 1, uses the flash to direct a beam of light at the subject prior to the actual exposure and before the flash fires in the normal way. This beam causes the pupils to narrow so that red-eye is reduced. When red-eye reduction is enabled and either the built-in or external flash is switched on, the exposure compensation scale -2..1..0..1..+2 at the bottom of the viewfinder is replaced by **IIIIII** when focus is confirmed.

The use of direct flash should always be considered carefully. It is worth noting that many press photographers keep a Sto-fen Omnibounce diffuser on their camera-mounted flashguns at all times to soften the harsh appearance of direct flash.

Attaching an EX Speedlite

1) With both camera and Speedlite switched off, mount the Speedlite on the camera's hotshoe and tighten the locking ring.

2) Turn the camera's power switch to **ON** and turn on the Speedlite.

3) On the camera, adjust the White balance setting to ⚡ Flash if using a Creative Zone mode. (Auto white balance will be selected automatically in Basic Zone modes and cannot be changed.)

First- and second-curtain flash explained

A focal-plane shutter works by two shutter curtains moving across the frame. Both move across the focal plane at the same speed, but there is a small gap between them which is how the sensor is exposed to the image projected by the lens. With a higher shutter speed, the curtains don't move any faster but the gap between them gets narrower. With an extremely slow shutter speed, the entire frame may be exposed before the second curtain begins to follow the first. This makes it possible to control shutter speeds precisely and reach speeds of up to 1/4000 second. With the E-TTL flash system the flash actually fires twice. The first burst is a preflash in the sense that it fires just before the shutter opens in order to determine exposure. The second burst is the one which illuminates the subject.

When first-curtain synchronization is selected, the illuminating burst occurs as soon as the travel of the first curtain opens the gap between it and the second curtain. This second burst is normally so soon after the metering burst that, to the naked eye, the two are indistinguishable.

When second-curtain synchronization is selected, the illuminating burst is fired at the end of the exposure, just before the second curtain catches up with the first. Because there is a longer time lag between metering and illumination, it may be more obvious that the flash has fired twice.

The duration of the flash is extremely short and, like using a fast shutter speed, it has the effect of freezing movement. However, the exposed image is subject to two light sources: flash and the ambient light. If the exposure is long enough for the ambient light levels to record subject detail, the final image will be illuminated by of a mixture of flash and ambient light. The subject will be seen as being frozen and sharp but there will also be a ghost image which is not, and there may also be light trails from moving highlights.

Imagine a subject moving across the frame from left to right. With first-curtain sync, the flash will fire immediately the shutter opens and freeze the image toward the left of the frame. Any ambient light will continue to expose the subject as it moves across the frame. The end result is a sharp subject with light trails extending into the area into which it is moving, making it appear as if it is moving backwards. With second-curtain sync, the subject is lit by the ambient light first and then frozen by the flash at the end of the exposure. This adds to the impression of forward movement and looks much more natural.

Wireless and multiple flash

When a single flash head is no longer sufficient, either in terms of power or to control highlights and shadows, you can use multiple flash units with either wired or wireless connectivity. Wired connection can be achieved using the accessories listed on pages 176–7, but with the exception of the Off-camera shoe cord, the benefits of E-TTL II metering will be lost.

A wireless system will retain full E-TTL II compatibility and can be established using either the Wireless Transmitter ST-E2 as the camera-mounted control unit or an EX Speedlite (550EX upward) as the master unit. All other flash units will be deemed "slave" units. The ST-E2 is purely a control unit and transmitter and does not incorporate a flash head.

EX Speedlites

Canon's EX Speedlites are fully compatible with E-TTL II metering. The range runs from the cheapest 220EX to the high-powered 580EX II. The model number is a quick and easy indication of the power of each unit, with the 580EX having a guide number of 58 (meters at ISO 100) or the 430EX having a guide number of 43 (meters at ISO 100), for example. If you are interested in wireless flash photography, check whether the model is capable of acting as a master unit or only as a slave unit.

220EX Speedlite

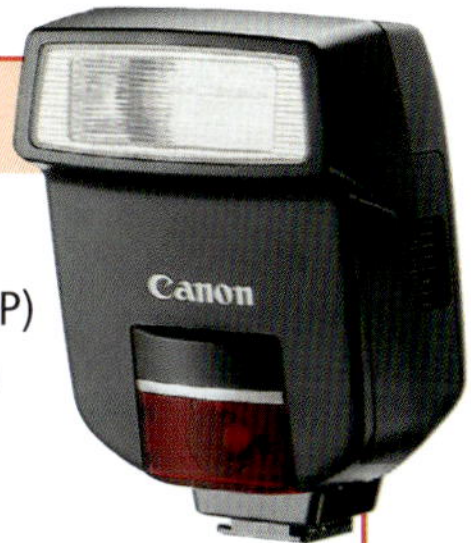

The 220EX Speedlite is the smallest and least expensive of Canon's range. It includes flash exposure lock compatibility and high-speed (FP) synchronization. However, this model is not compatible with use as a wireless slave unit, and it can't take Canon's external power pack.

Max. guide number 72/22 (ISO 100 ft/m)
Zoom range 28mm fixed
Tilt/swivel No
Recycling time 0.1–4.5 seconds
AF-assist beam Yes
Weight (w/o batteries) 160g

270EX Speedlite

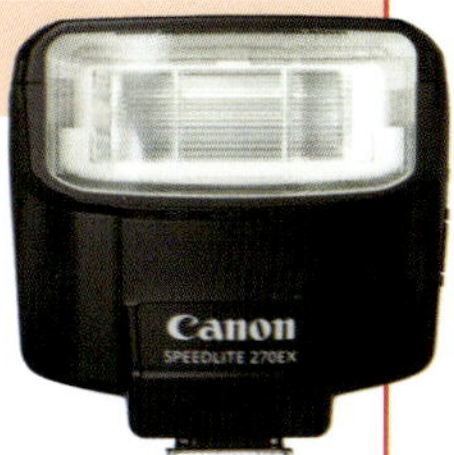

The 270EX Speedlite is the most recent introduction to Canon's range and is compatible with recent models starting with the EOS 50D. Firmware updates permit its use on a range of slightly older models. It has a handy Quick Flash function for use during continuous shooting, and communicates color temperature information to the camera for optimal white balance correction.

Max. guide number 89/27 (ISO 100 ft/m)
Zoom range Two step (fixed) 28mm and 50mm
Tilt/swivel Yes
Recycling time 0.1–3.9 seconds
AF-assist beam Yes
Weight (w/o batteries) 320g

430EX II Speedlite

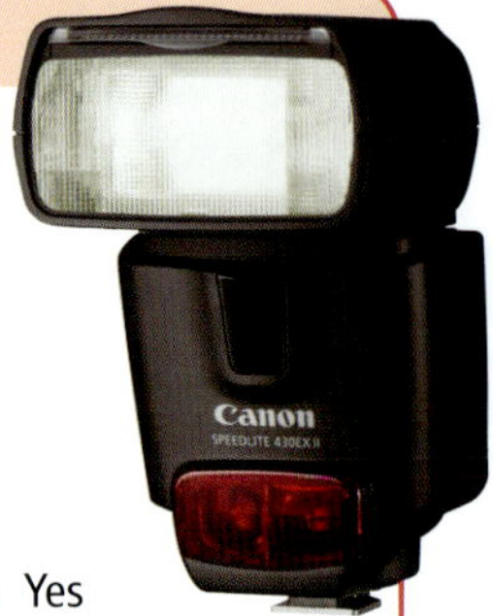

The 430EX II Speedlite includes flash exposure lock compatibility and high-speed (FP) synchronization and can be used as a wireless slave unit with the 550EX, 580EX, 580EX II, Speedlite Transmitter ST-E2, Macro Twin Lite MT-24EX, and Macro Ring Lite MR-14EX. Its zoom range has been extended from 24mm on the 420EX down to a very useful 14mm.

Max. guide number 141/43 (ISO 100 ft/m) at 105mm
Zoom range 24–105mm (14mm with wide panel)
Tilt/swivel Yes
Recycling time 0.1–3.7 seconds
AF-assist beam Yes
Wireless channels 4
Weight (w/o batteries) 320g

580EX II Speedlite

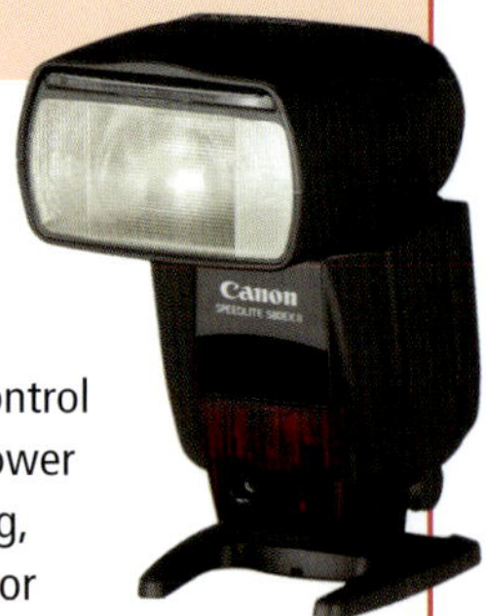

The 580EX II Speedlite provides flash exposure lock, high-speed (FP) synchronization, 14 custom functions, flash exposure bracketing, automatic or manual zoom head, and strobe facility. It can be used as either a master or slave unit for wireless flash photography. It even provides color temperature control for optimal white balance and manual settings down to 1/128 power in ⅓-stop increments. The Mk II version has added weathersealing, 20% faster recycling, a PC socket, and external metering sensor for non-TTL flash to the already popular EX 580.

Max. guide number 190/58 (ISO 100 ft/m) at 105mm
Zoom range 24–105mm (14mm with wide panel)
Tilt/swivel Yes
Recycling time 0.1–6 seconds
AF-assist beam Yes
Custom functions/settings 14/32
Wireless channels 4
Catchlight reflector panel
Weight (w/o batteries) 375g

MR-14EX Macro Ring Lite

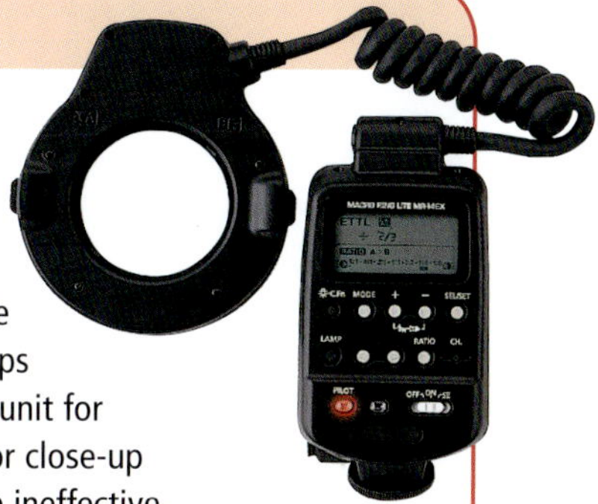

This unit consists of a control unit which is mounted on the hotshoe and a ring-flash unit which is mounted on the lens. The ring-flash unit has two flash tubes on opposite sides of the lens and the lighting ratio between these can be adjusted to provide better shadow control. It also has built-in focusing lamps and modeling flash and is capable of acting as master unit for wireless flash photography. The Ring Lite is designed for close-up photography where a hotshoe-mounted flash would be ineffective due to the short camera-to-subject distance.

Max. guide number 46/14 (ISO 100 ft/m)
Designed for use with EF macro lenses
Tilt/swivel No
Modeling flash Yes
Recycling time 0.1–7 seconds
Weight (w/o batteries) 404g

MT-24EX Macro Twin Lite

The Twin Lite consists of a control unit mounted on the camera's hotshoe plus two small flash heads which are mounted on either side of the lens and which can be adjusted independently. This model offers far more flexibility than the Ring Flash. It has the same wireless capabilities as the Ring Flash and is designed for use with the same EF Macro lenses.

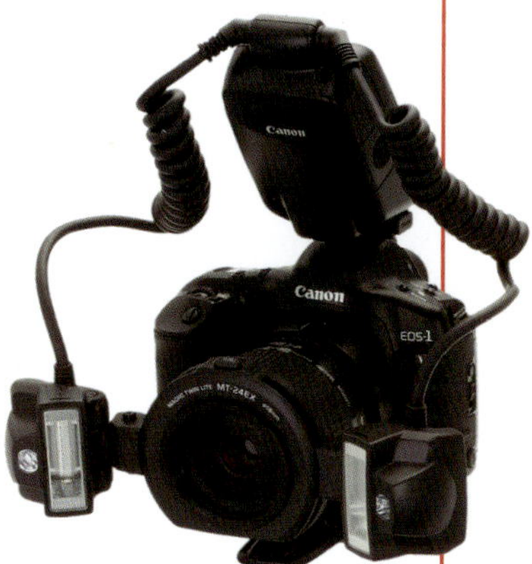

Max. guide number 79/24 (ISO 100 ft/m) (with both heads firing)
Zoom range N/A
Tilt/swivel Yes
Recycling time 4–7 seconds
Weight (w/o batteries) 404g

FLASH

Flash accessories

One of the great advantages of using a system camera is the range of accessories available, and Canon produce a wide range of useful additions for its flash units. These will increase the range of situations in which you can work and give you maximum control of the end result. In particular, they will help you to use the flash off-camera to reduce red-eye when shooting people and animals and for improved shadow placement, giving a more natural appearance to your photographs.

Speedlite Transmitter ST-E2
This unit acts as an on-camera wireless transmitter for 430EX, 550EX, and 580EX Speedlites. It can control two groups of slave flash heads with flash ratio variable between the two groups. The ST-E2 is not entirely necessary for wireless flash as some EX models can also act as master units, with or without the master unit firing.

Off-camera Shoe Adapter OA-2
This is a simple hotshoe socket for a Speedlite and incorporates a ¼-inch tripod socket, to be used with either of the connecting cords.

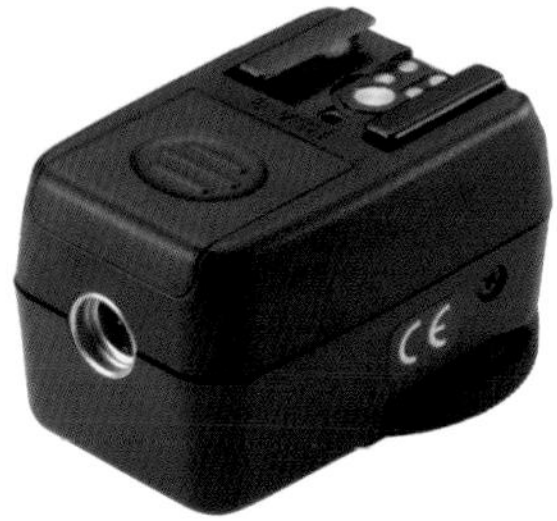

TTL Hotshoe Adapter 3
This can be used with either the Connecting cords and the TTL distributor, or the off-camera shoe cord to connect up to four separate Speedlites.

Connecting Cords 60 and 300
These cords consist of either a 2ft (0.6m) coiled lead or a 10ft (3m) straight lead to connect the TTL Distributor and TTL Hotshoe Adapter 3.

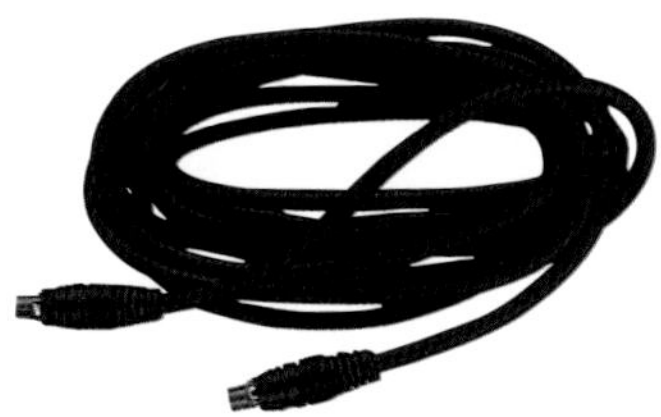

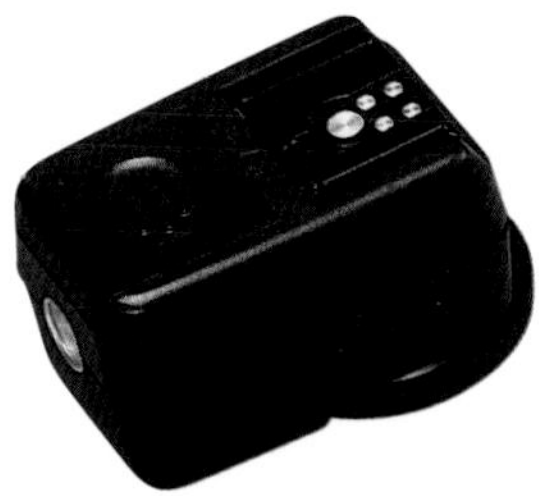

TTL distributor

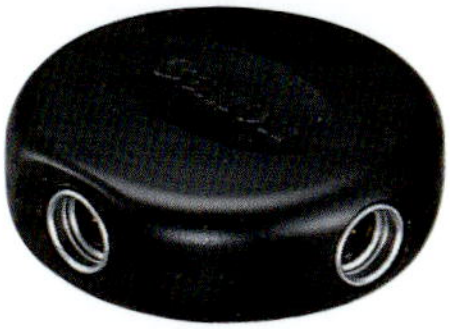

This accessory provides four connection sockets: one to connect to the TTL Hotshoe Adapter 3 and three for connecting to off-camera shoe adapters via Connecting cords 60 and 300.

Off-camera shoe cord OC-E3

This is one of the first accessories many people buy, enabling an EX Speedlite to be used up to 2ft (0.6m) away from the camera while retaining all normal functions. It is ideal for close-ups with a small light cube or Lastolite ePhotomaker, as well as improving bounce flash capability and helping to avoid red-eye.

Speedlite L bracket SB-E2

This allows a Speedlite to be positioned to the side of the camera rather than on the hotshoe, helping to reduce red-eye by taking the flash head off the camera-lens axis. It requires an off-camera shoe cord.

Tips

Wired flash accessories are not compatible with E-TTL II metering, irrespective of the capabilities of the flash unit you are connecting. For full E-TTL II compatibility, use a wireless system with the 550EX, 580EX, 580EX II, or ST-E2 transmitter as the master unit.

In order to ensure maximum compatibility, new accessories are often released at the same time as new Speedlites. Sometimes, but not always, these will also be compatible with discontinued flash units. To check compatibility, consult the Canon website or, even better, obtain a copy of EOS Magazine's annual products supplement, which lists all current and discontinued Canon products, in some cases as far back as the late 1980s.

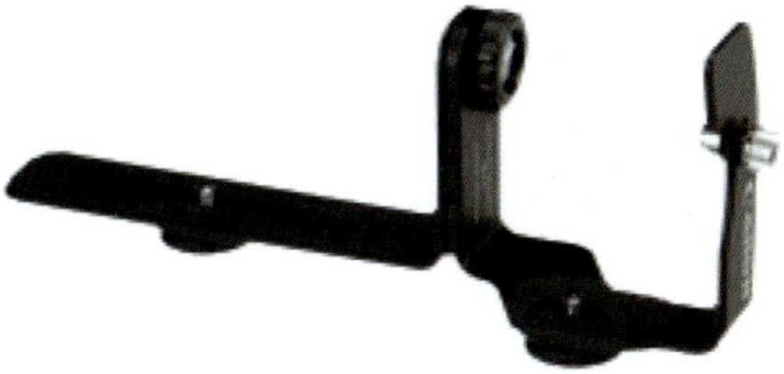

Compact battery pack CD-E4

The CD-E4 improves recycling times and the number of flashes available. It also permits the fast changeover of CPM-E4 battery magazines.

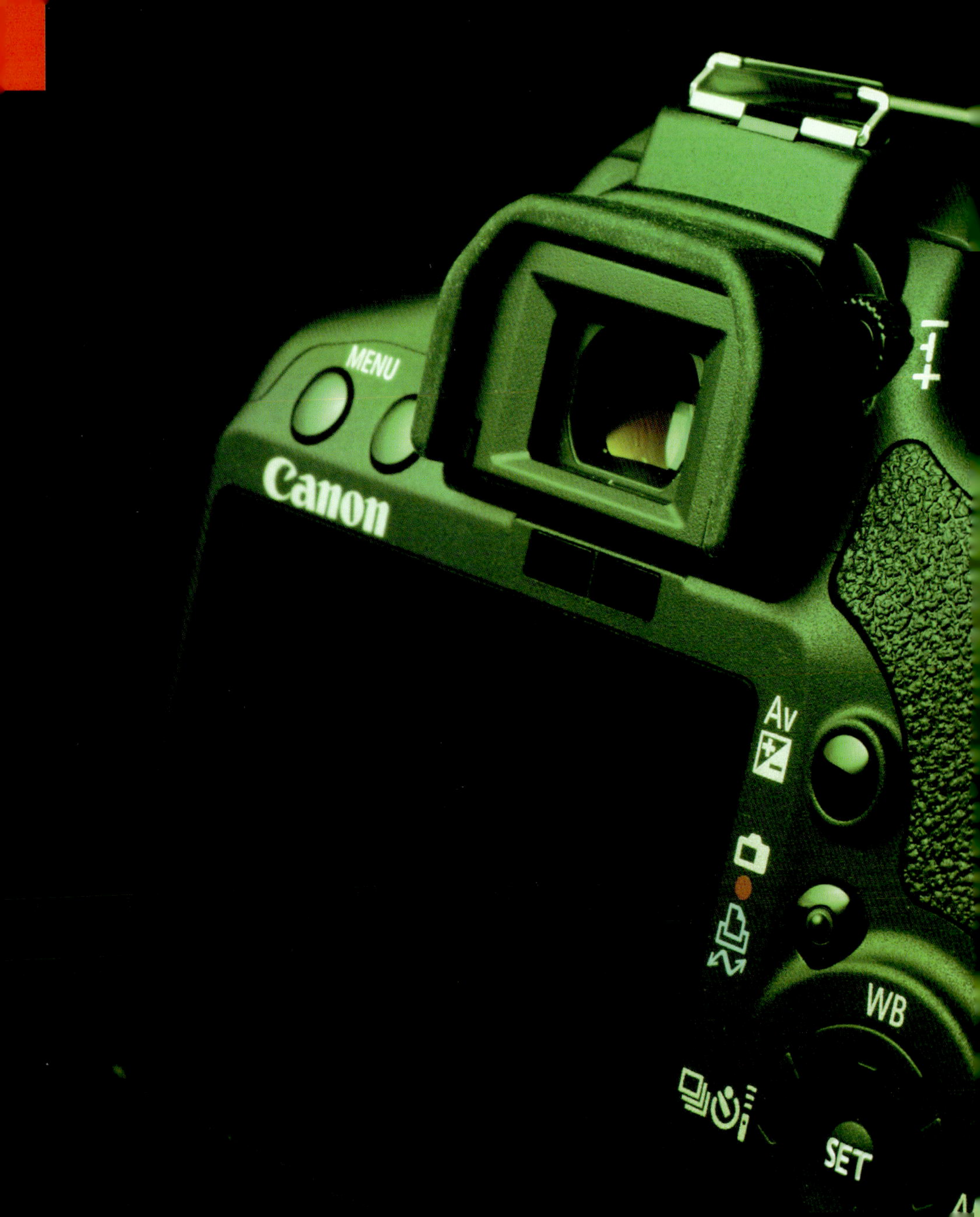
MENU
Canon
Av
WB
SET

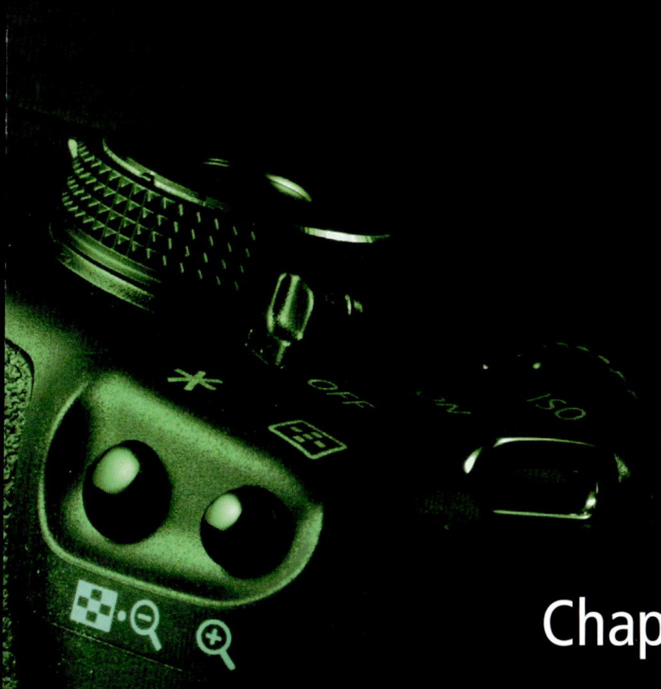

Chapter 6

Close-up

The revealing world of close-up photography is both fascinating and rewarding, and is available to all photographers with the minimum of additional equipment. What it does require, however, is great attention to technique and rock-solid camera support. The high magnifications involved mean that a slight error in focusing or the smallest camera movement will be immediately noticeable.

Lighting and depth of field are of the greatest importance in close-up photography. The latter is easily dealt with by choosing a very narrow aperture, and for this reason, purpose-built macro lenses often have a narrower aperture than usual, perhaps f/32 or f/45 rather than f/22. As well as making the use of depth of field preview more difficult, apertures like these require even slower shutter speeds, making lack of camera movement even more crucial. This is one of the reasons why so much extreme close-up photography requires flash.

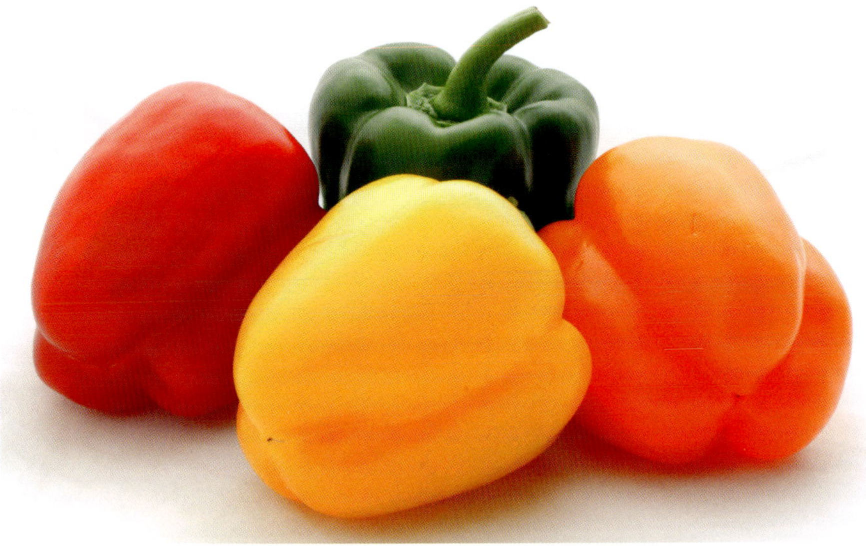

PEPPERS
A simple close-up using off-camera flash in Live View mode.

Lighting for close-ups

Lighting is one of the most difficult aspects of extreme close-up work. The very narrow apertures and slow shutter speeds necessary cannot be overcome by using a high ISO speed unless quality is to be sacrificed, so diffuse ambient lighting is often not sufficient unless working outdoors, when the additional problem of wind has to be considered.

Flash might seem the obvious solution, but it has its own problems. To start with, a flashgun mounted on the camera's hotshoe cannot be tilted down sufficiently to illuminate the subject at close proximity.

Off-camera flash

The starting point, then, for lighting close-ups is off-camera flash. This requires the Canon Off-camera shoe cord OC-E3 (see page 177) that will retain all E-TTL II features. However, direct flash will produce a rather harsh light at such short distances so it is best to diffuse it.

The two simplest ways to diffuse light from the flash are to either bounce the light off a white or near-white surface such as a sheet of white card or a Lastolite reflector, or to put translucent material between the flash and the subject. The oldest trick in the book is to drape a white handkerchief over the flash head.

This raises the issue of the size of the light source. One reason why bounce flash is so effective is that the effective size of the light source has been increased dramatically. If you bounce the light off a standard Lastolite reflector you have a light source 3ft (0.9m) in diameter, rather than a couple of inches.

The best inexpensive solution for photographing small objects with just one off-camera flash is some form of light tent or light cube. Lastolite's ePhotomaker, originally designed to help people photograph items for sale on eBay, is a small light tent with one internal side consisting of reflective material and the rest being translucent white material which will act as both diffuser and reflector.

By mounting the off-camera flash outside the ePhotomaker on the opposite side to the reflective material, a good balance of light and shadow can be achieved quickly and easily. All the product shots in this book were taken using this technique, using a 580EX Speedlite with an off-camera shoe cord, sometimes with a 550EX as wireless slave unit. A specially made Lastolite ePhotomaker with a black base and rear panel was also used for some shots.

Ring flash

For maximum control of shadows, two or more flash heads are better than one. One solution in the field is to use a ring-flash unit, which has two small flash heads within a circular reflector that fits on the front of the lens with the flash heads on opposite sides of the lens. Canon and Sigma offer similar models.

However, this brings us back to the problem of the harsh effects of direct flash, and ring flash can also produce small doughnut-shaped reflections in shiny surfaces. Ring flash is best reserved for matte subjects and for shooting flowers and similar subjects outdoors.

Canon also manufacture a very expensive lens-mounted two-head unit. This consists of a control unit that mounts on the hotshoe and has two independently adjustable heads. The ratio of one flash to the other can be adjusted for better three-dimensional modeling.

There are also many proprietary products that enable you to use two separate flash heads in a similar configuration using either wired or wireless flash. Remember that a wireless setup is necessary for full E-TTL II compatibility and, if at all possible, this is the most flexible choice when working in controlled conditions indoors. With a Canon 430 EX, 550EX, or 580EX Speedlite (or Mk II equivalent) acting as a master, other flashguns (580EX, 550EX, 430EX, 420EX) can be used as wireless slave units to control highlights and shadows while continuing to benefit from E-TTL II exposure control.

Live View

Because depth of field is so limited in close-up photography, it is often impossible to get the whole of the subject, from front to back, in acceptably sharp focus. Subjective decisions may need to be made about which parts of the subject need to be in sharp focus and which can be sacrificed. This means that there are great advantages to be had from adopting manual focus for the task. This is where the Live View feature comes into its own.

With Live View on the Canon Rebel T1i/EOS 500D you have the advantage of a large image on the camera's monitor on which you can check depth of field. By making use of the ×5 or ×10 magnification function you can check focus in detail. The small white rectangle on the monitor shows the area currently selected for magnification. Note also the grid lines which are useful for lining up the camera but which can also be disabled.

Working distance

The nature of the subjects you plan to photograph will play a large part in determining the working distance between the camera and subject, which in itself will help to determine the focal length(s) of the lens you use. Inanimate objects can be photographed from mere inches away, whereas live subjects will require a greater distance. If you plan to photograph live subjects that are camera-shy or dangerous, you should opt for a longer focal length to increase the working distance.

Because the Canon Rebel T1i/EOS 500D's sensor is only 22.3 × 14.9mm in size, any lens which is designed for use on a full-frame camera will have its field of view cropped by a factor of 1.6. This means that you can fill the frame from slightly farther away than would be the case with a 35mm or full-frame camera body. This is useful if you plan to use extension tubes on a conventional lens. Extension tubes bring the front element of the lens closer to the subject (see page 185).

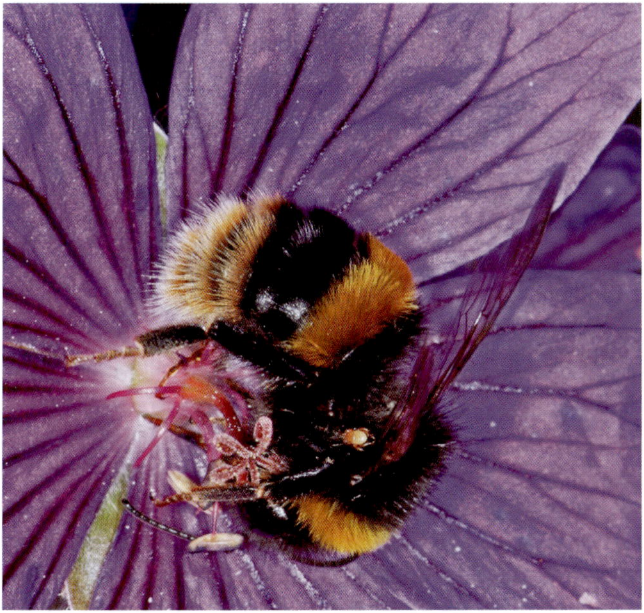

COLLECTING NECTAR
Your working distance needs to be great enough not to frighten off your subject. Bees are usually so engrossed in collecting nectar that you can get extremely close. A ring flash was used for this particular shot.

Close-up attachment lenses

These are one of the easiest routes into close-up photography and screw onto the lens thread just like filters. If you are not planning significant enlargements of your photos, close-up attachment lenses are good value and can produce great results.

They are best used with prime lenses such as a 50mm standard lens or a moderate wide-angle with close focusing capability, and work by reducing the minimum focusing distance even further. Magnification is measured in diopters, generally +1, +2, +3 or +4, and their great advantage for the novice is that all the camera functions are retained.

Close-up attachments can be used two or more at a time, for example combining a +2 with a +3 attachment to obtain +5 diopters. However, the optical quality will not be of the same standard as your lens and using two or more will reduce image quality more noticeably. This is another reason to use prime (fixed focal length) lenses—their image quality, despite many advances in zoom lens quality, still tends to be better.

There are some very inexpensive close-up attachment lenses on the market, but as with filters, you will have to pay more for better quality. Canon produce both 2 diopter (Type 500D) and 4 diopter (Type 250D) lenses in both 52mm and 55mm fittings, plus a 2 diopter (Type 500D) lens in both 72mm and 77mm fittings. All are double-element construction for higher quality. The Type number indicates the greatest possible lens-subject distance in millimeters. The 250D is optimized for use with lenses between 50mm and 135mm; the 500D is designed for lenses between 75mm and 300mm.

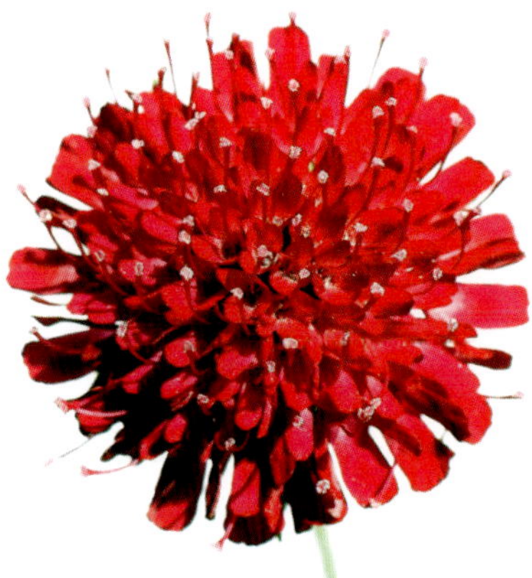

ISOLATED SUBJECT
A small Lastolite reflector is a useful and versatile aid to take into the field with you for close-up work. It folds up very small, can be stuffed in a pocket, and can be used to keep the wind off a subject as well as to reduce shadows. Perhaps best of all, it can be placed behind a subject to isolate it from its background, as shown in this image.

Extension tubes

Extension tubes fit between the lens and the camera body and can be used singly or in combination. Canon produce two: Extension Tube EF 12 II and Extension Tube EF 25 II. The former provides 12mm of extension and the latter 25mm. By increasing the distance from the lens to the lens mount and thus the focal plane, the minimum focusing distance and the magnification of the image are both increased. Both of Canon's extension tubes retain autofocus capability. They are compatible with most EF and EF-S lenses.

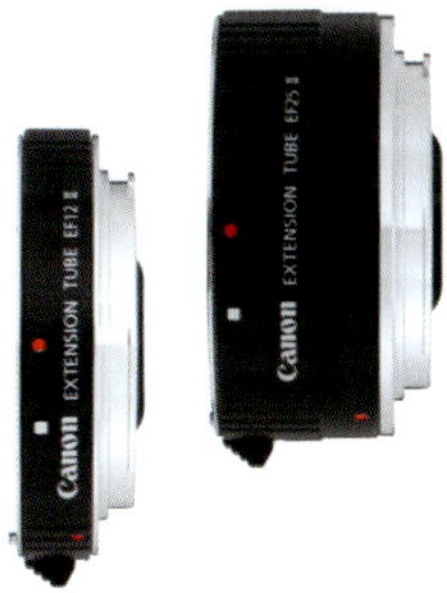

EXTENSION TUBES
Extension tubes EF 12 II and EF 25 II.

Bellows

Bellows work on the same principles as extension tubes, but are much more flexible. The basic concept is simplicity itself—a concertina-style lightproof tube mounted on a base which allows minute adjustment. This facilitates better control over the magnification ratio and focusing. Their greatest benefit is that bellows do not employ any glass elements at all and consequently can be used to deliver maximum image quality. The downside is that there is a significant loss of light, resulting in a darker viewfinder image.

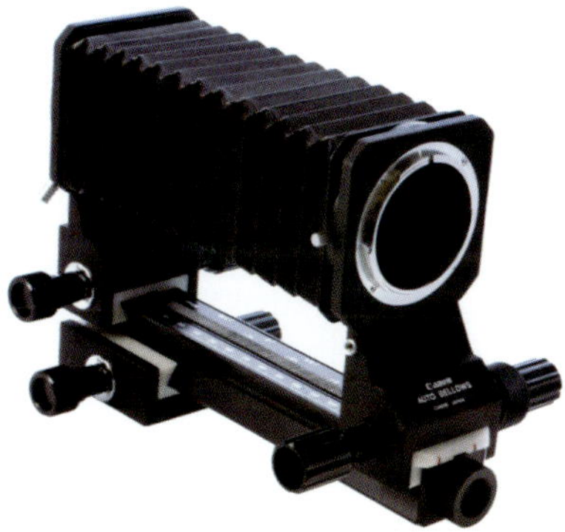

CANON FD BELLOWS
Although discontinued, this bellows can still be found regularly on eBay.

Canon no longer produce bellows but alternatives are available from independent manufacturers, notably Balpro/Novoflex, whose range includes the expensive but highly versatile tilt-and-shift bellows (see page 186). It is also still possible to find mint-condition examples of Canon's FD bellows (above) which can be mounted on an EOS

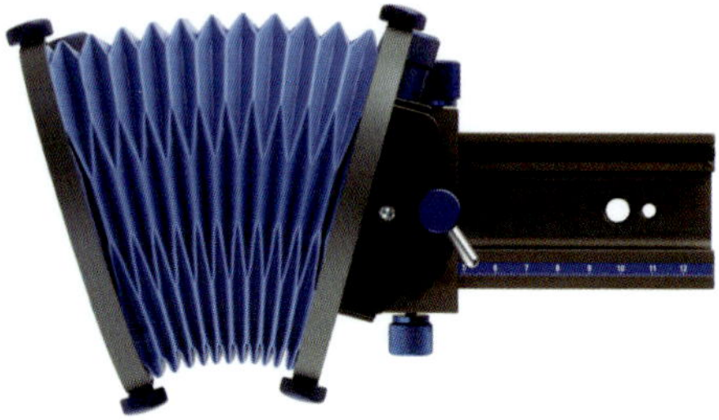

BALPRO TILT & SHIFT BELLOWS
The ultimate close-up accessory, this set of bellows features tilt and shift adjustments for maximum control of perspective and depth of field. Metering is still possible with the appropriate adapter.

body using an adapter. Canon used to make two such adapters. The first incorporated a lens element in order to permit focusing to infinity, and was manufactured so that professionals could mount their often extensive range of FD lenses onto EOS bodies when the range was first launched. The second adapter had no such lens element but could be used for macro work. The former adapter can still occasionally be found for sale, but the latter is now quite rare. However, the British company SRB-Griturn (see page 237) can provide their own version of either adapter. Autofocus is lost but metering is still possible. The sharp end of the bellows can be used with FD lenses, or with any brand of lens if reversed. Enlarger lenses, especially reversed, are popular with macro enthusiasts when using a bellows setup. SRB also manufacture adapters for mounting different lenses on the front of a set of bellows, and can also manufacture adapters to order.

Reverse adapters

Another simple solution for close-up work involves the use of a reverse adapter which allows you to mount your lens back-to-front on the camera to increase the possible magnification. The wider the normal focal length of the lens, the greater the magnification will be. (The same is also true when using reversed enlarging lenses with bellows or extension tubes.) With this method, there is no loss of light reaching the sensor. However, as the lens contacts are now at the front of the lens, all the information they normally transmit will no longer be usable unless you use an adapter that is specially designed to transmit that information. One such adapter is produced by Novoflex.

Macro lenses

There are three types of lens that tend to be sold as macro lenses. The first is a specialized lens designed for extremely high magnifications, such as Canon's MP-E65 f/2.8 Macro lens which has a maximum magnification of an astonishing 5× life-size. The second is a purpose-built conventional macro lens with a maximum reproduction ratio of 1:1, though half life-size is now commonly accepted in this category. These are excellent lenses for everyday use too, often giving crisp and contrasty results in everyday situations. Finally, there are those lenses that boast what they refer to as a "macro setting," which may offer a magnification ratio of up to perhaps 1:4, or one quarter life-size.

For close-up photography in general, a dedicated fixed focal-length macro lens is the ideal choice and provides excellent image quality at close focusing distances. Canon manufacture several such lenses.

There are two with shorter focal lengths—the full-frame but only half life-size EF 50mm f/2.5 and the 1:1 true macro EF-S 60mm f/2.8 USM. Both of these will fit the Rebel T1i/EOS 500D but the 50mm version lacks the faster and quieter Ultra Sonic Motor. The 50mm version can achieve 1:1 magnification with the addition of extension tubes or by using the dedicated four-element Life-size Converter. The EF 12 II and EF 25 II extension tubes are also compatible with the 60mm lens to achieve magnifications even greater than life-size. The 60mm lens is the first true macro lens in the EF-S range, designed specifically for digital photography with APS-C sensors, and will focus as close as 8in (20cm). Two longer close-up lenses are also available from Canon, allowing greater working distances: the EF 100mm f/2.8 Macro USM and the EF 180mm f/3.5L Macro USM. Both of these lenses provide a reproduction ratio of 1:1 and, like Canon's two other conventional macro lenses, have a minimum aperture of f/32. The 180mm version is designated an L-series lens and as such comes with the build quality associated with these legendary pieces of equipment, though it does weigh in at over two pounds (1kg).

To find out the maximum magnification ratio of any current Canon lens, visit Canon's website and check its specifications.

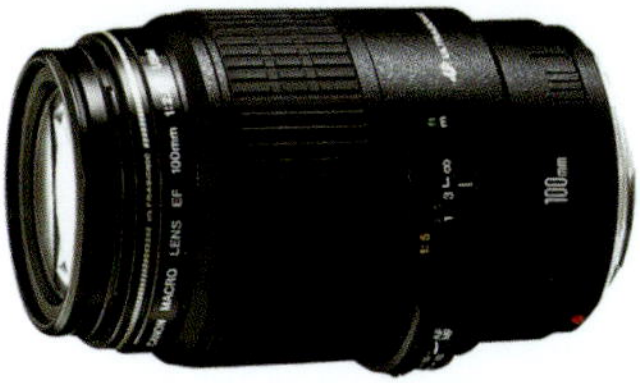

EF 100mm f/2.8 Macro lens

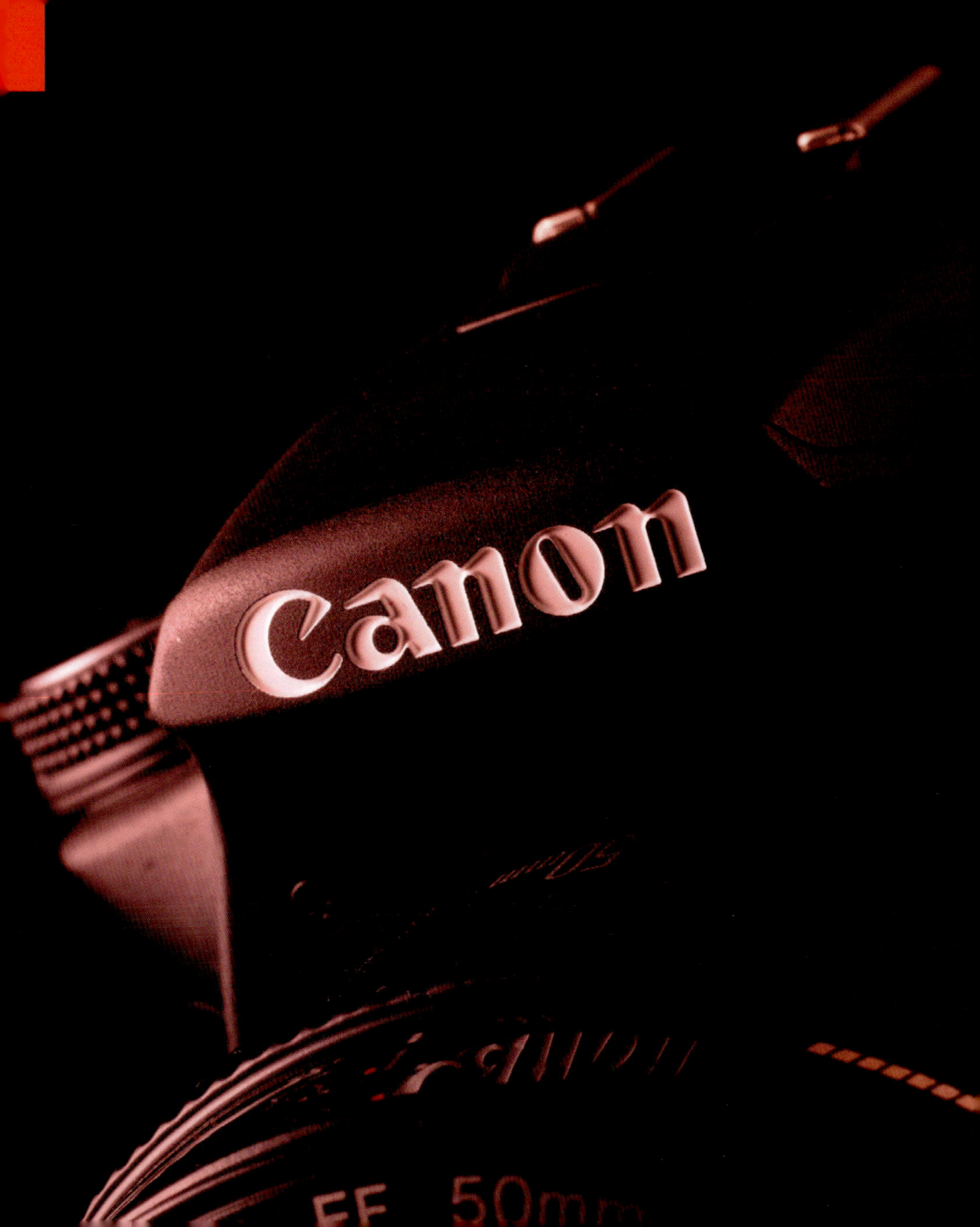
Canon
EF 50mm

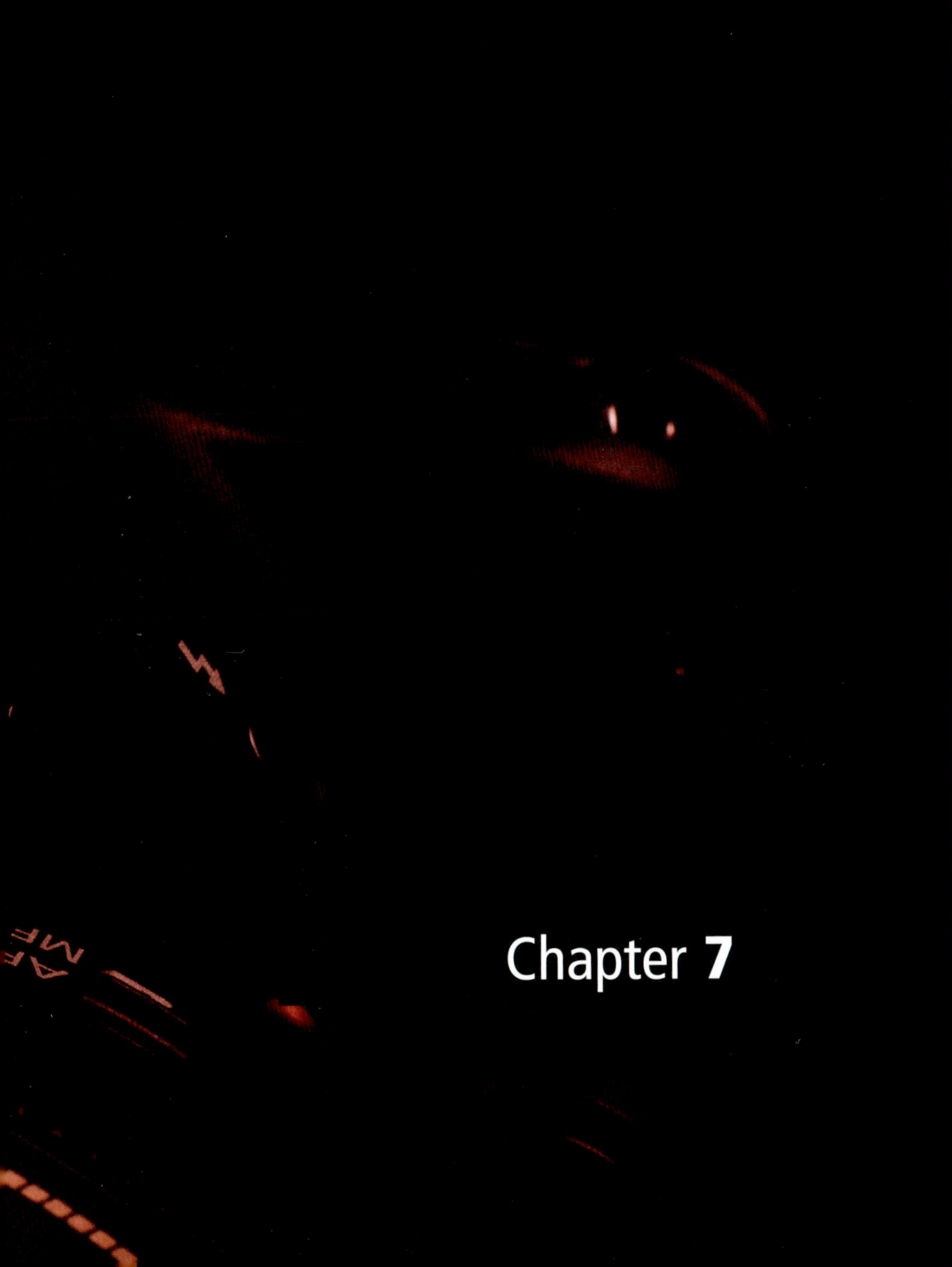

Chapter 7

Lenses

One of the main reasons photographers choose a manufacturer such as Canon is the extensive range of lenses and other accessories available. At the time of writing Canon offer no fewer than 70 lenses, including specialized items such as tilt-and-shift lenses.

The range encompasses Canon's standard EF lenses, which fit all EOS cameras; EF-S lenses, which have a smaller image circle and are optimized for APS-C digital bodies (from 20D and 300D onward); and their renowned L-series lenses, which are popular with professionals due to their rugged design, weather-proofing, and high optical quality. All three ranges feature ultrasonic (USM) motors on most lenses, and IS (Image Stabilization) is slowly being added model by model.

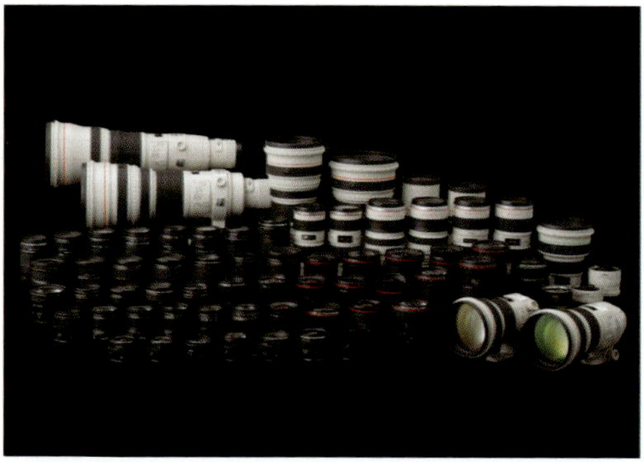

EF-S lenses

The EF-S lens series was developed to accompany the smaller body of the 300D and later 350D and 400D, and they are consequently very light in weight. The "S"designation identifies them as having shorter back focus, a smaller image circle, a specific mount not compatible with a standard EF mount, and a difference in build quality to reduce weight. The EF-S mount was included in addition to the EF mount on the EOS 20D, a feature retained for subsequent updates. The only prime lens in this series is the EF-S 60mm f/2.8 macro and at first only wide–standard zooms were on offer. These are now complemented by the superwide 10–22mm and more extensive 55–200mm models.

EF lenses

This is Canon's standard range. It stretches from a 15mm fisheye up to 400mm and includes the macro lenses, with the exception of the 180mm and 100mm L-series. It also includes two of the four manual-focus-only tilt-and-shift lenses and the 1.4× and 2× teleconverters. Zooms range from 16–35mm to 100–400mm. Some EF lenses, such as the EF 70-300mm f/4–5.6 IS USM, use L-series technology and represent terrific value for money.

L-series lenses

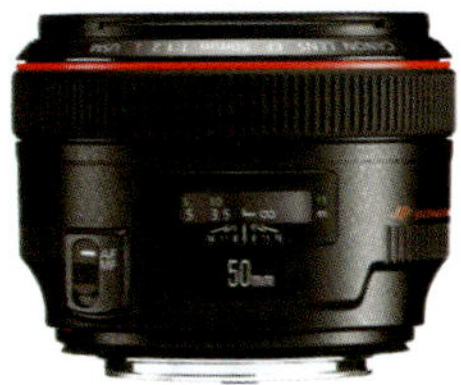

These are considered the cream of the line-up. The L-series prime lenses stretch from 14mm f/2.8 to 800mm. This range includes all the super-fast Canon lenses such as the 24mm f/1.4, 35mm f/1.4, 50mm f/1.2 (above), 85mm f/1.2, and 200mm f/2.

The build quality of the L-series is superb and later lenses have a rubber skirt on the mount to improve weather- and dustproofing. Longer focal lengths and extended zooms are off-white in color, allowing the world to see the extent to which Canon are dominant in the fields of news and sports photography, as can be witnessed at major events like the Olympics. The rest of the line-up has a black finish with a telltale red line.

Image stabilization (IS)

For decades photographers have relied on either very fast lenses or some form of camera support to cope with the slow shutter speeds necessitated by low lighting. Fast lenses have always meant greater weight and significantly higher cost: for example, the EF 50mm f/1.2 is thirteen times the price of the EF 50mm f/1.8. However, in 1995 Canon introduced an IS lens design for their EF 75–300mm which revolutionized low-light photography.

Canon's IS system uses tiny gyro sensors to detect lens vibration. They send signals to a microcomputer which controls a shifting lens group that can compensate for vertical and lateral movement. With the further developments since, it is now possible to shoot at speeds up to five stops slower than would previously have been possible, without loss of image quality. In order to facilitate panning when shooting action, some IS lenses have a second IS mode. While IS lenses are more costly than their non-IS counterparts, the price differential is nowhere near as great as when purchasing very fast lenses.

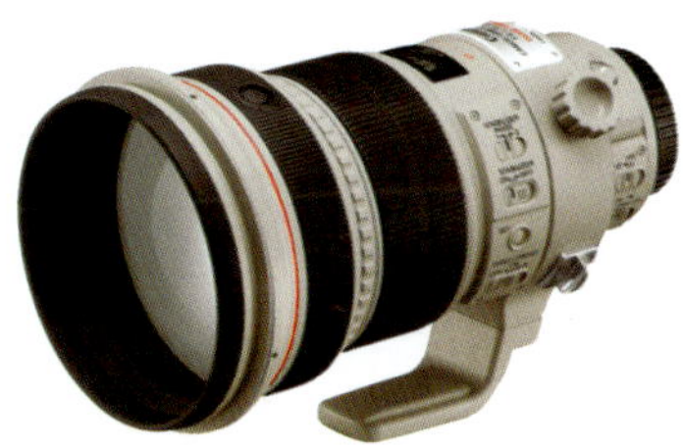

EF 200mm f/2 L IS
A sports photographer's dream, this lens has a very fast maximum aperture of f/2 plus a groundbreaking five-stop image stabilizer.

Focal length and angle of view

No matter how much is written, nor how often, about the focal length of lenses in this new age of "less than full-frame" DSLRs, confusion and debate continue to fill internet forums with threads about related topics on a daily basis. These pages should clarify a few of those points.

Focal length

When parallel rays of light strike a lens that is focused at infinity, they converge on a single point known as the focal point. The focal length of the lens is defined as the distance from the middle of that lens to the focal point. Photographic lenses are a little more complicated because the lens is comprised of multiple elements, but the principle holds good and the measurement is taken from the effective optical center of the lens group. The focal point is referred to in photography as the "focal plane" and this is the plane on which the film or sensor lies. Focal length is an absolute characteristic of any lens; it can be measured and replicated in laboratory conditions. The focal length of a lens always remains the same, irrespective of any other factor such as the type of camera it is mounted on.

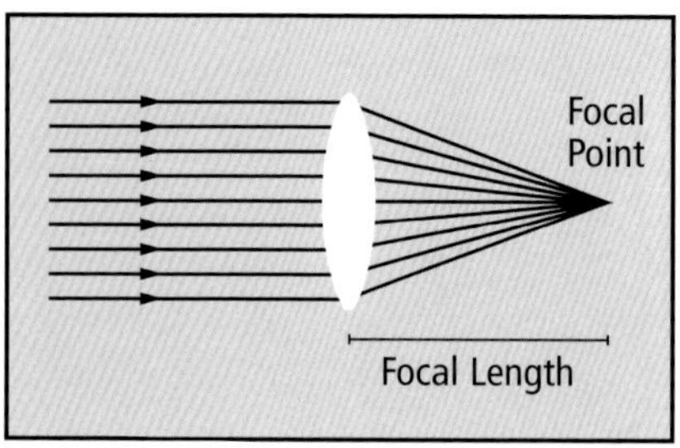

Crop factor

This term refers to the digital multiplier that must be used with less than full-frame sensor cameras when making comparisons with 35mm/full-frame sensor cameras. The "crop factor" on the Rebel T1i/ EOS 500D is 1.6×. It refers only to the field of view that the sensor covers (see pages 140–1). Technically speaking, the term should not be applied to the focal length of a lens used with the smaller sensor. Remember, a 300mm lens is always a 300mm lens, no matter what type of camera it is used on.

Field of view

In photographic terms, the field of view of a lens is the arc through which objects are recorded on the film or sensor. This arc of coverage is measured in degrees (°).

Although the image projected by the lens is circular, we are only really concerned with the usable rectangle within that circle (see page 141), and consequently the field of view of a camera lens can be found quoted as three figures: horizontal field of view, vertical field of view, and diagonal field of view. Where only one figure is quoted, it is generally assumed to be the diagonal field of view.

The field of view of a lens is not an absolute measurement and depends on two factors: the focal length of the lens and the area of the sensor or film which is to record the image.

As the focal length of a lens is fixed, the angle of view should be quoted alongside the image area it is intended for, but unfortunately this practice is not followed by lens manufacturers. Lenses continue to be marketed using the focal-length designation which would be applied to a full-frame (36mm × 24mm) sensor or 35mm film. One reason for this is that lenses designed to fill full-frame sensors/35mm can be used on a smaller format too, so at least three sets of figures would need to be given for Canon lenses alone.

Another reason is that different camera manufacturers make their sensors in different sizes, so the angle of view for, say, a 24mm Nikon lens is not exactly the same as that for a 24mm Canon lens when used on their respective "less than full-frame" sensor cameras.

Focal length comparison

When the focal length is doubled, the area covered is one quarter of the previous area. This image below was captured using a lens with a focal length of 20mm. If 40mm (i.e. double the focal length) had been used, the image area would have been that shown by the larger dotted rectangle. Similarly, had an 80mm focal length lens been used, the image area covered would have been that shown by the smaller dotted rectangle. The solid rectangle in the center appears to be a logical progression (i.e. 160mm) but it isn't. It actually represents 320mm in focal length. This is due to the fact as the focal lengths get longer, the numerical difference in the angle of view is reduced as you double the focal length.

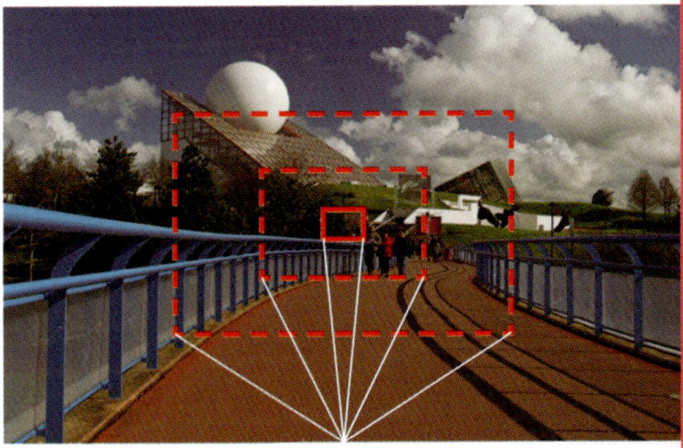

Standard lenses

The term "standard lens" dates back to the early days of 35mm photography, long before today's extensive range of prime lenses and, particularly, zoom lenses were even conceived of. The working photographer would carry three bodies equipped with a moderate wide-angle lens of 28mm or 35mm, a 50mm standard lens and a short telephoto of up to 135mm. The standard 50mm lens was sold with the camera and approximated the field of view of the human eye.

With APS-C sensor bodies like the Rebel T1i/EOS 500D, because of the crop factor explained on page 192, it is necessary to divide the 50mm focal length by 1.6 in order to arrive at a focal length that may be considered "standard." This means we're looking at a focal length of approximately 30mm. Today, the zoom lenses that are packaged with new cameras instead of the old 50mm prime lens tend to straddle this 30mm figure. Canon's 18–55mm EF-S lens is a classic example.

Historically, the standard lens was always the least expensive in any line-up, unless it was a particularly fast version, because it could be manufactured more cheaply and in greater quantities. But standard zooms have come down in price, size, and weight, and have increased in quality. Add to this the shift toward APS-C bodies by huge numbers of Canon users and it may seem that the 50mm standard lens is turning into a museum piece. Or is it?

Canon still produce 50mm f/1.4 and f/1.2 versions to act as standard lenses for 35mm film and full-frame sensor cameras. For users of APS-C Canon bodies such as the Rebel T1i/EOS 500D, these serve as really fast portrait lenses, with a field of view similar to an 80mm lens on 35mm, for a very competitive price in the case of the 50mm f/1.4.

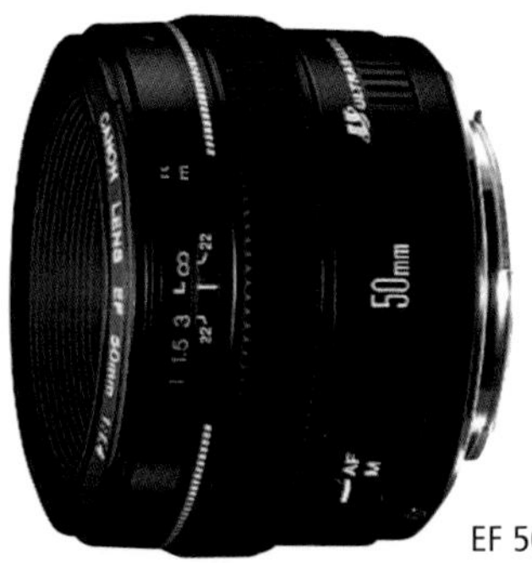

EF 50mm f/1.4 USM lens

Wide-angle lenses

The net effect of using APS-C sensor bodies has been a real boon for telephoto users because the field of view can be reduced by a factor of 1.6, but at the opposite end of the focal-length scale, wide-angle users have suffered. Even a 17–40mm lens provides the field of view of only a 27–64mm equivalent, and 27mm is definitely not considered wide-angle by today's standards.

However, in 2004, Canon introduced the EF-S 10–22mm lens which, for the first time, meant that there was an affordable Canon option that offered real wide-angle characteristics. Prior to this the only choice for those determined to stick with Canon lenses was the very expensive 14mm f/2.8L introduced way back in 1991—a rectilinear lens that gave largely distortion-free images as opposed to a fisheye lens of the same focal length.

Three independent manufacturers (Sigma, Tamron, and Tokina) produce numerous lenses between them which compete with the EF-S 10–22mm. Some of these are full-frame lenses and some have been designed to work with smaller sensors. Their quality varies but several of these lenses are serious competitors to Canon's own models.

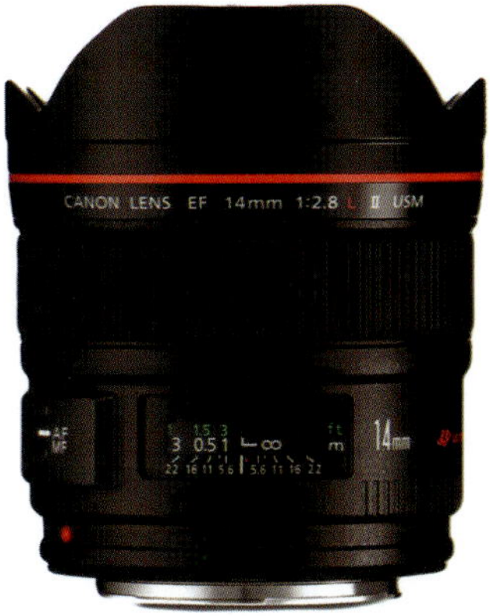

EF 14mm f/2.8 L II lens

The fast moderate wide-angle, a 35mm f/1.4 on 35mm for example, was always a photojournalist's mainstay, but the chances of an APS-C equivalent of 21mm f/1.4 being brought out are probably nil, so anyone wanting that sort of lens performance will be looking at a full-frame body.

Today's wide zooms are really quite slow: for the best performance it is usually necessary to stop down a couple of stops from the maximum aperture. This means working with an aperture of at least f/5.6 and more probably f/8—which places limits on working in low light because the shutter speeds will be very slow, making Image Stabilization an even more desirable feature.

Telephoto lenses

Telephoto users, whether using prime lenses or zooms, gain hands down from using APS-C sensor bodies like the Rebel T1i/EOS 500D because the field of view is reduced by ×1.6. My own favorite long lens combination is a 300mm f/2.8 with a ×1.4 converter, giving the equivalent field of view on the Rebel T1i/EOS 500D as a 672mm f/4.0. With a ×2 converter instead of the ×1.4 this equates to a staggering 960mm f/5.6, still with AF capability. Such possibilities are incredibly cost-effective.

Telephoto lenses give the appearance of compressing the different planes in an image, making distant subjects look closer than they are. The longer the focal length, the more this is true. However, telephotos also require faster shutter speeds, which is why you will see sports photographers carrying huge lenses along the touchline. It is not the focal length alone that results in such huge lenses so much as the combination of focal length and fast maximum apertures. But doesn't Image Stabilization remove the need for fast maximum apertures? No. Image Stabilization is designed to compensate for camera shake but has no impact on the need for a high shutter speed, and therefore fast maximum aperture, when trying to freeze a moving subject.

One of the bonuses of using longer lenses is the attractive out-of-focus background (known as"bokeh") which can result. This effect is determined to some degree by the number of blades in the diaphragm and by the extent to which they create a perfect circle when open.

EF 70–300mm IS lens

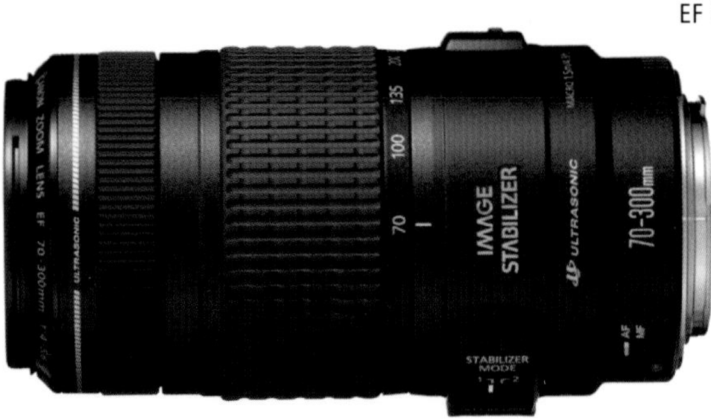

Perspective

There are several reasons why we might choose a lens of a particular focal length: angle of view, depth of field, and perspective chief among them. Perspective is the term used to describe the relationships between the different elements that comprise an image, in particular the apparent compression or expansion of planes within the image.

Let's start with the most obvious examples. With a very wide-angle lens, taking a head and shoulders portrait will involve a very short camera-to-subject distance, and the nearest facial features will appear quite distorted and overly large. Conversely, try photographing a line of parking meters with a long telephoto lens and the meters will give the impression that they are spaced only a couple of feet apart.

Between these two extremes are a host of options, especially if you use zoom lenses. There are no hard-and-fast rules except to say that if you want natural-looking portraits, it is best to opt for a slightly longer than standard focal length, traditionally 50mm on the Rebel T1i/EOS 500D.

Canon's own prime lenses in this bracket are excellent value (not counting the fabulous but expensive 85mm f/1.2), with wide maximum apertures and superb image quality.

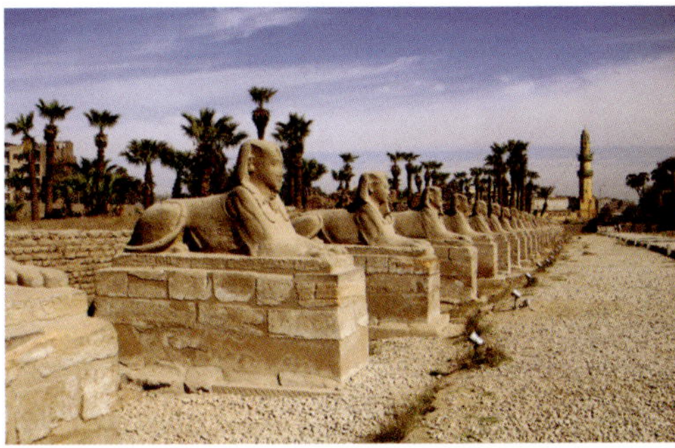

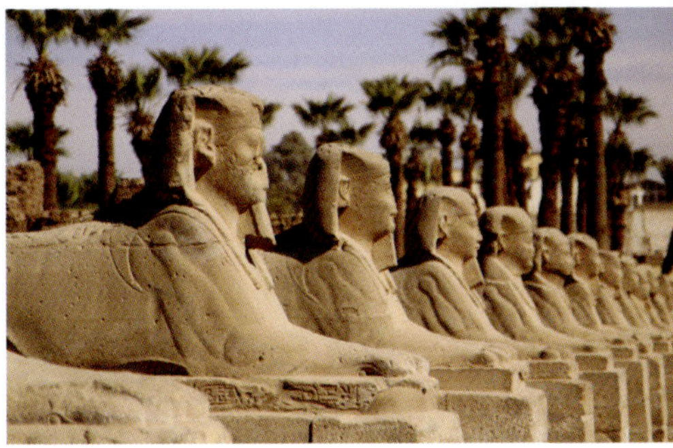

CHANGE OF PERSPECTIVE
The perspective with any given focal length will change according to the camera-to-subject distance and the viewpoint. The two images here were taken from the same spot at 24mm (top) and 105mm (below).

Teleconverters

Canon use the term "extenders" to describe their two teleconverters. The first is the 1.4× extender which is fitted between the camera body and the lens to increase the focal length by a factor of 1.4 and which causes the loss of one stop of light. The 2× extender doubles the focal length with a loss of two stops.Both Canon and Sigma manufacture 1.4× and 2× versions.

While teleconverters are an inexpensive way of increasing the pulling power of your telephoto lenses, they are not going to provide the same quality as a lens of the same focal length, especially a prime lens. Autofocus will also be slower and you may find that the AF will "hunt" unless it can lock onto a suitably contrasty part of the image.

Tip

It is important to pay attention to the maximum aperture of your lens if you are considering purchasing an extender. If the recalculated maximum aperture with an extender fitted is smaller than f/5.6, you will lose autofocus capability.

Warning!

Only selected lenses can be used with extenders without causing damage to the rear element of the lens. To check which of the current range of lenses can be used, visit the Canon website and check the specification of the lens concerned.

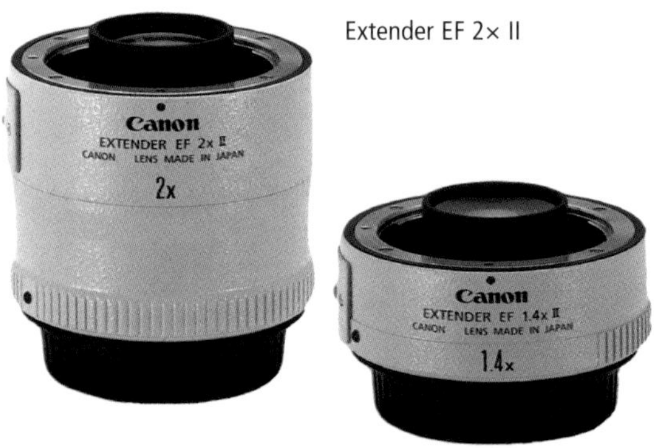

Extender EF 2× II

Extender EF 1.4× II

Tilt and shift lenses

One of the main drawbacks of using normal lenses for any architectural subject is that tilting the camera and lens to accommodate the height of the building results in the convergence of vertical lines, usually the sides of the building. You can get around this by finding a viewpoint that is at roughly half the height of the building. However, a more satisfactory solution comes in the shape of a tilt-and-shift lens.

Canon manufacture four such lenses—the TS-E 17mm f/4 L, TS-E 24mm f/3.5 II L, TS-E 45mm f/2.8, and TS-E 90mm f/2.8. The latter was the world's first 35mm-format 90mm lens with tilt-and-shift movements. All of these lenses are manual focus only and adopt the same principles as a view camera but are much more portable. They work by allowing the lens to perform three different movements (tilt, shift, and rotate) in relation to the plane of focus, with the added benefit of improving (or reducing) depth of field without changing the aperture. Tilt and shift locks on the L-series lenses prevent unwanted slipping.

TS-E 17mm f/4 L lens

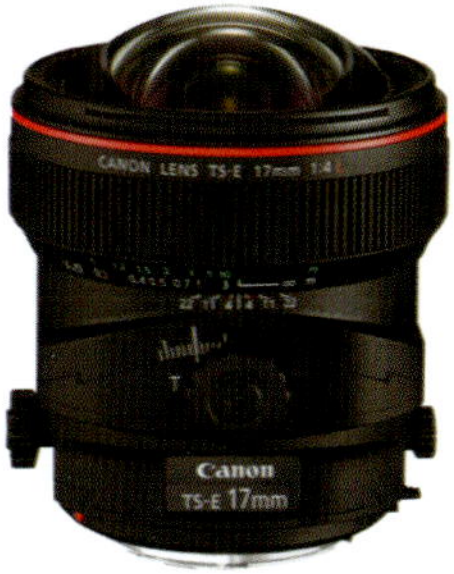

Both the 17mm and 24mm Mark II versions allow independent rotation of the tilt and shift axes. The earlier versions of the 24mm, the 45mm, and the 90mm could be set up as either parallel or at right angles by a Canon service center but could not be changed in the field. The two new versions also boast a greatly increased image circle.

Lens	Field of view	Tilt	Shift	Rotation	Image circle
TS-E 17mm f/4 L	104° (diag.)	+/- 6.5°	+/- 12mm	+/- 90°	67.2mm
TS-E 24mm f/3.5 II L	84° (diag.)	+/- 8.5°	+/- 12mm	+/- 90°	67.2mm
TS-E 45mm f/2.8	51° (diag.)	+/- 8°	+/- 12mm		58.6mm
TS-E 90mm f/2.8	27° (diag.)	+/- 8°	+/- 12mm		58.6mm

EF lens chart

Lens (USM* = Ring USM)	Construction (elements/ groups)	Diaph. blades	Min. f/no.	Closest focus (m)
Fixed focal length lenses				
EF 14mm f/2.8L II USM*	14/11	6	22	0.20
EF 15mm f/2.8 Fisheye	8/7	5	22	0.20
TS-E 17mm f/4L	18/12	8	22	0.25
EF 20mm f/2.8 USM	11/9	5	22	0.25
EF 24mm f/1.4L II USM*	13/10	8	22	0.25
EF 24mm f/2.8	10/10	6	22	0.25
TS-E 24mm f/3.5L	11/9	8	22	0.30
TS-E 24mm f/3.5L II	16/11	8	22	0.21
EF 28mm f/1.8 USM	10/9	7	22	0.25
EF 28mm f/2.8	5/5	5	22	0.30
EF 35mm f/1.4L USM	11/9	8	22	0.30
EF 35mm f/2	7/5	5	22	0.25
TS-E 45mm f/2.8	10/9	8	22	0.40
EF 50mm f/1.2L USM*	8/6	8	16	0.45
EF 50mm f/1.4 USM	7/6	8	22	0.45
EF 50mm f/1.8 II	6/5	5	22	0.45
EF 50mm f/2.5 Macro	9/8	6	32	0.23
EF-S 60mm f/2.8 Macro USM	12/8	7	32	0.20
MP-E 65mm f/2.8 1–5× Macro	10/8	6	16	0.24
EF 85mm f/1.2L II USM*	8/7	8	16	0.95
EF 85mm f/1.8 USM	9/7	8	22	0.85
TS-E 90mm f/2.8	6/5	8	32	0.50
EF 100mm f/2 USM	8/6	8	22	0.90
EF 100mm f/2.8L Macro IS USM*	15/12	9	32	0.30

Max. mag. (× life size)	Filter (mm) *drop in	Width × Length (mm)	Wgt (g)	Lens hood	Introduced
0.15	n/a	80 × 94	645	Built-in	2007
0.14	n/a	73 × 62	330	Built-in	1987
0.14	77	89 × 107	820	n/a	2009
0.14	72	78 × 71	405	EW-75II	1992
0.17	77	94 × 87	650	EW-83K	1997
0.16	58	68 × 87	270	EW-60II	1988
0.14	72	78 × 87	570	EW-75BII	1991
0.34	82	89 × 107	780	EW-88B	2009
0.18	58	74 × 56	310	EW-63II	1995
0.13	52	67 × 42	185	EW-65II	1987
0.18	72	79 × 86	580	EW-78C	1998
0.23	52	67 × 42	210	EW-65II	1990
0.16	72	81 × 90	645	EW-79BII	1991
0.15	72	86 × 66	580	ES-78	2006
0.15	58	74 × 51	290	ES-71 II	1993
0.15	52	68 × 41	130	ES-62	1990
0.50	52	68 × 63	280	n/a	1987
1.00	52	73 × 70	335	ET-67B	2005
5.00	58	81 × 98	710	n/a	1999
0.11	72	92 × 84	1025	ES-79 II	2006
0.13	58	75 × 72	425	ET-65 III	1992
0.29	58	74 × 88	565	ES-65 III	1991
0.14	58	75 × 74	460	ET-65 III	1991
1.00	67	78 × 123	625	ET-73	2009

Lens (USM* = Ring USM)	**Construction (elements/ groups)**	**Diaph. blades**	**Min. f/no.**	**Closest focus (m)**
EF 100mm f/2.8 Macro USM	12/8	8	32	0.31
EF 135mm f/2L USM	10/8	8	32	0.90
EF 135mm f/2.8 Soft Focus	7/6	6	32	1.30
EF 180mm f/3.5L Macro USM	14/12	8	32	0.48
EF 200mm f/2L IS USM*	17/12	8	32	1.90
EF 200mm f/2.8L II USM	9/7	8	32	1.50
EF 300mm f/2.8L IS USM	17/13	8	32	2.50
EF 300mm f/4L IS USM	15/11	8	32	1.50
EF 400mm f/2.8L IS USM	17/13	8	32	3.00
EF 400mm f/4 DO IS USM	17/13	8	32	3.50
EF 400mm f/5.6L USM	7/6	8	32	3.50
EF 500mm f/4L IS USM	17/13	8	32	4.50
EF 600mm f/4L IS USM	17/13	8	32	5.50
EF 800mm f/5.6L IS USM*	18/14	8	32	6.00
Zoom lenses				
EF-S 15–85mm f/3.5–5.6 IS USM*	17/12	7	22–38	0.35
EF-S 10-22mm f/3.5-4.5 USM	13/10	6	22–27	0.24
EF 16–35mm f/2.8L II USM*	16/12	7	22	0.28
EF 17–40mm f/4L USM	12/9	7	22	0.28
EF-S 17–55mm f/2.8 IS USM*	19/12	7	22	0.35
EF-S 17–85mm f/4-5.6 IS USM	17/12	6	22–32	0.35
EF-S 18–135mm f/3.5–5.6 IS	16/12	6	22–38	0.45
EF-S 18–55mm f/3.5-5.6 IS	11/9	6	22–38	0.25
EF-S 18–200mm f/3.5-5.6 IS	16/12	6	22–38	0.45
EF 20–35mm f/3.5–4.5 USM	12/11	5	22–27	0.34

Max. mag. (× life size)	Filter (mm) *drop in	Width × Length (mm)	Wgt (g)	Lens hood	Introduced
1.00	58	79 × 119	600	ET-67	2000
0.19	72	83 × 112	750	ET-78 II	1996
0.12	52	69 × 98	390	ET-65 III	1987
1.00	72	83 × 187	1090	ET-78 II	1996
0.12	52*	128 × 208	2520	ET-120B	2008
0.16	72	83 × 136	765	ET-83BII	1996
0.13	52*	128 × 252	2550	ET-120	1999
0.24	77	90 × 221	1190	Built-in	1997
0.15	52*	163 × 349	5370	ET-155	1999
0.12	52*	128 × 233	1940	ET-120	2001
0.12	77	90 × 257	1250	Built-in	1993
0.12	52*	146 × 387	3870	ET-138	1999
0.12	52*	168 × 457	5360	ET-160	1999
0.14	52*	163 × 461	4500	ET-155	2008
0.21	72	82 × 88	575	EW-78E	2009
0.17	77	84 × 90	385	EW-83E	2004
0.22	82	89 × 112	635	EW-88	2007
0.24	77	84 × 97	500	EW-83E	2003
0.17	77	84 × 111	645	EW-83J	2006
0.20	67	79 × 92	475	EW-73B	2004
0.21	67	75 × 101	455	EW-73B	2009
0.34	58	69 × 70	200	EW-60C	2007
0.24	72	79 × 102	595	EW-78D	2008
0.13	77	84 × 69	340	EW-83 II	1993

Lens (USM* = Ring USM)	Construction (elements/ groups)	Diaph. blades	Min. f/no.	Closest focus (m)
EF 24–105mm f/4L IS USM*	18/13	8	22	0.45
EF 24–70mm f/2.8L USM	16/30	8	22	0.38
EF 24–85mm f/3.5–4.5 USM	15/12	6	22–32	0.50
EF 28–90mm f/4–5.6 III	10/8	5	22–32	0.38
EF 28–105mm f/3.5–4.5 II USM	15/12	7	22–27	0.50
EF 28–135mm f/3.5–5.6 IS USM	16/12	6	22–36	0.50
EF 28–200mm f/3.5–5.6 USM	16/12	6	22–36	0.45
EF 28–300mm f/3.5–5.6L IS USM*	23/16	8	22–40	0.70
EF 55–200mm f/4.5–5.6 II USM	13/13	6	22–27	1.20
EF-S 55-250mm f/4-5.6 IS	12/10	7	22–32	1.10
EF 70–200mm f/2.8L USM	18/15	8	32	1.50
EF 70–200mm f/2.8L IS USM*	23/18	8	32	1.40
EF 70–200mm f/4L USM	16/13	8	32	1.20
EF 70–200mm f/4L IS USM*	20/15	8	32	1.20
EF 70–300mm f/4.5–5.6 DO IS USM*	18/12	6	32–40	1.40
EF 70–300mm f/4–5.6 IS USM	15/10	8	32–45	1.50
EF 75–300mm f/4–5.6 III USM	13/9	7	32–45	1.50
EF 100–300mm f/4.5–5.6 USM	13/10	8	32–38	1.50
EF 100–400mm f/4.5–5.6L IS USM	17/14	5	32–38	1.80

Max. mag. (× life size)	Filter (mm) *drop in	Width × Length (mm)	Wgt (g)	Lens hood	Introduced
0.23	77	84 × 107	670	EW-83H	2005
0.29	77	83 × 124	950	EW-83F	2002
0.16	67	73 × 70	380	EW-73 II	1996
0.30	58	67 × 71	180	EW-60C	2004
0.19	58	72 × 75	375	EW-63 II	2000
0.19	72	78 × 97	540	EW-78B II	1998
0.28	72	78 × 90	500	EW-78D	2000
0.30	77	92 × 184	1670	ET-83G	2004
0.21	52	70 × 97	310	ET-54	2003
0.31	58	70 × 108	390	ET-60	2007
0.16	77	85 × 194	1310	ET-83 II	1995
0.17	77	86 × 197	1470	ET-86	2001
0.21	67	76 × 172	705	ET-74	1999
0.21	67	76 × 172	760	ET-74	2006
0.19	58	82 × 100	720	ET-65B	2004
0.26	58	77 × 143	630	ET-65B	2005
0.25	58	71 × 122	480	ET-60	1999
0.20	58	73 × 122	540	ET-65 III	1990
0.20	77	92 × 189	1380	ET-83C	1998

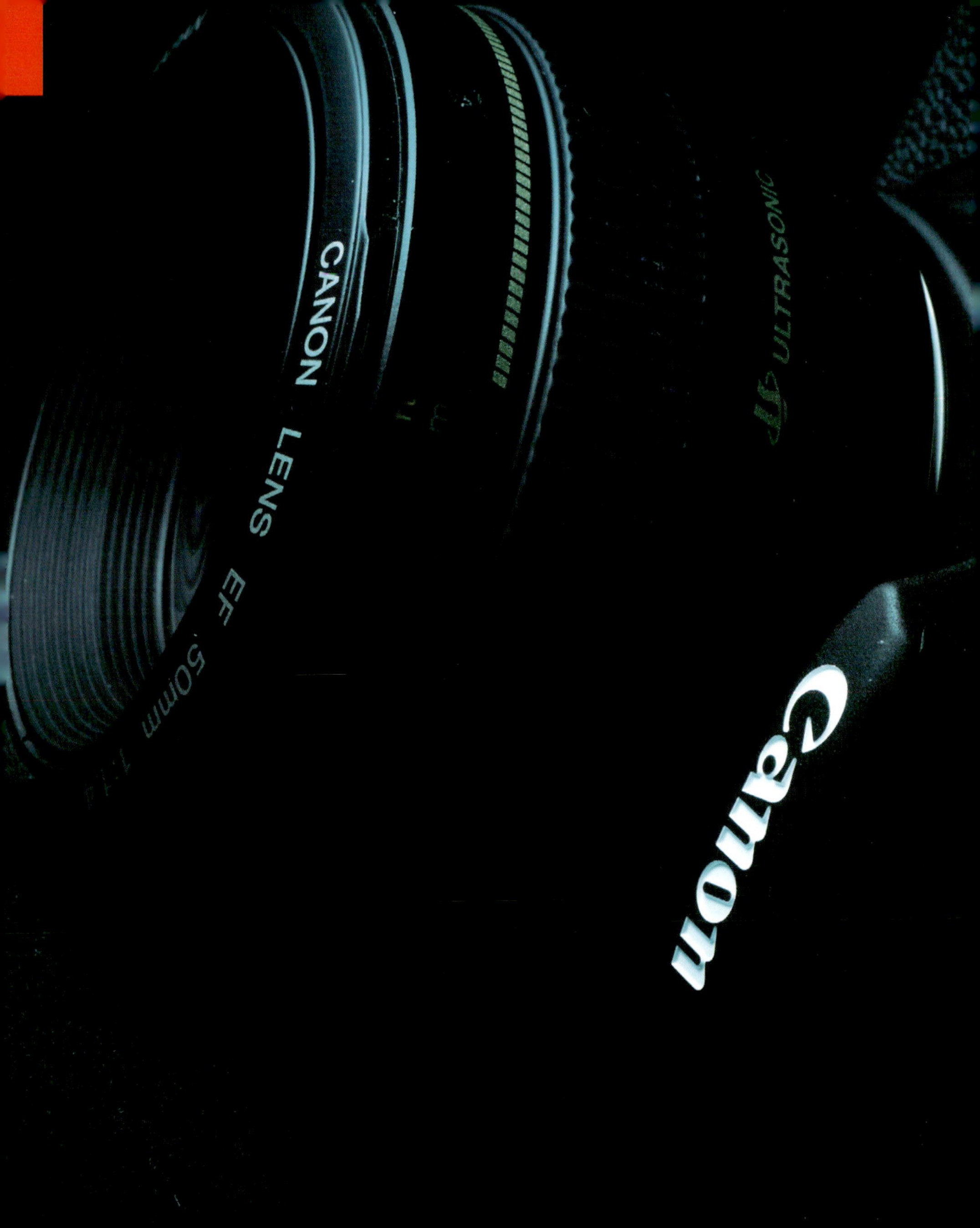
CANON LENS EF 50mm
ULTRASONIC
Canon

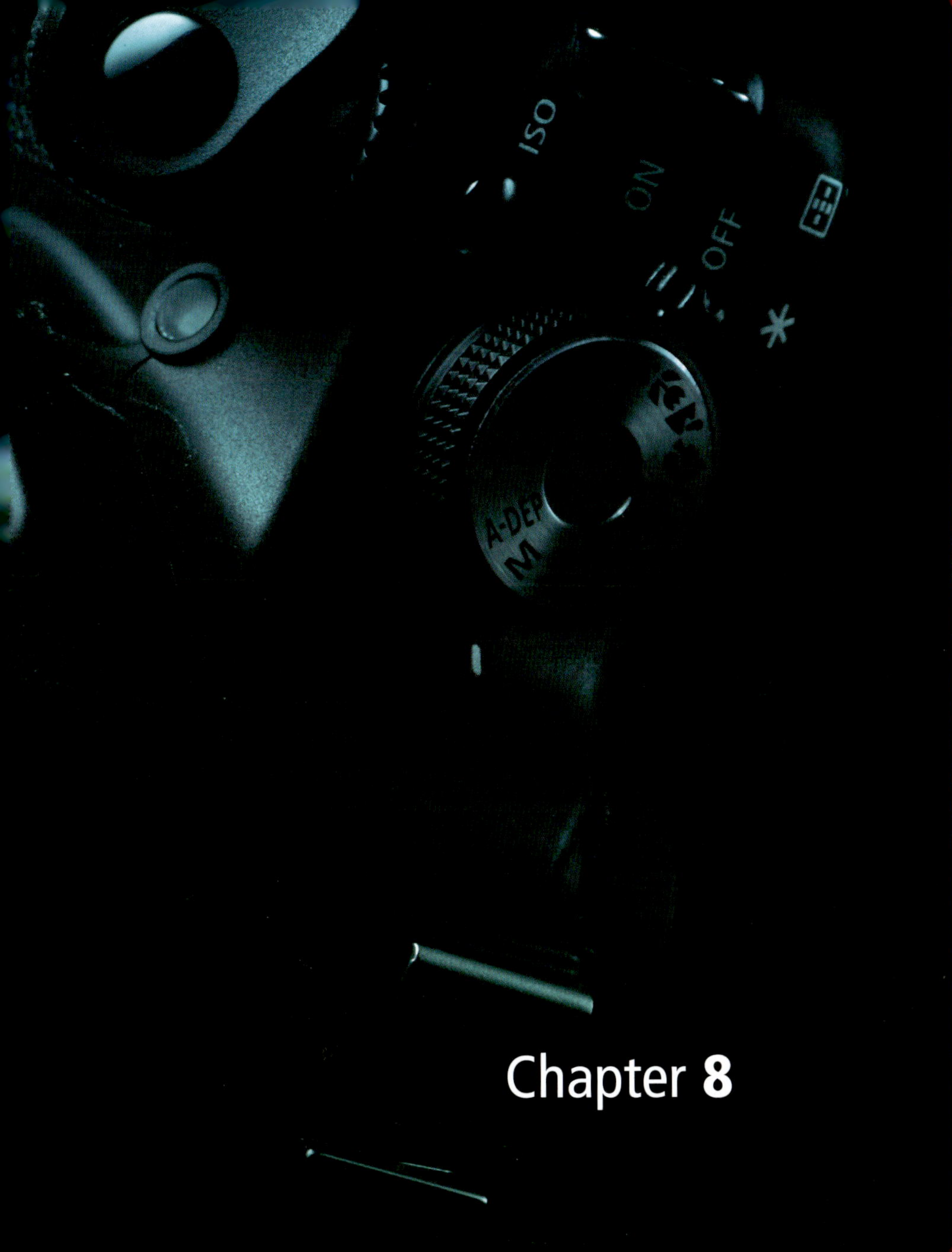

Chapter 8

Accessories

All photographers have a mental shortlist of accessories they can't live without. Here we examine some of the most popular items, covering a range of techniques and photographic styles, but concentrating largely on filters, as these are very popular with almost all photographers.

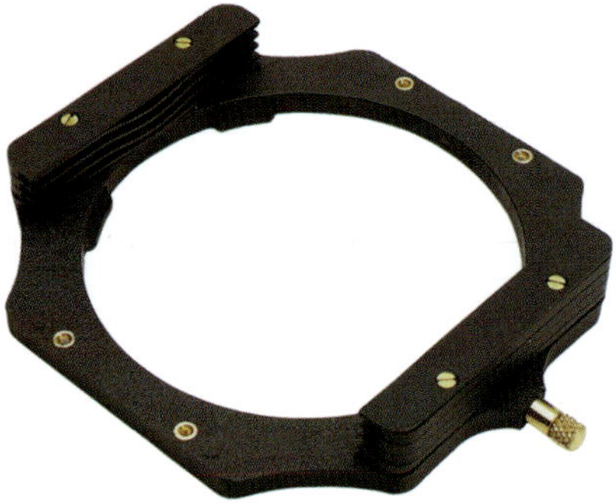

LEE FILTER HOLDER
Lee's filter holders and filters are considered by many to be the ultimate filter system.

Filters

There are essentially four types of filter: color-correction filters used on the lens, color-correction filters used on the light source, filters that help to enhance an existing characteristic but preserve a fairly natural feel to the photograph, and special-effects filters. In some circumstances a mixture of these types may be used.

The materials that are used in the construction of filters range from gelatine (usually reserved for lighting), through resins, to glass. The quality may vary widely and, generally speaking, you get what you pay for. A major factor to consider when purchasing glass filters is the number of additional coatings to reduce flare. Glass filters come with no coating at all, single-coated, and multi-coated, the latter being considerably more expensive.

The alternative to glass is one of the rectangular filter systems that make use of resin filters and a special holder into which the filters are inserted. The filter holder, which will accept two or three filters, fits onto an adapter ring which screws into the lens's filter thread, and it is a simple matter to carry several adapter rings for different lenses as well as numerous filters.

Tip
The larger rectangular filter systems are very versatile, and the same filters will fit multiple lenses using inexpensive adapter rings.

Special-effects filters

An astonishingly wide range of effects filters is available, far too many to even begin to describe here. It is suggested that you explore the websites of filter manufacturers such as Lee, Cokin, Formatt, and Hoya to get some idea of what is available. Their website addresses can be found on page 236.

Drop-in glass and gelatin filters

Some lenses require drop-in filters. These are literally dropped into a slot in the lens which is located near the back and therefore only requires a relatively small filter. Canon produces them in two sizes, namely 48mm and 52mm. They also make drop-in holders for gelatine filters in the same sizes. Unfortunately, the glass versions are restricted to polarizing filters. Many fisheye lenses, which tend to have a bulbous protruding front element and built-in petal-shaped lens hood, will take gelatin filters mounted on the back of the lens.

Tips

To retain the best possible image quality, filters should be treated like lenses and kept clean, free from dust, and protected from scratches.

Filters can be expensive, so take time to research the different systems and their compatibility with your existing equipment. The outlay on a professional system such as Lee can be considerable, but once you have made that decision you will never regret it.

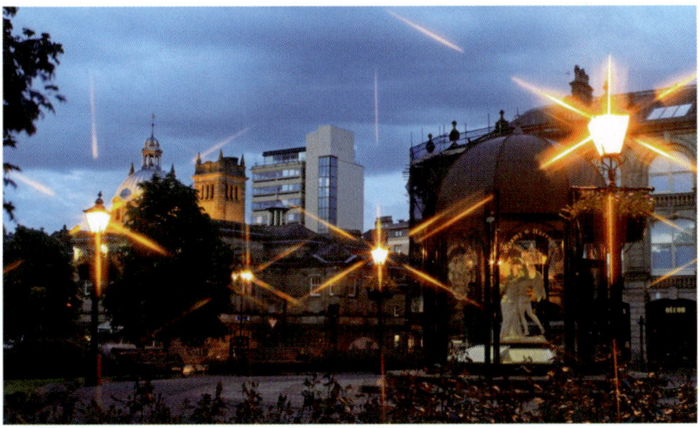

SIX-POINT STAR
A B+W six-point star filter was used at dusk for this photograph of Harrogate, Yorkshire, UK.

Polarizing filters

Polarizing filters are best known for boosting the depth of blue skies and making white clouds stand out, and are most effective when used at 90° to the sun. Of the hundreds of filters available, the polarizing filter is the one that landscape photographers would least like to do without—and, coincidentally, it is also the most expensive. The filter is mounted in a holder that allows it to be rotated using a knurled ring on the front of the filter mount. The filter effect is transitional, shifting through maximum effect at 90° and 270° to the direction of the sun and minimum effect at 180° and 0/360°, bearing in mind that the sun's height in the sky also plays its part.

A polarizing filter always reduces the light reaching the camera sensor and therefore requires a degree of exposure adjustment, though this will be achieved automatically in any auto exposure mode. The degree of exposure adjustment required is not constant and varies according to the extent to which the filter blocks the polarized light waves.

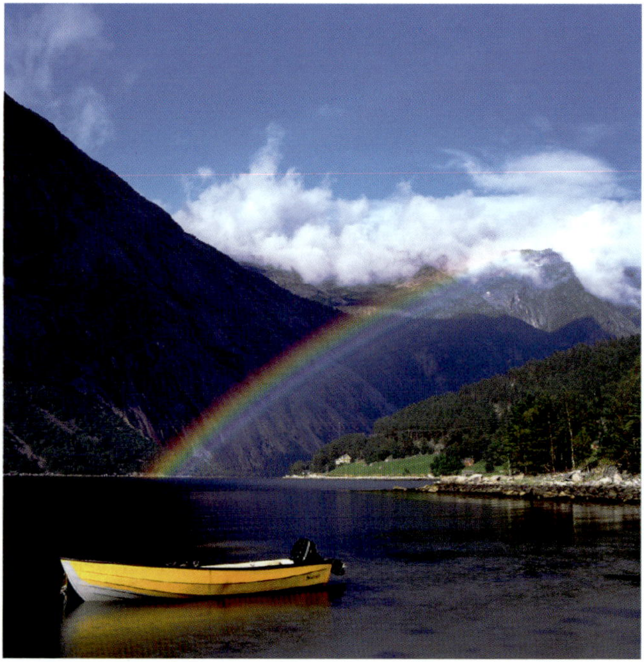

NORWEGIAN FJORD
Polarizing filters are well-known for boosting blue skies and clouds, but they can also significantly intensify the colors of rainbows.

In some cases the combination of side-lighting (ie the sun at 90°) and maximum filter effect can produce images which have far too much contrast with a lot of deep shadow. In these circumstances it should be remembered that the polarizing filter's effect is not "all or nothing" and it does not necessarily have to be rotated to achieve maximum effect when partial effect will do.

The other main function of a polarizing filter is to control reflections in an image. While its most obvious use is to reduce unwanted reflections from shiny surfaces and water, it is also highly effective at reducing the light reflected by foliage, producing richer green tones.

There are two types of polarizing filter: circular and linear. These terms refer to light-wave behavior and the word "circular" has nothing to do with the shape of the filter. Both types are equally effective but linear polarizers don't work well with autofocus cameras that employ beam-splitter technology, so you should use a circular polarizing filter with the Rebel T1i/EOS 500D.

Tips

A polarizing filter can be used instead of a plain neutral density filter to reduce exposure by approximately two stops.

Used in conjunction with Landscape Picture Style on clear blue skies, a polarizing filter may produce an oversaturated result.

Vignetting

This is the term given to the loss of image detail at the outer edges of the frame, starting at the corners, and may have several causes—one of which is the use of filters on wide-angle lenses. Manufacturers expect filters to be used on their lenses or they wouldn't incorporate filter threads on them. The problems usually start when you "stack" filters, using two or more screw-in filters together, especially if you then screw a lens hood onto the front of them. Vignetting can also occur when using rectangular filter holders, especially if you add a second one to allow for rotation.

This problem is highly unlikely to manifest itself if you are using full-frame lenses on the Rebel T1i/500D because the sensor is not making full use of the image circle projected by the lens (see pages 140–1).

UV and skylight filters

These are designed to absorb ultraviolet light, thus reducing the blue color cast which can be a nuisance in landscape shots at high altitude and on hazy days. The UV filter renders a natural result and the skylight version provides a warmer, slightly pinkish tone. In reality, far more photographers use these to protect the front element of the lens from wear and tear than to filter out ultraviolet light. Others wouldn't dream of unnecessarily using a filter on their expensive high-quality lens as the optical quality of the filter cannot match that of the finest lenses. Nevertheless, a UV filter is a worthwhile accessory as its benefit cannot be effectively replicated in computer software.

Color correction filters

Most color-correction filters have become largely redundant, because even entry-level cameras now have a facility to adjust color temperature. In addition, Canon's own software provides the option to adjust the color temperature of RAW images in post-processing. There is one particular filter, however, which is worth mentioning here: a combined polarizing and warm-up filter.

Traditionally, warm-up filters have been available in several densities, with 81A being the weakest and 81E being the densest. An 81A or 81B can provide a slightly tanned skin tone, with an 81B or 81C providing a distinct earthy appearance to landscapes. Several years ago an American landscape photographer hit on the idea of combining a polarizing filter with a warming filter, and this combined filter is still available, its effect being not quite the same as using a polarizing filter combined with in-camera color-temperature control.

JERSEY SUNSET
With film, color-correction filters are usually needed to produce images like this. With the Rebel T1i/EOS 500D, however, you can make the necessary adjustments to color temperature in-camera or during post-processing.

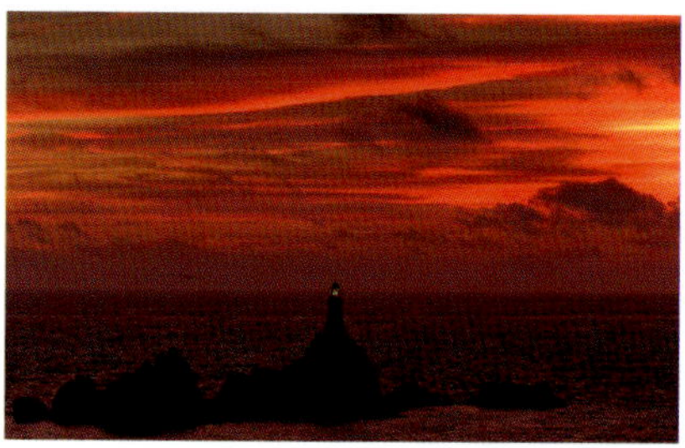

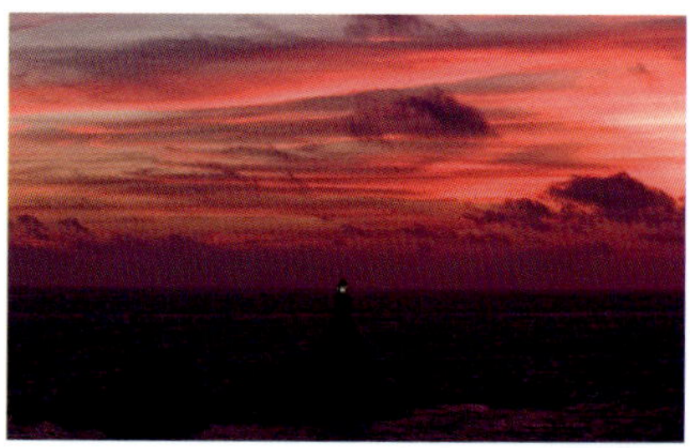

Neutral density filters

Sometimes there can be too much available light. The most common scenario is when a very slow shutter speed is needed to create blur—when shooting a waterfall, for example. In these circumstances a neutral density (ND) filter, which reduces the light passing through the lens equally across the frame, is a valuable aid. ND filters come in a range of strengths and are available in 1- to 4-stop versions in both glass and resin varieties. Strength may be indicated as ND2 for 1 stop, then ND4 for 2 stops, and so on; or ND0.3 for 1 stop, ND0.6 for 2 stops and so on, with ND0.45 being 1½ stops.

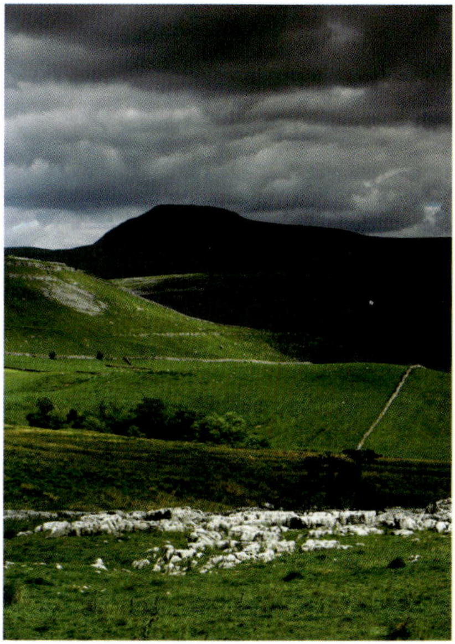

Graduated neutral density filters

Second only to a polarizing filter in the landscape photographer's tool kit, graduated neutral density (GND) filters are half clear, with the other half having a neutral density coating that is increasingly dense as it approaches the upper edge of the filter. Like plain ND filters, they are available in various strengths.

A GND filter's strength relates to the maximum light reduction at the upper edge. The area in the center, where the clear half merges with the weakest edge of the neutral-density coating, can have different grades of transition: commonly soft, hard, or razor. Hard- or razor-edged graduations are useful when you are photographing a flat horizon.

GND filters are used to balance exposure in different areas of the image. You can vary the effect by how far you slide the filter into the holder, or insert a filter upside down to darken the bottom of the image.

PIGGY BACK

Making use of two Lee filter holders in tandem, three soft graduated neutral density filters were used for this image. One was used on an angle to darken the brooding cloud at top right. Another was used across the top half of the image to accentuate the profile of the mountain and add depth to the clouds. The third was inverted to cover the pale limestone in the foreground to stop it from burning out.

Camera supports

Two aspects of digital technology that are continually being improved are image stabilization (IS) and noise reduction, both of which have some impact on the need to provide additional support for your camera.

Canon now claim an effective 4-stop reduction in shutter speeds for their latest IS lenses, meaning that a previous shutter speed of, say, 1/250 sec could now be reduced to 1/15 sec without significant loss of sharpness due to camera shake. Improved noise reduction also means that a higher ISO setting can be used, again reducing the need for additional camera support.

Tripods

Despite these advances, there will always be circumstances in which a tripod or other form of support is necessary. The tripod remains the primary form of support and relies on three things for its effectiveness: weight, appropriate feet for the situation, and leg angle. Much recent development has gone into reducing the first of these factors using materials like carbon fiber.

Tripod feet aren't something you think about about too often, but if you own a tripod that offers various alternatives, such as a Manfrotto, you may be aware of the difference they can make. Spiked feet are good for using on soft ground but no use on a wooden floor, for example, as they will scratch it and—more importantly in this context—the entire setup will be balanced on three tiny points. The usual compromise consists of threaded spikes with rubber feet which can be screwed up or down according to your requirements. There are also wider, flat feet designed for use on snow or soft ground.

As for leg angle, the broader the base of the tripod, the more stable it will be. This concept has been extended to produce models like the Benbo, which offers unlimited leg movement in any direction for absolute stability. Miniature tripods and tabletop tripods are a lightweight solution out in the field, and there are some intriguing versions with flexible legs that can be manipulated to improve stability.

Note

Image stabilization is effective in reducing the effects of camera shake but will have no impact on blur caused by subject movement.

Alternative supports

The monopod is a firm favorite for action photography, especially when used with the tripod collar that is attached part-way along some longer focal-length lenses. There are also clamps that can be mounted in birdwatching hides or over a partly opened car window; ball heads mounted on short columns with a large suction pad at the base; chestpods; clamps for screwing onto trees; and even bean bags on which to rest the lens or camera body when using a wall or other feature for support.

No single camera support will serve in every situation and most photographers end up collecting a variety over the years.

Tip

Bean bags are a particular favorite of birdwatching enthusiasts as they can be filled with bird seed, some of which can also be used to attract birds into a photogenic setting.

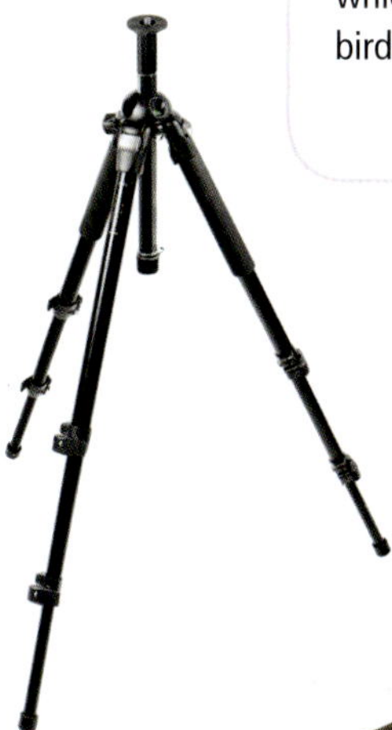

(Right) The central column of this Manfrotto professional tripod can also be used as a horizontal arm.

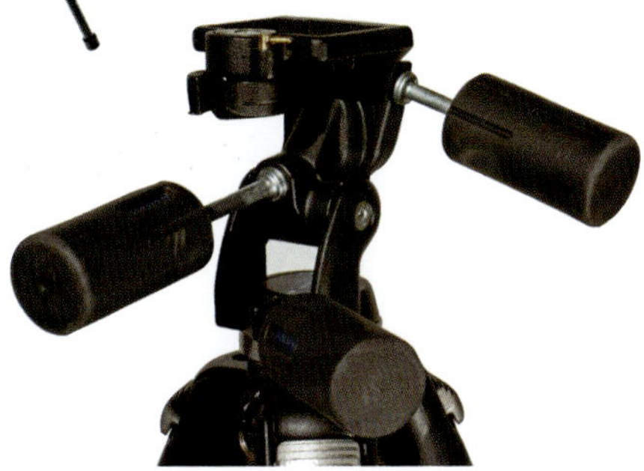

(Below) This tripod head has a three-way pan-and-tilt mechanism to allow easy adjustment in both the horizontal and vertical planes.

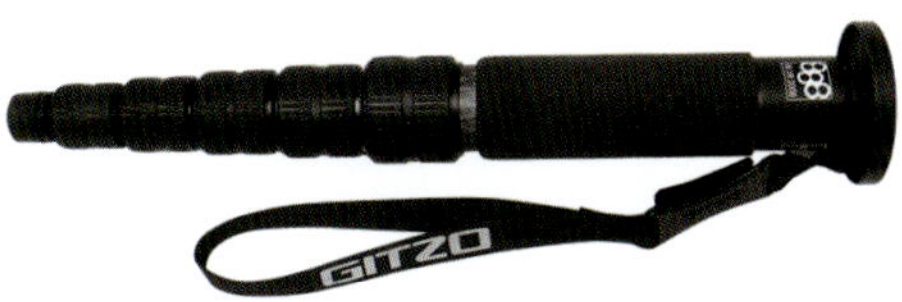

(Below) Monopods such as this Gitzo model are widely used in action photography and are very light and easy to carry when closed.

Other accessories

Canon manufacture a wide range of accessories to support the Rebel T1i/EOS 500D and a full brochure can be downloaded from their website (see page 236). Here we will examine some of the most useful accessories available.

AC Adapter kit ACK-E5
A mains adapter enabling the use of household power directly on the Rebel T1i/EOS 500D.

Battery charger LC-E5E
A mains charger for use with LP-E5 batteries.

Battery pack LP-E5
A rechargeable lithium-ion battery for the Rebel T1i/EOS 500D. Beware of using non-Canon products.

Car battery charger CBC-E5
A useful accessory for charging LP-E5 batteries when away from home and on the move.

Battery grip BG-E5
This grip attaches to the base of the camera, doubles shooting time by carrying two batteries, and provides an additional shutter release when shooting vertical images. The battery grip significantly improves handling, especially with heavier lenses.

EX Speedlites
EX Speedlite is the name given to Canon's wide range of hotshoe-mounted or off-camera flashguns, designed to work intelligently with EOS bodies using their own E-TTL II auto flash system. Full details of EX Speedlite models and their supporting accessories can be found in Chapter 5.

Speedlite transmitter ST-E2
This can be used to control wireless flash using two groups of compatible EX Speedlites.

Remote switch RS-60 E3
A short electronic remote-release cable. The shutter-release switch can be half-depressed to activate autofocus and metering just as on the camera.

Eyepiece extender EP-EX15 II
Extends the eyepiece by 15mm to provide more comfortable viewing. The extender also reduces contact with the LCD monitor.

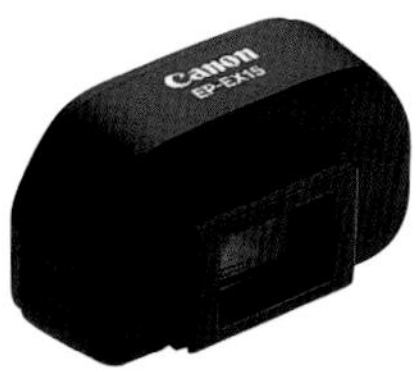

E-Series dioptric adjustment lenses
Removes the need to wear spectacles while shooting. Available in ten strengths between +3 and -4 diopters.

Angle finder C
Allows viewing at right angles to the camera eyepiece for low-viewpoint photography.

Portable storage devices
Canon manufacture the Media Storage M30 and M80 storage devices, each with a 3.7in (9cm) LCD screen and offering 30GB and 80GB storage respectively. These are portable hard drives onto which memory cards can be downloaded, and can be less expensive than carrying several high-capacity CF cards.

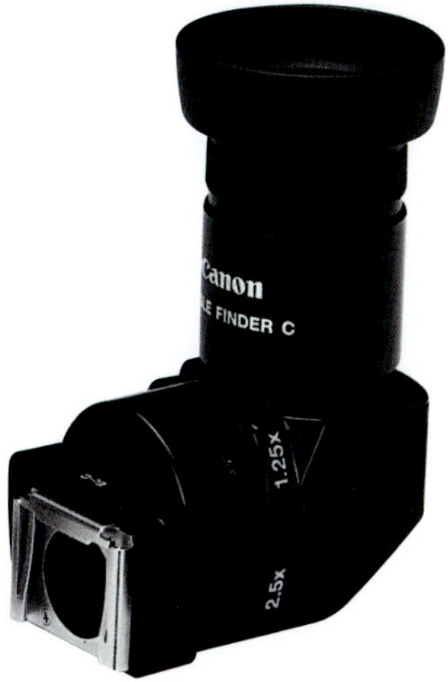

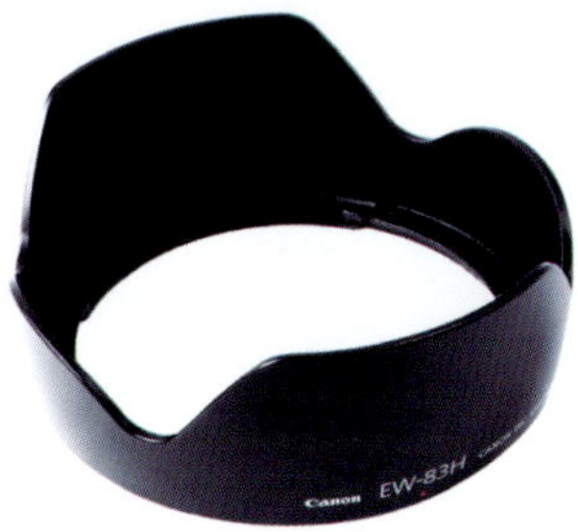

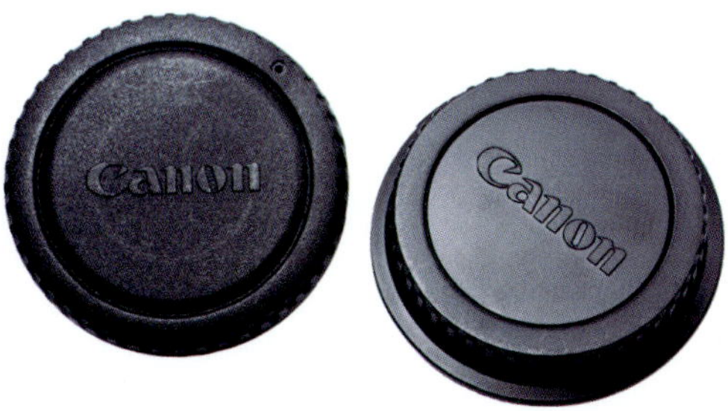

Lens hoods
L-series lenses come with hoods, but they need to be purchased separately for other lenses.

Body and lens end caps
It is always worth carrying one of each of these.

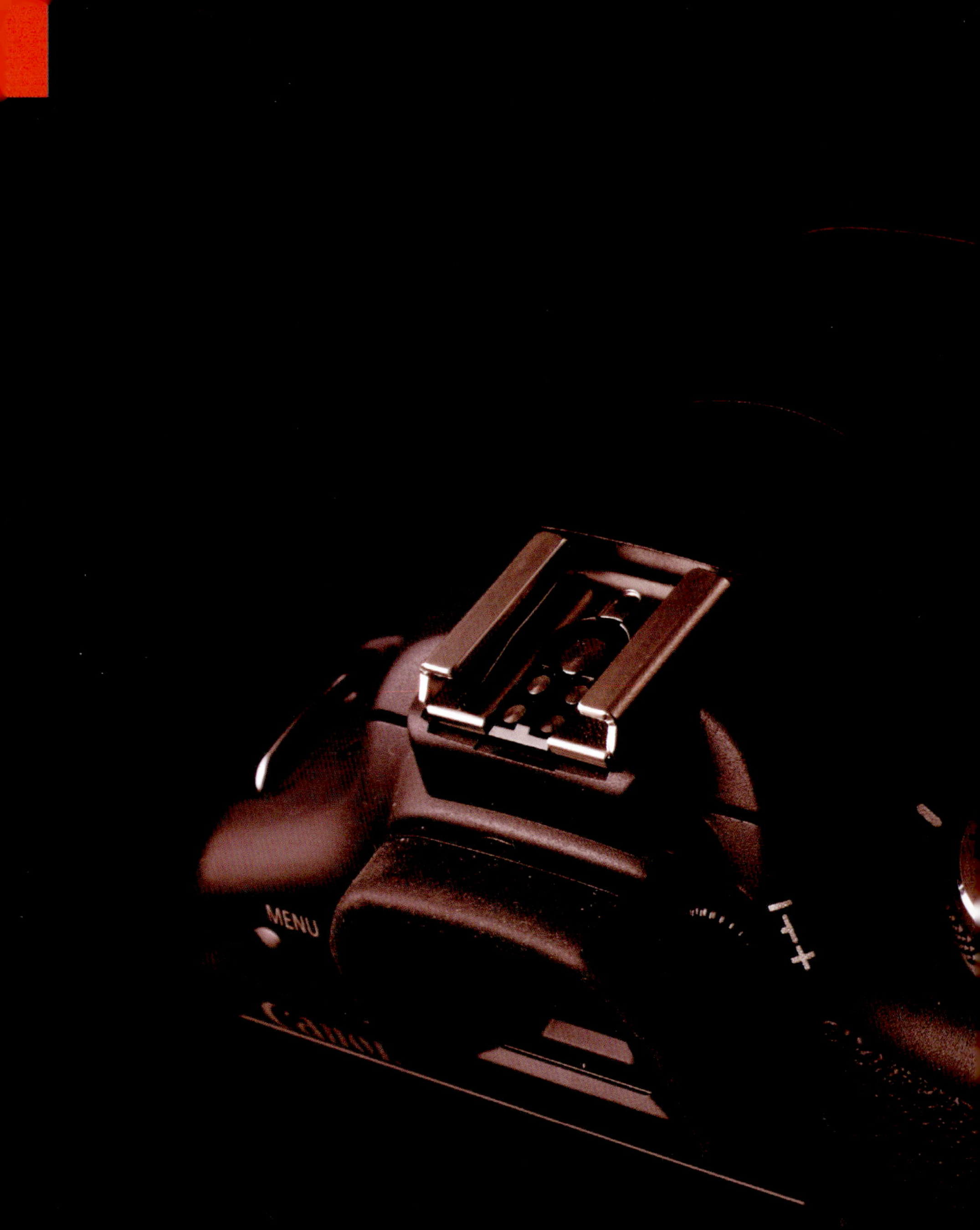
MENU

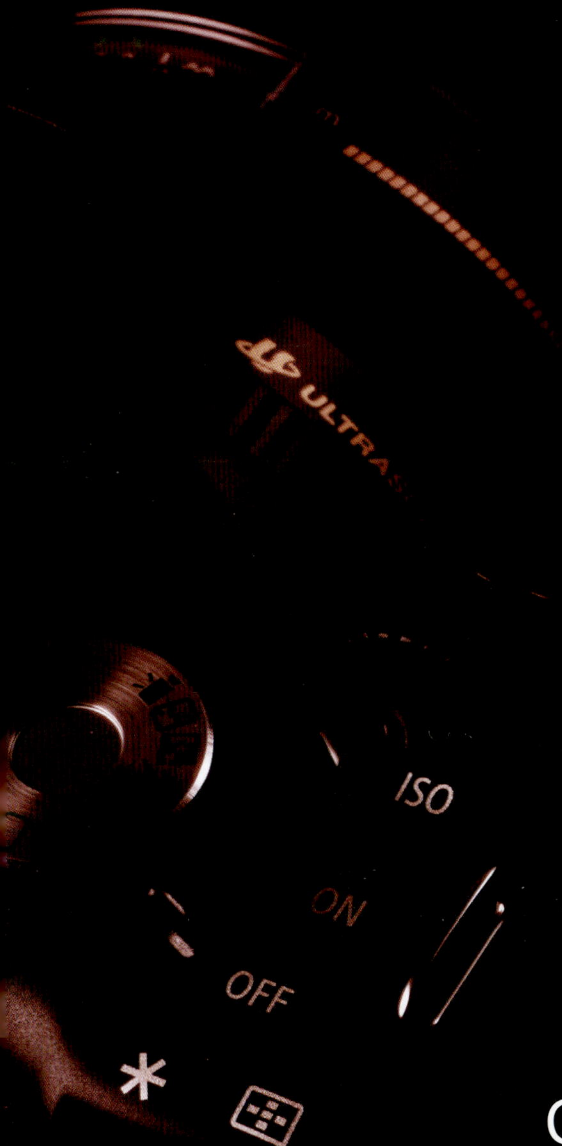

Chapter 9

Connection

If you want to save and organize your images, print them, or show them to others on your television, you need to be able to connect your camera to a variety of other devices. These devices would usually include a computer, printer, and TV. When the Rebel T1i/EOS 500D is connected to a computer, it is also possible to control shooting remotely via the keyboard.

Viewing images on TV

Non-HD TV sets

1) Make sure that both the TV and the camera are turned off.

2) Connect the AV cable provided with the Rebel T1i/EOS 500D to the **AV OUT/ DIGITAL** terminal on the camera.

3) Connect the AV cable to the television, with the yellow plug to the TV's **VIDEO IN** terminal and the black plug to the **AUDIO IN** terminal.

4) Turn on the television and select the appropriate setting/channel for video input.

5) Turn on the camera and press the ▶ playback button.

> **Note**
> For playback controls when viewing movies, see page 135.

HD TV sets

Note: Connecting to an HD TV requires an additional HDMI cable, sold separately.

1) Make sure that both the TV and the camera are turned off.

2) Connect the HDMI cable (sold separately) to the **HDMI OUT** terminal on the camera.

3) Connect the HDMI cable to the television's **HDMI IN** port.

4) Turn on the television and select the appropriate setting for the connected port.

5) Turn on the camera and press the ▶ playback button.

Common problems

If the video system selected in Set-up menu 2 does not match that of the television, images will not be displayed properly. Change the camera setting.

Connecting to a computer

Screen calibration

Before manipulating images on your computer, make sure that your monitor is calibrated for brightness, contrast, and color using dedicated software or graphics freely available on the internet. You should be able to discern a good range of tones from pure black to pure white. If the dark gray tones blend into black, the screen is too dark. If the light gray tones blend into white, the screen is too bright.

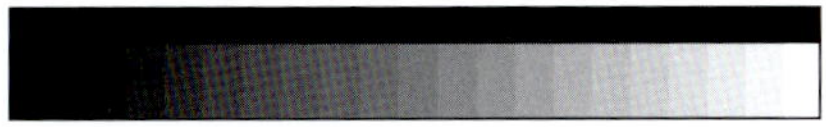

Correct calibration

Too dark

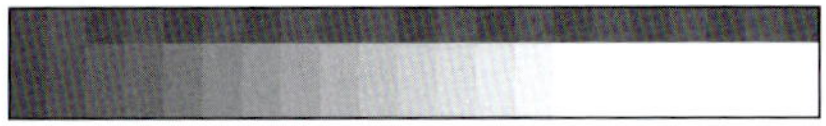

Too light

Typical color calibration image (courtesy of Digital Masters)

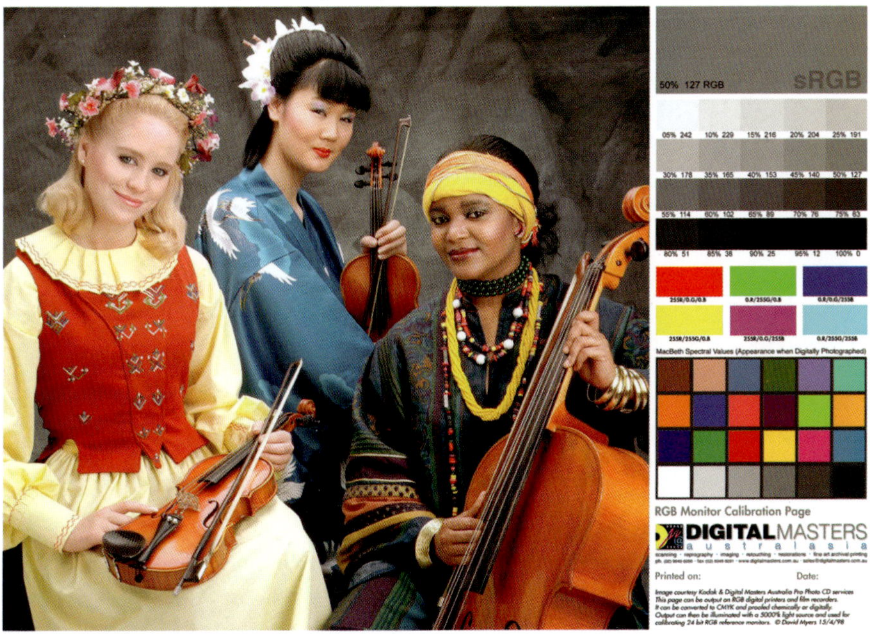

Installing the software

EOS Digital Solution Disk

1) Make sure that your camera is NOT connected to your computer.

2) Insert the EOS Digital Solution Disk (provided).

3) Follow the onscreen prompts through the installation procedure.

4) When installation is completed, you will be prompted to restart the computer. Leave the CD in the drive.

5) When your computer has rebooted, remove the CD from the drive.

Warning!

Do not connect your camera to your computer before installing the software provided.

EOS Digital Software Instruction Manuals Disk

1) Insert the disk into the CD drive of your computer.

2) Open the CD in **My Computer** (or in the **Finder** if using a Mac).

3) Click on **START.pdf files**.

Warning!

All Canon's software instruction manuals are in PDF format so make sure you have the necessary reader software installed before you start. You can download Adobe Reader free from www.adobe.com.

4) Adobe Reader will display the Instruction Manuals index.

5) Save each PDF file to your computer in the location of your choice.

Note

Software updates for the programs on the EOS Digital Solutions Disk are available to download from Canon's website (see page 236).

Connecting the camera

Warning!
Before connecting the camera to a computer, install the EOS Digital Solution Disk and make sure the camera battery is fully charged.

1) Make sure the camera is switched off.

2) Connect the USB cable (provided) to the camera's **AV OUT/DIGITAL** terminal with the ⭠⭢ symbol facing the front of the camera. Connect the other end of the cable to a USB port on the computer.

3) On the camera select any shooting mode except 🎥. Turn the camera's power switch to **ON**. If **EOS Utility** does not start automatically, select **EOS Utility** from the program selection screen.

4) The **EOS Utility** screen will be displayed on the computer and the Direct Transfer menu will be shown on the camera's LCD monitor.

Transferring images

Unless you have specified otherwise, images will be saved in My Pictures (Windows) or Pictures (Mac) and organized by shooting date. You can choose to transfer **All images**, **New images**, **Transfer order images**, **Select & transfer**, or **Wallpaper**.

1) Select the required images and press the 🖨∿ button. The button's blue lamp will blink to indicate the transfer process and a progress screen will be displayed on the camera's monitor.

2) Press **MENU** to exit.

3) Transferred images will automatically open in Digital Photo Professional ready for editing.

Tip
If you choose **Select & transfer**, you can use the **Transfer order** function in ▶ Playback menu 1 to select the images beforehand. Use the ◀ and ▶ buttons to scroll through the images and ▲ and ▼ to select or deselect an image. Press **MENU** twice to save the selection to the memory card. Up to 999 images can be selected. An image which has been captured as both RAW and JPEG will count as a single image.

Canon software

Canon produce their own software specifically designed to work with their digital cameras. It is largely aimed at EOS digital SLR users but also works with certain Powershot models. It is sometimes possible to launch one program from within another. Due to the complexity of this integration, and because programs such as Digital Photo Professional and Picture Style Editor now represent significant pieces of software in their own right, only a brief outline of their capabilities can be given here. For detailed information, refer to the instruction manuals on the CD provided with your camera.

Digital Photo Professional

Digital Photo Professional is a standalone RAW workflow tool that links with or incorporates other Canon software such as PhotoStitch and Picture Style Editor. It can be used to adjust RAW images, apply Picture Styles, and convert RAW to JPEG or TIFF files both singly and through batch processing. It also supports the use of JPEG and TIFF files as base images with which to work. Digital Photo Professional includes sophisticated color-management techniques including CMYK simulation.

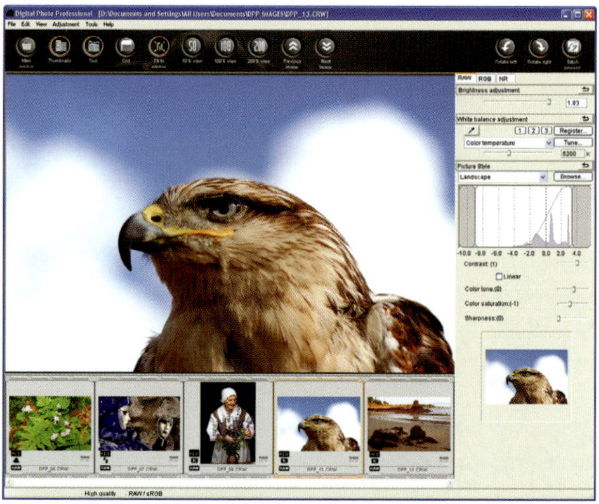

EOS Utility

EOS Utility facilitates batch downloading of your images from the camera to the computer, also allowing you to only download selected images. It also enables you to capture images remotely by controlling the camera from the computer. The latter supports Live View shooting in EOS cameras and links with Digital Photo Professional in order to view and work with remotely captured images.

Picture Style Editor

Picture Style Editor can apply six Picture Styles to base images, saving you from repeatedly making the same adjustments to each one. Each Picture Style can be customized and registered in order to fine-tune the desired results. Changes to color tone, saturation, contrast, sharpness, and gamma characteristics can all be applied. Picture Styles that have been defined in-camera can also be saved onto the computer. Picture Styles can be even applied to images that have been shot previously on cameras which do not support Picture Styles.

ZoomBrowser EX

ZoomBrowser EX is used for viewing, organizing, and editing images and folders via a variety of windows. It also facilitates the printing of images with Canon inkjet printers. Secondary software such as Camera Window and Raw Image Task may be started from within ZoomBrowser. The program's editing suite supports adjustments to brightness, color, cropping, sharpness, and red-eye correction, adding images to emails or using them as wallpaper or screensavers, and the insertion of text into images. It also facilitates the transfer of images to Canon iMAGE Gateway.

Canon iMAGE Gateway

Canon iMAGE Gateway provides 100MB of web space, allowing you to share photos with friends and family by creating online albums. It even supports the customization of your camera by adding startup images and sound effects as well as downloadable Picture Styles.

PhotoStitch

PhotoStitch permits the opening and arranging of JPEG images to be merged, saved, and printed. It is frequently used to create panoramic images from a sequence.

Using a printer

You can connect the Canon Rebel T1i/EOS 500D directly to a printer and print the images held on the memory card. You can also preselect which images you wish to print. The camera is compatible with PictBridge. Printing is controlled directly from the camera using the LCD monitor to view the operation. If your printer has slots for memory cards, you may also be able to simply insert your memory card into the printer without connecting the camera.

Warning!

Printers which are only compatible with CP Direct or Bubble Jet Direct cannot be used with the Canon Rebel T1i/EOS 500D.

Connecting to a printer

1) Check that the camera's battery is charged or use the AC Adapter Kit ACK-E2 (sold separately) to use AC power.

2) Make sure the camera is switched off.

3) Connect the USB cable provided with the camera to the Rebel T1i/EOS 500D's **AV OUT/DIGITAL** terminal. The symbol must face the front of the camera.

4) Connect the cable to the printer according to the printer's manual.

5) Turn on the printer.

6) Turn the camera's power switch to **ON**.

At this point some printers may emit a beep. If this beep is prolonged, there is a problem with the printer. To discover the error, press the ▶ playback button on the camera. When the image is played back, press **SET**. On the Print Setting screen, select **Print** and the error message should be displayed on the LCD monitor.

Possible error messages include Paper Error, Ink Error, Hardware Error, and File Error. These messages may also be displayed at any time during the printing process. Press **SET** to pause printing while you resolve the issue, then select **Continue**.

Canon PIXMA iP4600 printer

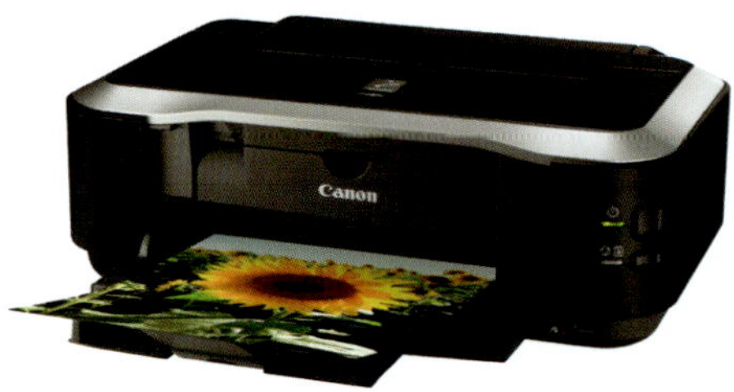

7) Press the [▶] playback button to bring up the first image. The symbol will be shown on the monitor at top left to indicate camera-printer connection. The button's blue lamp will illuminate.

8) If this is not the image you wish to print, use the ◀ or ▶ buttons to scroll through the images on the card. Press **SET**.

9) The LCD monitor will display the **Print Setting** screen with the selected image reduced in size plus a list of settings covering printing effects, date, file number, quantity, trimming, paper size, and layout. Amend these settings as desired using the ▲ and ▼ buttons to scroll through the menu and pressing **SET** to select an item to change.

At this point you may wish to go to step 10 on page 228 where you can find the full setting procedure followed by Trimming instructions. If you want to skip the full Print Settings procedure and Trimming at this stage, or are already familiar with them, go to step 26, above right.

26) When you are ready to begin printing, select **Print** and press **SET**.

27) The button's blue lamp will blink and printing will take place.

28) While **Stop** is displayed you can stop printing by pressing **SET** and then **OK**.

29) To print further images using the same settings, select each image and press the button. Repeat as necessary.

30) When you have finished printing, turn off the camera.

31) Turn off the printer.

32) Disconnect the USB cable.

Warning!

The extent to which your printer supports the functions described will determine whether or not some functions will be displayed or can be performed.

Print settings

10) From the **Print setting** menu reached in step 9 (see page 227), select **Paper settings** and press **SET**.

11) The **Paper size** screen will be displayed first. Select the paper to be loaded into the printer and press **SET**.

12) The **Paper type** screen will be displayed next. Select the type of paper to be used and press **SET**.

13) Finally, the **Page layout** screen will appear. Select and press **SET**. Depending on the printer in use, possible page layouts may include: Bordered, Borderless, Bordered with info, Index, or Default. In addition you can opt for 2,4,8,9, or 16 images on a single sheet. (Bordered with info prints will have shooting information printed on the border for prints 9 × 13cm and larger. Default prints on a Canon printer will be borderless.)

14) The display will now revert to the Print Setting screen.

Common problems

If your printer cannot print borderless prints it will probably rescale the image and print it with a border.

Printing Effects

15) On the **Print Setting** screen, select the symbol and press **SET**. The default setting is **Off** but the options in the tables which follow may be available.

16) Select the effect you wish to apply and press **SET**.

17) If the icon is displayed next to **DISP**, additional options are available if you press the camera's **DISP** button.

Preset Printing Effects Item	 Description
Off	Same as the printing characteristics turned **On**. No automatic correction will be performed.
On	The image will be printed according to the printer's standard colors. The image's Exif data is used to make automatic corrections.
Vivid	The image will be printed with higher saturation to produce more vivid blues and greens.
NR	The image noise is reduced before printing.
B/W B/W	Prints in black and white with true blacks.
B/W Cool tone	Prints in black and white with cool, bluish blacks.
B/W Warm tone	Prints in black and white with warm, yellowish blacks.
Natural	Prints the image in the actual colors and contrast. No automatic color adjustments will be applied.
Natural M	The printing characteristics are the same as the **Natural** setting. However, this setting enables finer printing adjustments than with the **Natural** setting.
Default	The printing will differ depending on the printer. For details, see the printer's instruction manual.

The LCD screen display may differ depending on the printer.
When the printing effects are changed, the changes will be reflected on the LCD screen. However, the actual result of the printing effects might look different from what you see on screen. The LCD screen only shows an approximate rendition.

Tip
Images can also be printed as thumbnails, as either a set of 20 or a set of 35 on Letter or A4 paper. A set of 20 will also print shooting information. See DPOF printing on page 231.

Adjustable Printing Effects

Brightness	The image brightness can be adjusted.
Adjust levels	When you select **Manual**, you can change the histogram's distribution and adjust the image's brightness and contrast. With the **Adjust Levels** screen displayed, press the **DISP** button to change the position of the indicator. Use the ◀ ▶ buttons to adjust the shadow level (0–127) or highlight level (128–255).
Brightener	Effective in backlit conditions which can make the subject's face look dark. When **On** is set, the face will be brightened for printing.
Red-eye corr.	Effective in flash images where the subject has red-eye. When **On** is set, the red-eye will be corrected for printing.

The **Brightener** and **Red-eye corr.** effects will not show up on the screen.
When you select **Detail set.** you can adjust the **Contrast**, **Saturation**, **Color tone** and **Color balance**.
When you select **Clear all**, all the printing effects will revert to the default.

Date / Time / File Number

18) Select ⌚, then press **SET**.

19) Select the desired setting and press **SET** again.

Number of copies

20) Select ⧉ then use the ▲ or ▼ buttons to set the number of copies required. Press **SET**.

21) Unless you want to trim images, go back to step 26 on page 227 to start printing.

Trimming the image

Trimming should only be done after all other print settings are complete.

22) On the **Print Setting** screen, select **Trimming**.

23) Use the ⊞/🔍 Enlarge and ✱/⊞• 🔍 Reduce buttons to adjust the size of the trimming frame and the ◀ ▶ ▲ ▼ buttons to move the frame.

24) Press the **DISP** button to rotate the image through 90°.

25) Press **SET** to exit Trimming and go back to step 26 on page 227.

Digital Print Order Format (DPOF)

Commonly abbreviated to DPOF, this is a system for recording printing instructions to the memory card. The DPOF system is managed through the **Print Order** option in ▶ Playback menu 1.

With the camera connected to a printer, you can use the **Print Order** menu to manage the direct printing of your images from the camera's CF card. Because the DPOF data is stored on the memory card, it is also possible to simply take the card to an instore photo printing facility.

Digital Print Order Format (DPOF) settings can be applied to all JPEG images on the memory card or to selected images. (RAW images are not compatible.) However, different settings cannot be applied to individual images in the same batch and therefore the same print type, date, and file number settings will be applied.

Print ordering

First set up the print type, date, and file number to be applied to all the images to be printed. File number and date settings are restricted to **On** or **Off**. **Standard** print type prints a single image per sheet. **Index** prints thumbnail images.

1) Select ▶ Playback menu 1 and press **SET**.

2) Select **Set up** and press **SET**.

3) A menu showing print type, date, and file number options will be displayed. Select the option required and press **SET**. On the submenu, select the option desired and press **SET**.

4) Press **MENU** to return to the Print order menu and select either **All images** or **Select images** to finalize your settings.

Before printing with DPOF you will need to select the images you wish to print. You can do this with single images displayed on the monitor or a group of three images. Use the ✱/▦•🔍 Reduce button and the ▤/🔍 Enlarge button to toggle between the two different display formats.

5) If you have opted for **Sel. Image** in step 4 above, you can add images one by one to the print order.

6) For **Standard** or **Both** settings, use the ▲ or ▼ buttons to change the required number of copies of the image displayed.

7) For **Index** printing, use the ▲ or ▼ buttons to check the box so that the image is included.

Direct printing with DPOF

Having determined your print order, you can use DPOF to print directly to a PictBridge printer.

1) Connect the camera and printer as described in steps 1–6 on page 226.

2) Select ▶˙ Playback menu 1 and then **Print order**.

3) Select **Print**.

4) Set the **Print settings** as in steps 10–14 on page 228.

5) Set the **Printing effects** as in steps 15–17 on page 228.

6) Select **OK**.

General hints on printing

Even with **Date** or **File number** selected, some printers may not print this information. With **Index** printing (see page 231) you cannot print both **Date** and **File number**.

Up to 400 images can be selected for a single print order with a PictBridge printer.

Unless it has been reformatted, do not insert a memory card which has already had DPOF settings applied in a different camera and try to apply new print order settings.

Do not view images on a television screen when trimming (see page 230) as the trimming frame may not be represented accurately.

The smaller the trimmed image, the greater the magnification of the final image will be. This may result in loss of apparent sharpness or an increase in noise in the printed image.

Some televisions incorporate different screen formats. When viewing images on your TV screen, you may need to consult your television's instruction manual to change the screen format.

For more detailed information on using Canon EOS software, refer to *Canon EOS Software for Windows*, ISBN 978-1-906672-17-1.

Glossary

Aberration An imperfection in the image caused by the optics of a lens.

AE (auto exposure) lock A camera control that locks in the exposure value, allowing an image to be recomposed.

Angle of view The area of a scene that a lens takes in, measured in degrees.

Aperture The opening in a camera lens through which light passes to expose the CMOS sensor. The relative size of the aperture is denoted by f-stops.

Autofocus (AF) A through-the-lens focusing system allowing accurate focus without manually rotating the focusing ring.

Bracketing Taking a series of three identical pictures—changing only the exposure—at, above, and below the nominal exposure.

Buffer Temporary memory that stores image data while it is written to the memory card.

Burst size The maximum number of frames that a digital camera can shoot before its buffer becomes full.

Cable release A device used to trigger the shutter of a tripod-mounted camera at a distance to avoid camera shake.

Center-weighted average metering A metering mode which takes into account the whole image area but places greater importance on the central area.

Chromic aberration The inability of a lens to bring spectrum colors into focus at one point.

CMOS (Complementary Metal-oxide Semi-conductor) A type of image sensor which converts an optical image to an electrical signal, as opposed to the CCD (Charge Coupled Device) used in earlier models.

Color temperature The color of a light source expressed in degrees Kelvin (°K).

CompactFlash card A digital storage mechanism offering safe, reliable storage.

Compression The process by which digital files are reduced in size.

Contrast The range between the highlight and shadow areas of an image, or a marked difference in illumination between colors or adjacent areas.

Depth of field (DOF) The amount of an image that appears acceptably sharp. This is controlled by the aperture: the smaller the aperture, the greater the depth of field.

Diopter Unit expressing the power of a lens.

dpi (dots per inch) Measure of the resolution of a printer or a scanner. The more dots per inch, the higher the resolution.

Dynamic range The ability of the camera's sensor to capture a full range of shadows and highlights.

EF (Extended Focus) lenses Canon's range of fast, ultra-quiet autofocus lenses.

Evaluative metering A metering system whereby light reflected from several subject areas is calculated based on algorithms.

Exposure The amount of light allowed to hit the CMOS sensor, controlled by aperture, shutter speed, and ISO-E. Also the act of taking a photograph, as in "making an exposure."

Exposure compensation A control that allows intentional over- or underexposure relative to the meter reading.

Extension tubes Hollow spacers that fit between the camera body and lens, typically used for close-up work. The tubes increase the focal length of the lens.

Fill-in flash Flash combined with daylight in an exposure. Used with naturally backlit or harshly side-lit or top-lit subjects to prevent silhouettes forming, or to add extra light to the shadow areas of a well-lit scene.

Filter A piece of colored, or coated, glass or plastic placed in front of the lens.

f-stop Number assigned to a particular lens aperture. Wide apertures are denoted by small numbers such as f/2, and small apertures by large numbers such as f/22.

Focal length The distance, usually in millimetres, from the optical center point of a lens element to its focal point.

Focal length and multiplication factor The CMOS sensor of the Rebel T1i/EOS 500D measures 22.3 × 14.9mm—1.6× smaller than full-frame. The angle of view of any full-frame lens is reduced by the same factor.

fps (frames per second) The ability of a digital camera to process one image and be ready to shoot the next.

Histogram A graph used to represent the distribution of tones in an image.

Hotshoe An accessory shoe with electrical contacts that allows synchronization between the camera and a flashgun.

Hotspot A light area with a loss of detail in the highlights. This is a common problem in flash photography.

Incident-light reading Meter reading based on the light falling on the subject.

Interpolation A way of increasing the file size of a digital image by adding pixels, thereby increasing its resolution.

ISO-E (International Organization for Standardization) The sensitivity of the CMOS sensor measured in terms equivalent to the ISO rating of a film.

JPEG (Joint Photographic Experts Group) JPEG compression can reduce file sizes to about 5% of their original size.

LCD (Liquid Crystal Display) The flat screen on a digital camera that allows the user to preview digital images.

Macro A term used to describe close focusing and the close-focusing ability of a lens.

Megapixel One million pixels equals one megapixel.

Memory card A removable storage device for digital cameras.

Microdrives Small hard disks that fit in a CompactFlash slot, resulting in larger storage capabilities.

Mirror lock-up A function that allows the reflex mirror of an SLR to be raised and held in the up position, before the exposure is made.

Pixel Short for "picture element"—the smallest bits of information in a digital image.

Predictive autofocus An autofocus system that can continuously track a moving subject.

Noise Colored image interference caused by stray electrical signals.

Partial metering A metering system that is unique to Canon, it meters a relatively small area at the center of the frame.

PictBridge The industry standard for sending information directly from a camera to a printer, without having to connect to a computer.

Red-eye reduction A system that causes the pupils of a subject to shrink by shining a light prior to taking the flash picture.

RAW The file format in which the raw data from the sensor is stored without permanent alteration being made.

Resolution The number of pixels used to capture or display an image. The higher the resolution, the finer the detail.

RGB (Red, Green, Blue) Computers and other digital devices understand color information as combinations of red, green, and blue.

Rule of thirds A rule of thumb that places the key elements of a picture at points along imagined lines that divide the frame into thirds.

Shading The effect of light striking a photosensor at anything other than right angles, incurring a loss of resolution.

Shutter The mechanism that controls the amount of light reaching the sensor by opening and closing.

SLR (single lens reflex) A type of camera (such as the Rebel T1i/EOS 500D) that allows the user to view the scene through the lens, using a reflex mirror.

Spot metering A metering system that places importance on the intensity of light reflected by a very small portion of the scene.

Teleconverter A lens that is inserted between the camera body and main lens, increasing the effective focal length.

Telephoto lens A lens with a large focal length and a narrow angle of view.

TTL (Through The Lens) metering A metering system built into the camera that measures light passing through the lens at the time of shooting.

TIFF (Tagged Image File Format) A universal file format supported by virtually all relevant software applications. TIFFs are uncompressed digital files.

USB (Universal Serial Bus) A data transfer standard, used by the Rebel T1i/EOS 500D when connecting to a computer.

Viewfinder An optical system used for composing and sometimes focusing the subject.

White balance A function that allows the correct color balance to be recorded for any given lighting situation.

Wide-angle lens A lens with a short focal length and consequently a wide angle of view.

Useful websites

CANON
www.canon.com
www.usa.canon.com
www.canon.co.uk
www.canon-europe.com
www.canon.com.au
www.canoneos.com
www.canon.com/camera-museum

Canon Professional Network
http://cpn.canon-europe.com

Canon Picture Style Special Site
www.canon.co.jp/imaging/picturestyle

Seminars
www.eos-experience.co.uk

SOFTWARE
Adobe USA
www.adobe.com
Adobe UK
www.adobe.co.uk

FILTERS
www.leefilters.com
www.tiffen.com
www.cokin.com
www.formatt.co.uk
www.hoya-online.co.uk

DIGITAL FILTERS
www.tiffen.com/dfx_essentials
www.niksoftware.com

PUBLICATIONS
Photography books
www.pipress.com

Black & White Photography magazine
Outdoor Photography magazine
www.thegmcgroup.com

www.eos-magazine.com

TECHNIQUE / TECHNICAL
www.digitalphotopro.com
www.sphoto.com
www.northlight-images.co.uk
www.luminous-landscape.com
www.outbackphoto.com
www.dxomark.com
www.clarkvision.com

Hyperfocal distance calculator
www.cambridgeincolour.com/tutorials/hyperfocal-distance.htm

Depth of field calculator
www.dofmaster.com

NEWS / RUMORS
www.canonrumors.com
www.dpreview.com
www.photorumors.com
www.photographybay.com
www.ephotozine.co.uk

RETAILERS
ACE index of US/Canada photo retailers
www.acecam.com/chains.html

www.adorama.com
www.ritzcamera.com
www.bhphotovideo.com
www.calumetphoto.com
www.blackphoto.com

www.speedgraphic.co.uk
www.bristolcameras.co.uk
www.calumetphoto.co.uk
www.camerapricebuster.co.uk
www.fotosense.co.uk
www.jacobsdigital.co.uk
www.mathersoflancashire.co.uk
www.provisualdirect.co.uk
www.warehouseexpress.com

Leasing
www.photolease.co.uk

Extensive UK used stock & commission sales
www.ffordes.com

OTHER
SanDisk
www.sandisk.com

Sigma lenses
www.sigma-imaging-uk.com
www.sigmaphoto.com

Lens / body adapters
www.srb-griturn.com/

Bureau of Freelance Photographers
www.thebfp.com

Photography discussion forum
www.photo.net

Index

accessories 208–17
camera supports 214–15
close-up photography 185–6
filters 208–13
flash 176–7
AC power 29, 216
add original decision data 121
AE lock button 120
AI focus 35–6
AI Servo mode, focusing 35
aliasing 151
angle finder C 217
aperture 62
teleconverters 198
Aperture Priority mode (Av) 74–5
attachment
lenses 27
strap 27
auto exposure (AE) lock 64
auto exposure bracketing (AEB) 92
auto focus (AF) 35–6
assist beam 69, 119
Live mode 128
lock 69
Movie mode 133
points 68–9
Quick mode 127
teleconverters 198
Auto Lighting Optimizer 45, 118
Automatic Depth of Field mode (A–DEP) 78–9
Live View 126
auto rotate 110
average metering 89
background blur 48
balance
composition 145
white 40, 94–7
Basic Zone 45–61
Mode Dial 33
preset adjustment 98–102
batteries 29–30
charging 29, 216
grip 216
insertion 29
life 30
bean bags 215
beep 86
bellows 185–6
blurring
background 48
motion 144
bounce flash 169–70
bracketing
auto exposure 92
flash 89, 167
white balance 96–7
brightness
histograms 106–7
LCD displays 112
built-in flash 38, 89

camera
care 159–61
layout 14–17
preparation 27–30
settings display 44
shooting without memory card 87
supports 214–15
switching on/off 31
Canon iMAGE Gateway 225
center–weighted average metering 39, 94
charging batteries 29
circle of confusion 139–40
clipping 151
Close-up mode 54–5
close-up photography 180–7
accessories 93–6
lenses 184, 187
lighting 181–2
working distance 183
cold temperatures 159–60
color
correction filters 212
lighting 148–9
space 98
composition 145–7
perspective 197
computer connection 221–5
computer software 13, 222–5
connection
to computer 87, 105, 221–5
to printer 226–30
to television 113, 220
contact lenses 30, 217
continuous file numbering 109
contrast 149
converging lines 146
Creative Auto mode 48–9
Creative Zone 70–9
Mode Dial 33
settings 115–21
crop factor 192
Custom Functions 13, 115–21

date/time settings 113
deleting images 43, 104
depth of field 139–41
ISO 74
maximization 78–9
depth-of-field preview 36
dials
Main 34
Mode 33
Digital Photo Professional software 224
Digital Print Order Format (DPOF) 231–2
diopter 30, 217
direct flash 169, 171
directing the eye 145–6
direction of light 149
Drive mode 32
drop-in filters 209
dust
changing lenses 161
delete data 102
dynamic range 153

EF lenses 190, 200–5
EF-S lenses 190, 200–5
EOS digital disks 222
EOS Utility software 225
erasing images 104
evaluative metering 39, 89, 94
evaluative through-the-lens metering (E-TTL II) 89, 164–5
exposure 12, 62–6
AE lock 64
compensation 65–6, 91, 154
flash 166–71
ISO settings 37
modes 70–9
settings 116
EX Speedlites 173–5
attaching 171
control 88, 90

extension tubes 185
eyepiece extenders 216

face detection 128–9
features
full 14–23
main 12–13
field of view 192–3
files
formats 12
numbering 109–10
quality 85–6
filters 208–13
firmware updates 121
first-curtain flash 171–2
flare 150–1
flash 13, 164–77
accessories 176–7
bounce 169–70
bracketing 89, 167
built-in 38, 89
direct 169, 171
exposure calculation 166, 168
exposure compensation 89, 168
EX Speedlites 88, 90, 171, 173–5
macro photography 175
No Flash mode 60–1
ring 175, 182
settings 88–90
sync speed 116
wireless 172, 216
flash exposure lock 167
focal length 192–3
focusing 12, 35–6
autofocus 68–9
live mode 127–9
formatting memory cards 110
f-stops 62
Full Auto mode 46–7
functions 26–121
availablity 22–3
basic 31–44

gelatin filters 209
glass filters 209
graduated neutral density (GND) filters 213
guide numbers (GN) 166

HD televisions 220
High Dynamic Range (HDR) software 65
high ISO noise reduction 117
highlight tone priority 118
high temperature 125, 160–1
histograms 106–7
playback 41
humidity 160–1
hyperfocal technique 140
hyperopia 30, 217

Image jump 42, 107
images
aliasing 151
clipping 151
deletion 43
dynamic range 153
flare 150–1
magnification 42,129
noise 150
perspective 197
playback 41–3
printing 227
properties 150–3
protection 44, 103
reduction 42
rotation 43, 104
sharpening 151–3
transfer 105, 223
image stabilization (IS) lenses 191
in the field 138–61
composition 145–7
depth of field 139–41
lighting 148–9
motion 142–4
inserting memory cards 28
inverse square law 168
ISO 62
depth of field 74
expansion 116
noise reduction 117
settings 37, 116

JPEG files 12, 85–6, 151–2

Landscape mode 52–3
landscapes 78
language settings 113
LCD monitor 13, 15
auto off 111
brightness 112
lenses 190–205
attachment 27
caps 217
changing 161
close-up 184, 187
concepts 192–3
depth of field 140
hoods 217
image stabilization 191
macro 187
removal 27
standard 194
teleconverters 198
telephoto 196
tilt-and-shift 199
wide-angle 195
lighting 148–9
close-up photography 181–2
light metering 63
Live mode auto focus 128
Live View 124–30
close-up photography 182
information display 130
settings 114
long exposure noise reduction 38, 117
L-series lenses 191

macro lenses 187
magnifying images 42
Main Dial 34
Manual Exposure mode (M) 76–7
memory cards 13
formatting 110
insertion/removal 28
portable storage devices 217
using without 87
menus 20–1, 80–121
selection 80
summary 81–3
metering 63–4
modes 39
Movie mode 132
settings 94
mirror lock-up 119
Mode Dial 33
moisture 160–1
monochrome 100
monopods 215
motion 142–4
lenses 191
Movie functions menu 132
Movie mode 131–5
shooting stills 134–5
sound 133
movies
playback 135
shooting 131–3
multiple flash 172
My Menu 83, 84

nature 54, 78, 156–7
neutral density (ND) filters 213
Night Portrait mode 58–9
No Flash mode 60–1
noise 150
  reduction 117
NTSC 113

One Shot mode 35

PAL 113
panning 143
  lenses 191
panoramic image stitching 225
partial metering 39, 94
peripheral illumination correction 87
perspective 197
photo essays 156–7
PhotoStitch software 225
Picture Style Editor software 225
Picture style preset adjustment 98–102
playback
  images 41–3
  Jump function 42
  movies 135
Playback menu 1 82, 103–5
Playback menu 2 82, 106–7
polarizing filters 210–11
portable storage devices 217
Portrait mode 50–1
power on/off 31
  auto 108
printing 226–30
  effects 228–30
Print ordering 105, 231
processor 12
Program mode (P) 70–1
  Live View 126
protecting images 44, 103

quality
  images 85–6
  movies 132
Quick control screen 19
Quick mode auto focus 127

RAW files 12, 85–6, 151–3
  exposure 65
red-eye correction 88
remote control 216
  Movie mode 133
removal
  lenses 27
  memory cards 28
reset file numbering 110
reverse adapters 186
review time 87
RGB histograms 107
ring flash 182
rotation
  auto 110
  images 43, 104

screen color 111
second-curtain flash 171–2
sense of depth 158
sensor 12
  cleaning 114
  confusion 140–1
SET button settings 120
settings
  clear 121
  display 44
  printing 228
Set-up menu 1 82, 108–11
Set-up menu 2 83, 112–14
Set-up menu 3 83, 115–21
sharpening 151–3
shooting
  in the field 138–61
  movies 131–3
  stills in Movie mode 134–5
Shooting menu 1 81, 85–90
Shooting menu 2 81, 91–102
Shutter Priority mode (Tv) 72–3
shutter-release button 34
  settings 120
shutter speed 62–4
skylight filters 212
slide shows 107
software 13, 224–5
sound 133
special-effects filters 209
Sports mode 56–7
spot metering 39, 94
standard lenses 194
strap attachment 27
sunsets 155
switching on/off 31
  auto 108

teleconverters 198
telephoto lenses 196
temperature 159–61
tilt-and-shift lenses 199
time/date settings 113
Time value 72
Transfer Order 105
transferring images 105, 223
tripods 214
turning on/off 31
  auto 108

User-defined picture styles 102
UV filters 212

video settings 113
viewfinder display 18
  metering modes 39
vignetting 87, 211

water protection 161
white balance 40, 94–7
  bracketing 96–7
wide-angle lenses 195
wireless flash 172
working distance, close-up photography 183

ZoomBrowser EX software 225

CANON REBEL T1i / EOS 500D

THE EXPANDED GUIDE

SYMBOLS USED

- Main Dial
- Shooting menu 1
- Shooting menu 2
- Playback menu 1
- Playback menu 2
- Set-up menu 1
- Set-up menu 2
- Set-up menu 3
- My Menu
- Playback button
- Single frame advance
- Continuous advance
- Self-timer 10-second delay
- Self-timer 2-second delay
- Self-timer plus continuous advance
- Full Auto mode
- Portrait mode
- Landscape mode
- Close-up mode
- Sports mode
- Night Portrait mode
- Flash off mode
- Movie mode
- Focus confirmation light
- Flash exposure compensation
- Flash ready indicator
- Flash exposure lock/ bracketing indicator
- Evaluative metering mode
- Center-weighted metering mode
- Partial metering mode
- Spot metering mode
- AF point selection button
- FE lock/Index button
- AF lock button
- Enlarge button
- Reduce button
- Erase button
- Image protected
- Auto rotate image (camera & PC)
- Auto rotate image (PC only)
- Image quality fine
- Image quality normal
- Custom white balance
- AWB Auto white balance
- Daylight white balance
- Shade white balance
- Cloudy white balance
- Tungsten white balance
- Fluorescent white balance
- Single face detection
- Multiple face detection
- AF Quick Live View Quick AF mode
- AF Live Live View Live AF mode
- AF Live View Live face detection AF mode
- Exit
- Play
- Slow motion
- First frame
- Previous frame
- Next frame
- Flash white balance
- Flash high-speed sync
- 2..1..0..1..2 Exposure level indicator
- Picture Style
- Sharpness parameter
- Contrast parameter
- Saturation parameter
- Color tone parameter
- Filter effect parameter
- Toning parameter
- High temperature warning
- Live View and Movie mode
- Live face detection mode
- Last frame
- Volume
- USB connection
- Print share
- PictBridge direct printing
- Printing effects
- Printing effects options
- Printing date/time settings
- Printing number of copies
- Print single image
- Print multiple thumbnails

PHOTOGRAPHER'S
GRAY CARD

CAMERA RAW
WHITE BALANCE